Distant Corners

In the series **Sporting**
edited by Amy Bass

David Wangerin

Distant Corners

American Soccer's History of
Missed Opportunities and Lost Causes

TEMPLE UNIVERSITY PRESS
Philadelphia

TEMPLE UNIVERSITY PRESS
Philadelphia, Pennsylvania 19122
www.temple.edu/tempress

All attempts have been made to locate the owners of the photographs published in this book. If you believe you may own one of them, please contact Temple University Press so that appropriate acknowledgment may be included in subsequent editions of the book.

Library of Congress Cataloging-in-Publication Data

Wangerin, David.
  Distant corners : American soccer's history of missed opportunities and lost causes / David Wangerin.
     p.   cm. — (Sporting)
  Includes index.
  ISBN 978-1-4399-0630-9 (cloth : alk. paper)
   1. Soccer—United States—History.   2. Soccer—History.   I. Title.
GV944.U5W359 2011
796.3340973—dc22   2010045075

♾ The paper used in this publication meets the requirements of the American National Standard for Information Sciences—Permanence of Paper for Printed Library Materials, ANSI Z39.48-1992

Printed in the United States of America

2 4 6 8 9 7 5 3 1

Contents

A photo gallery begins on page 89

Preface

Worthy Diversions

I T SHOULD BE an upright headstone, the caretaker said; the trick will be finding it among the various blocks and gates. It's a big cemetery. But the sun was out and it was warm for April, and if I had to visit a graveyard, today was as good a day as any. I left my jacket in the car and made my way on foot to Section 28.

In one sense, I knew why I'd come to the Gate of Heaven Cemetery in East Hanover, New Jersey. I wanted to see Tom Cahill's grave. There might be a date of birth on the marker, and maybe too some sort of epitaph: how had he wanted to be remembered? It wasn't as if I had made an enormous sacrifice to get here; East Hanover was hardly even a detour on my route from Newark Airport to the National Soccer Hall of Fame, 200 miles to the north in Oneonta, New York. But in another sense it was wholly irrational. Why would the burial site of a man I wasn't related to and who'd died more than a half-century earlier merit an afternoon of my attention?

There are websites—of course there are—that tell you which famous people are buried in which cemetery. One that I came across for Gate of Heaven yielded a handful of names: congressmen, mafiosi, a run-of-the-mill baseball pitcher, the tragic figure of Karen Ann Quinlan. But even narrowing my search from "very famous" to "somewhat famous" produced no mention of Cahill, the "father of American soccer," the man whose life I'd spent the last several months trying to piece together. It wasn't a surprise. Only a few weeks earlier I had trawled the newspaper archives for his obituary and found one under the headline **Hockey Pioneer Dies.**

Finding his grave didn't turn out to be difficult, even if there probably isn't a more inconspicuous marker in the cemetery. But as I stood there, vaguely somber and uncomfortably self-conscious, it occurred to me that nobody aware of Cahill's place in soccer history might ever have stood here before, at least not since the day they laid him to rest in 1951. After all, how many even knew who he was when the sport itself seemed to struggle with honoring his memory?

As I walked back to the car, I remembered the minutes from the 1947 meeting of the United States Soccer Football Association, the last one Cahill attended. He was in his eighties, and they'd given him a standing ovation. A past president announced that a book would be written on Cahill's life and he was "going to go to St. Louis to get it all down." But he never did. I remembered, too, a letter Cahill had sent to Hap Meyer, the soccer obsessive from St. Louis in whose possession much of Cahill's paraphernalia would end up: scrapbooks bulging with press clippings; box upon box of photographs, match programs, and reports; trophies and trinkets from Scandinavia; tangible evidence of a life unparalleled in the history of the game. "None of my family are interested in Soccer," the letter said. "I would never part with any of what I am sending to you if my family would take good care of it after I passed away."

The family's loss was Meyer's gain. So, too, apparently, was a film reel of the 1923 National Challenge Cup final, footage Cahill had paid for out of his own pocket because no one else thought it worth the trouble. He promised Meyer he would ship it to him, but maybe he never did. Or maybe he never got the chance; maybe his indifferent family threw it out when he wasn't looking. Certainly, when Cahill's bequest—as well as Meyer's own prodigious collection—was given to Southern Illinois University Edwardsville, it was without any reels of film.

AMERICAN SOCCER has no Babe Ruth or Jack Dempsey; no Yankee pinstripes or Boston Gardens; no *Casey at the Bat* or *Monday Night Football.* But it most certainly has a history, ill-preserved and half-forgotten though it may be. Ever since I discovered the curious path the game has traced across the country's sporting landscape, I have wanted to chronicle it, to tell the story as best I can. The initial result, *Soccer in a Football World: The Story of America's Forgotten Game,* was first published in 2006. But in my research for that book, I soon became aware that the broad story I was aiming to tell would need to leave out a lot of important details. The more I thought about this, the more I realized that many of the details were actually themes in their own right—worthy diversions from the main narrative. Taken collectively, they, too, might tell the story of the game, in a less linear fashion.

For me—and for many others, I suspect—the history of soccer in America is more a story of what didn't happen than what did. It's especially true of its first hundred years, and it certainly applies to the seven chapters of this book, the notion of what might have been but couldn't ever be: a glass-roofed soccer stadium in St. Louis, the Oakland Clippers touring the world, 100,000 for an Open Cup final, soccer burning brightly in America's sporting firmament. There were those who thought it could happen.

And yet when Landon Donovan scored in the dying moments against Algeria at the 2010 World Cup, America screamed itself hoarse. This wasn't something it was used to doing for soccer, particularly for an event thousands of miles distant. All the same, much of the country had worked its Wednesday morning breakfast around the match or even taken the day off. Sports bars opened early to accommodate hordes of painted fans. People talked about the game in the office; they posted videos of their celebrations on YouTube and e-mailed, blogged, and Twittered just as they did for more familiar occasions.

That the World Cup has caught on in America is now beyond question—and the time it has taken to do so has followed a resolute logic. People my age who were impressionable teenagers when Pelé appeared for the New York Cosmos were carting their kids off to soccer practice when the United States hosted the 1994 World Cup. By the time Donovan was rescuing his team from elimination in Pretoria, some of us were looking after grandchildren. In the lifetime of our generation, soccer has changed from a sort of foreign perversity to a cause for national celebration. We are the first to have grown up with the game in much the way the rest of the world has been doing.

This evolution—it's certainly no phenomenon—would scarcely have been possible had the World Cup come out of nowhere, as it may seem to have done for many Americans. The tournament mattered so much in 2010 not just because it was bigger and the hopes of the United States were higher, but because the national team had appeared in each of the previous five tournaments, because twenty years had passed since Bob Gansler's squad of raw collegians made it to Italy in 1990. Without historical foundations, any sport struggles for recognition. The World Cup has helped to lay down some of them, but so, too, have the Cosmos and the Clippers, clubs that put a stake in the ground and dared to think big. And as I hope this book makes clear, there have been others like Cahill who tried to do the same, if with less enduring success.

As the desire to follow soccer has grown, so has interest in its history. A generation or two ago, few Americans were even aware that the United States had managed to defeat England at the 1950 World Cup. Now many fans can name every member of the team that did it. The more demonstrative can even purchase replicas of the jerseys they wore that day. If interest is measured by the things that you wear—and it certainly seems to be the case these days—then soccer in America has come a very long way indeed.

The headstone on Cahill's grave isn't upright. It bears only his surname, with no date of birth or death. There had been no need for me to visit. But as I pulled out of the cemetery parking lot and pointed the car toward Interstate 287, there wasn't a doubt in my mind the diversion had been worth it.

A Note on Terminology

FOR THOSE who are unfamiliar with American soccer history, a brief comment on terminology may be helpful. The national governing body has undergone a confusing number of name changes. The United States Soccer Federation (or US Soccer, as it likes to call itself) changed its name from the United States Soccer Football Association in 1974. It was known as the United States Football Association until 1945. The references in this book to the USFA, USSFA, and USSF are all to the same organization.

Acknowledgments

F OR ANY JOURNEY through American soccer history, there have been two obligatory stops: the National Soccer Hall of Fame in Oneonta, New York, and the Lovejoy Library at Southern Illinois University Edwardsville. I have managed to spend time in both these places but feel I have only begun to come to grips with the wealth of material they hold. I therefore owe a considerable debt of gratitude to Jack Huckel and George and Peggy Brown—three of the most obliging people I have ever met—for putting my time in Oneonta to maximum use, and to Steve Kerber and Amanda Bahr-Evola at Edwardsville, especially for the use of the photographs in this book. Unfortunately, since my last visit the Hall of Fame has been forced to close its doors; it is unclear at the time of writing where the obligatory stops will be in future.

For their help in providing research material, thanks are due to Robin Carlaw at the Harvard University Library; the Cincinnati Public Library; Mickey Cochrane and the University of Maryland Libraries; Wallace Dailey at the Harvard College Library; the Enoch Free Pratt Library in Baltimore; Sarah Hartwell at the Rauner Special Collections Library of Dartmouth College; Nancy Miller at the University of Pennsylvania Archives; Mary O'Brien of the Syracuse University Archives; and, in particular, Paul Dzyak of the Special Collections Library at Penn State University and the Wisconsin Historical Society Library in Madison, whose newspaper archive is surely one of the wonders of the Midwest. Up in Canada, Colin Jose continues to answer my e-mails with diligence and patience; I am grateful for the decades of work he has put into researching the game, which has made writing this book immeasurably easier. For their assistance here in Britain, I acknowledge the Bellfield Library in Kilmarnock, Jean Campbell at Thurso Library, Rob Cavallini, Denis Clarebrough, Graham Curry, Helen Darling at Galshiels Library, Margaret Heron at the Moray Heritage Centre, Peter Holme at the National Football Museum in Preston, and Michele Lefevre of the Leeds City Council. And for their help in various capacities, I am indebted to Derek Liecty, Zoran Mrdjenovic, Barbara Ryan, Edward Ryan, Heidi Saunders, Samo Toplak, Clive Toye, WSC Books, and Nick Zentner.

A number of people read through various parts of the manuscript, including Roger Allaway, Gabe Logan, Ross Parker, Gunnar Persson, Lee Stout, Mike Ticher, Alex Usher, and Michael Volkovitsch. I am very grateful for their advice and encouragement. I am also grateful to Sue Deeks and Lynne Frost for their help in knocking the pages into shape. And for their interest in American soccer history and for allowing me to write about it, thanks are due to Temple University Press and, especially, Micah Kleit.

My deepest gratitude, though, is to Anne, whose encouragement, forbearance, and support—through some indescribably dark days—have kept me upright, somehow, when I felt certain of falling. A remarkable achievement from a remarkable woman. And for far more than the room and board that helped me to finish the manuscript, I am very much indebted to my father, whose remarkable coaching career includes one rather less celebrated season in charge of the University of Chicago soccer team. It is to him this book is dedicated, with all my love.

1

"Here They Come!"

Pilgrims, Corinthians, and the "Foreign Game" as Invader

We have come over here not so much to win games, although we have managed to do that with pretty fair regularity. We are making this tour because we want to show Americans how football ought to be played.

—Fred Milnes

"ASSOCIATION FOOT BALL is by no manner of means a new game in this country," wrote a contributor to Spalding's *Association Foot Ball Guide* in 1904. "[It] can be said that more or less, it has been played for a number of years, and the words 'more or less' just about explain the situation, for just when it would appear that the game was booming, petty quarrels, and the inevitable spectator stepped in, newly organized clubs lost interest, and spasmodic was the life of this, one of the grandest winter sports."

Brighter days lay ahead, according to the *Guide*—they always would— yet the game teetered in the dark for some time to come. To most of the country, "foot ball" had come to mean Americanized rugby, in all its rugged, manly glory, and under its considerable weight soccer had all but suffocated. Nowhere was this more true than on college campuses, where sports were developing a telling significance. Well before the start of the twentieth century, many of the most enduring rivalries of the gridiron had been established: Georgia–Georgia Tech, Minnesota–Wisconsin, California–Stanford, and dozens of others—headed, of course, by Harvard–Yale.

Soccer hadn't simply missed out on this attention and excitement, it had proved incapable of so much as organizing any sort of intercollegiate play. After 1876, when Columbia, Harvard, Princeton, and Yale agreed to form a rugby football association and not a soccer one, the game faded from campuses—and most of the country would never get to see it. In places like Kearny, New Jersey, and Fall River, Massachusetts, British enclaves disconnected from elite institutions of higher learning, soccer would become all the rage. But that was part of its problem.

Perhaps more to the point, it lacked violence. In an industrialized country increasingly fearful of becoming effete, aggression on the gridiron, even at the risk of serious injury, had come to be perceived as a welcome demonstration of masculinity. This wasn't necessarily limited to headlong leaps and crunching tackles. Few saw much wrong with the occasional flying elbow or closed fist, or even with Frederic Remington, the future artist and sculptor, dousing his Yale uniform in slaughterhouse blood in preparation for Saturday's game. Though nominally proscribed, stamping, gouging, hair pulling, slugging—or jumping on an opponent and breaking his collarbone, as had occurred in the infamous Harvard–Yale encounter of 1894—had become furtive tactics. The sight of sideline doctors stitching dazed combatants back together was an accepted consequence of the pursuit of glory for the alma mater.

Not everyone had been swept along. A few college presidents—most notably, Charles Eliot of Harvard—wanted desperately for the game to be removed from campus. But popular sentiment weighed against it. Far more of Eliot's number echoed the sentiments of Notre Dame's John Cavanaugh that it was better for students to play football and suffer the occasional broken collarbone than "see them dedicated to croquet." Even the nation's rough-riding president stood firmly behind the game: Theodore Roosevelt was "utterly disgusted" by Eliot's desire to ban football and "would a hundred fold rather keep the game as it is now, with the brutality, than give it up."

Periodically, though, the level of carnage, as well as the use of protoprofessional and tramp athletes and football's bloated position on campus, sparked calls for reform. But the game's leading figures, headed by Walter Camp of Yale, resisted. Critics were mollified through disingenuous "statistical" analyses of casualties as well as propaganda initiatives, underlining what Camp and his counterparts professed to be the merits of playing the game: discipline and self-sacrifice, teamwork, endeavor, and the transformation of weedy boys into strapping young men.

Of course, such virtues could be applied to a number of sports, soccer among them. But as the "college game" had demonstrably won campuses over, it was assumed to possess inherently superior qualities. After watching a soccer match between teams from Philadelphia and New York in 1894, Penn's quarterback remained convinced of his sport's superiority:

Ours is a running and tackling game. The association game is an individual game. By this I do not mean that it is not one of team work, for there is plenty of this, and in some respects there is more than in the college game. What I mean by individual is that spectators can see who is doing a particular thing, as distinguished from our game, where the men are massed and it is impossible to see, in a jumbled-up heap, the ball or the man who has it. . . . The game is exciting, but not so much so as the college game. In the association game the goal is threatened oftener, the ball changes from one side of the field to the other very rapidly. In the college game the excitement is wrought up to a greater nervous tension.

Julian Curtiss, a Yale alumnus, was more unequivocal in 1903:

I venture to say that if an Association game was played on one field and a game under the college rules was played next door, the latter would so far outdraw the former that there would be no comparison. This "tag, you're it" style of play would not draw a corporal's guard when there was a game of the other sort going on.

At the start of the twentieth century, the most likely hope for soccer—assuming it would establish itself—was not of supplanting football but of coexisting with some toned-down version of it. Reporting in 1904 that Harvard's decision to form a soccer team had "been seconded at the University of Pennsylvania," the *New York Times* noted that "rugby and association football are both popular in England, and there is no reason why they should not work together in this country."

Intercollegiate play finally arrived in April 1904, when Harvard and Haverford College of Pennsylvania faced each other in a home-and-home series. Some schools had fielded teams prior to then, but they had been left to compete against whatever opposition they could find. In 1895, the *New York Times* reported at length on Princeton's trip to Newark for a match with the Rangers club of Kearny. "Being used to [watching] a game where weight and strength count for everything," the paper noted, "they relied too much on charging, and passing and dribbling were neglected." They lost, 7–3.

But it was at Haverford where the college seed first found purchase, some two years before the encounter with Harvard. Its soccer team had taken part in matches against Philadelphia's cricket clubs and even helped them to form a league in 1903. The University of Pennsylvania could also attribute its comparatively early start to the profusion of teams in the city. Indeed, at the time, Philadelphia offered a more sympathetic home to the game than New York. In a report on a match between the Belmont club of Philadelphia and the Staten Island Cricket Club in 1902, the *New York Times* claimed that soccer was "not played much in this city" and that only around a hundred fans had attended a match that, according to the visiting team, would have brought a crowd of 500 or 1,000 to Philadelphia. Spalding's 1904 *Guide* even contended that "games are now played in Philadelphia which will compare favorably in skill and conduct with the average game in Britain."

In St. Louis, soccer was catching on just as keenly, if with less finesse. One official noted "while the St. Louis teams rated highly compared with clubs from Chicago and even Canada, it was apparent that the finer points of the game . . . were forgotten. Rough play featured almost every game and many former followers of the sport refused to continue their patronage."

The reasons for such capitulation to primitive play, in St. Louis and elsewhere, were not merely bloodlust and a lack of coaching. One of the perceived advantages of soccer was that it could—allegedly—be played right through the winter, a folly that consigned much of it to pools of mud or sheets of ice. Even in the best weather, the marginal places in which the game was played were small, uneven, and rutted, and the best chance of success on them wasn't always in maneuvering the ball methodically along the ground. Not surprisingly, chasing down ambitious long passes and beating a more direct path to the goal worked very well; in turn, this made the game seem easy enough to learn. Yet it also attracted criticism that soccer lacked the necessary "science" of the gridiron.

Fortunately, the emerging incidence of international competition—in particular, between North America and Great Britain—would begin to change perceptions. As early as 1888, a Canadian soccer team toured the British Isles; three years later, it did so again, taking part in no fewer than fifty-eight matches and including several American players in the squad. As British soccer teams were also crossing oceans with some regularity, a visit from some crack English or Scottish eleven seemed inevitable. In 1890, newspapers reported that an "international team of Scottish players" was likely to visit the eastern United States, taking on the likes of Yale, Harvard, and Columbia—whether they had teams or not—as well as more tangible opposition in Fall River and elsewhere. The plans were abandoned, apparently out of a "fear that a representative team could not be got together." But the idea was not. Sunderland, the English champion in 1892 and runner-up in 1893, announced its intention to make a North American tour in 1894, with stops from Boston to St. Louis. This, too, failed to materialize (or, at least, it took sixty years to do so; the club finally came across in 1955).

The sport of cricket was having better luck attracting British teams into the country, and a few of them, given a willing opponent and a spare afternoon, even indulged in soccer. Kent's county eleven did so against an all-Philadelphia selection during a 1903 tour. Yet the closest America had come to hosting a genuine international soccer match remained the two encounters it had staged in New Jersey with a representative Canadian team in the 1880s.

Things looked set to change the following year. Toward the end of 1904, it was reported that the Corinthians, "the foremost association football club in England" that "numbers among its members all the best known amateurs," had agreed to a North American tour. All seemed to be in order until the English Football Association got wind of the plans. One report somewhat cryptically claimed the governing body "did not look with too much favor upon the trip and probably feared that it would not be conducted on the principle of pure amateur sport, for which the Corinthians' name is so well known."

For the time being, the club stayed put. But on the heels of this disappointment, or perhaps even as a result of it, another English team announced its intention to make a North American tour and proved as good as its word.

The group, known as the Pilgrims Football Club, was more a collection of individuals than an enduring team. They bore no relation to the club of the same name from East London that had regularly entered the English Football Association Challenge Cup (the FA Cup) in the 1870s and 1880s, nor were they the former students of a college in Brighton who in 1902 had won an international tournament in Belgium as Pilgrims FC. They were, in fact, a band of "gentlemen amateurs" who, as was common at the time, played as little or as often as they cared to or as their professions permitted.

According to one U.S. publication, the sixteen players likely to feature in the squad were "not absolutely first-class" but did include "quite a number of well-known names in the football world." Among them were Tom Fitchie of Woolwich Arsenal (which became Arsenal in 1914) and Vivian Woodward of Tottenham Hotspur. Fitchie, a Scotland international, ended up staying at home, but it scarcely mattered: the nimble

Woodward, who according to the biographer Norman Jacobs was then "generally recognized as the best centre forward in the country," would average more than two goals a game on the tour. Woodward's most famous days were still to come. In the 1908 and 1912 Olympic Games, he captained England to the gold medal and over his career made seventy appearances for his country, including forty-four at an amateur level.

In America, though, not even the presence of a top-class striker could overshadow that of a baronet. As its goalkeeper, the Pilgrims had selected Sir Charles Sharpe Kirkpatrick of Closeburn, variously described as a representative of "the main line of the family to which the Empress Eugenie [wife of Napoleon III] belongs" and "a big fellow with a genial smile." As a soccer player, Kirkpatrick's pedigree seems open to question—one account describes him as "merely a spare man who butted into the team at his own request"—but to the smitten U.S. newspapers, this mattered little; he had supposedly "earned high honors at the game" and was "good at almost everything in the way of athletics."*

Preoccupied as they were with the nobleman in their midst—the *New York Times* even devoted 450 words to his hat falling off outside a hotel—the cosmopolitan press assumed Kirkpatrick to be captaining, directing, or otherwise leading his team. There are suggestions that the others became piqued by this star billing, an irritation doubtless exacerbated by the American promoters, who knew what sold newspapers. In truth, the driving force behind the Pilgrims was a twenty-seven-year-old Yorkshireman named Fred Milnes, who'd occasionally played fullback for Sheffield United but was also "in business with his father as an iron founder." Milnes's peripatetic soccer career would encompass appearances for several other clubs, including Manchester United, all of them fleeting. "He is a fair-haired young fellow of splendid physique," one account observed, "and so fond is he of the game that he has been known to play six strenuous matches in as many days."

Milnes's account of the tour, published in 1906 as *A Football Tour with the Pilgrims in America,* places the transatlantic competition firmly in the context of a sightseeing expedition rather than any mission to change America's sporting predilections, as some have claimed. The tour lasted virtually the whole of September and October, starting in Canada and swinging as far west as St. Louis. It also included excursions to Niagara

---

* The press also took a strong interest in another soccer-loving baronet, Sir Ernest Cochrane, a "noted patron of the game in England" who accompanied the Pilgrims in 1905 and donated a "valuable silver cup" for unspecified "international challenge play."

Falls and other natural wonders; visits to parks, libraries, and monuments; and tours of factories, breweries, and distilleries (to Milnes even the municipal water works of Detroit represented "one of the sights well worth seeing"). "Off the field they might be taken for members of the Moseley commission, which came from England some time ago to investigate commercial conditions," noted one of the tour's organizers. "Machine shops, car works, factories, and other industries appear to be their especial delight."

Clad in the same combination of white shirts and blue shorts as England's national team, the inquisitive visitors had little difficulty in asserting their superiority. After a 5–0 victory in Montreal, they did come unstuck against the Rangers club of Berlin (now Kitchener). Milnes, though, pointed to extenuating circumstances:

> Berlin is certainly German, and many of the residents are German, too. Our referee for this match, which was well attended, seemed more conversant with rules Made in Germany, than with English Football Association Rules, and thus his way of refereeing spoiled everything in the way of good football, and he would persist, after the first few minutes[,] in playing the game under Canadian Rules and his own thrown in. We offered to find a referee so that the game might be played correctly, but the knight of the whistle, who was also an official of the Berlin club, would not hear of it. Several times he would ask my decision on certain points, and especially what off-side was. During the game the ball was kicked out of touch, and until it came back the referee solicited more information on the rules. Imagine my surprise when suddenly an opponent came to us and said they'd scored a goal! Neither the referee nor I knew anything about the goal, but it was allowed to count as the winning goal of three, and thus our first defeat was administered.

The man in charge, a Mr. Radforth, would not be the last whistle-toting chevalier to aggravate the Englishmen. For the fifth match of the tour, against Galt FC of Ontario, Milnes asserted that although a "special referee had been chartered right away from Montreal," a local man ended up taking charge. "Of course as far as we were concerned we did not mind who the referee was, so long as he understood the rules," Milnes wrote. "However whether the 'tootler' knew our rules or not, I can't say, he certainly did not enforce them, and we soon found ourselves playing strictly Canadian rules." Urged on by a crowd of 5,000, the gold-medal winners from the previous year's Olympics managed a 3–3 draw. "We certainly got well kicked during the game," claimed Milnes, "but remembered that the best method of revenge is not to imitate the one who has done the injury."

Two days later, they crossed the border into Detroit to begin the American part of their tour. Rather ambiguously, Milnes refers to the match against a picked eleven there as the "most disappointing game of the tour . . . whether through lack of interest or some other cause I do not exactly know, although I have reason to believe it was not the former." The 10–2 trouncing may have contributed to his disappointment; or, perhaps, it was the fact that the referee turned up without a ball, leaving the players to sit around for the better part of an hour while he left to buy one. Woodward tormented the home defense, scoring five times to take his tally to thirteen goals in five games.

St. Louis, where two matches were scheduled, was expected to offer a sterner challenge, in every sense of the word. Indeed, the captain of the local all-star eleven, Phil Kavanaugh, seemed more concerned by the severity of the refereeing than the visiting team. "If the contest were fought out under the conditions which prevail in St. Louis during the regular football season, I would be almost certain of winning," he said, "but the Englishmen interpret the rules of charging differently, and do not, in general, conduct as spirited a game as we do." All the same, he believed his team had an "excellent chance to win both games," owing among other things to its "superior weight."

Certainly the St. Louisans were not light on their feet; their own season had not yet started, and most of the players appear to have been risibly out of shape. Years later, the team's center-half, "King" Finnegan, would claim that two teammates "were so obese they had to wear elastic abdominal supporters." Keeping up with the sprightly Englishmen, let alone putting the wood to them, proved a fanciful notion. The Pilgrims scored ten times without reply in the first game—and, as Finnegan recalled, left the home goalkeeper fearing for his life:

> "Gaspipe" Tully was our goalie, and what a day he had of it. Those English forwards hammered at him all afternoon. He fisted, headed and booted the shots away heroically during the first half, but the second found him exhausted. The terrific bombardment from British foes could not be held off and goals began to slip through Gaspipe's guard. Panting and all in, he fisted one away and shouted to his nearby teammates: "Say, come back here! What are you guys trying to do, get me killed?"

The intrepid Gaspipe survived the rematch—this time the score was 0–6—and was probably as relieved as anyone by a decision to shorten the halves to thirty-five minutes, apparently in deference to English complaints about the heat. Kavanaugh had complained after the first match that the referee had not been sympathetic in his interpretation of the rules. But after the second game—for which hopes had been high ("You can put all your money down that we will not only make a better showing, but will win")—he was left to concede the opposition had been "too fast and too clever for us."

The real story, though, had been the level of fan interest, which had benefited from the necessity of playing both games after major-league baseball contests. The 10,000 or so who attended the first match may have set a record for soccer in the Midwest; if so, it lasted barely a day. No one can be sure how many attended the second; it might have been 28,000, as Milnes wrote, or it may have been nearer to the 21,000 cited as the baseball attendance, which even for that sport represented the "greatest crowd seen in a St. Louis park this year." Years later, a St. Louis newspaper placed the figure at a precise 15,986, claiming that several thousand more had gate-crashed crumbling League Park after the baseball had finished. In a facility with a capacity of less than 16,000, this was no mean trick. What was clear, though, was that the Pilgrims had demonstrated a standard of play far beyond anything the city had ever witnessed—and whether through an appreciation of their talents, a fervent desire for revenge, or sheer curiosity, the public had responded in numbers soccer in America would not see again for decades. That Milnes should later reflect, "If there is a place in the U.S. where our Association game has a bright future, it is St. Louis," was hardly a surprise.

But early October was time for a major shift in the sporting calendar—or, as one newspaper mused, "It will not be long now before the gridiron will be the scene of many a fierce scrimmage, and the annual talk of whether football is a brutal game or not will be in full force." The conversations had become particularly animated that summer as a number of influential publications ran articles drawing attention to the less reputable elements of the game. It had even attracted presidential attention. Around the time the Pilgrims were leaving St. Louis, President Roosevelt met with Walter Camp and other gridiron chieftains and directed them to address the excesses of violence, cheating, and unsporting behavior he'd been reading about. The meeting had little effect (according to one account, "Camp made some considerable talk but was very slippery and did not allow himself to be pinned down to anything"), and it did little to point the sport in a new direction. Indeed, it might even have crystallized perceptions that the game was out of control. While there is no evidence to suggest the president threatened to abolish football, as is sometimes claimed, to many in the press the possibility seemed genuine.

The Pilgrims knew of the sport's perilous position. To the likes of Milnes, the American brand of football was rather superfluous ("We play the ball, not the man. There are plenty of other games where you can play the man—prize-fighting, for instance") and destined to lose out to the association game. While such an attitude may have reeked of British imperialism, soccer was certainly developing with alacrity in other parts of the world. Only the year before, the Fédération Internationale de Football Association (FIFA) had been formed.

But in Milnes's view, even American teams who had chosen the right code of football were playing it the wrong way. "The main difference in our style of play and that of the American teams we have played against is that we use heads—both literally and figuratively—to a far greater extent than they do," he claimed. "Both here and in Canada you seem to rely more upon the 'one man' play. You kick the ball much more than we and do about four times as much running." The British, naturally, knew best. Milnes wrote:

> Combined, or team play, is certainly the best method of succeeding in this game, each player working with his fellows, passing the ball from one man to another, to the disadvantage of the opposing team. Directly each player commences playing for himself and keeping the ball, the other side finds comparatively little difficulty in obtaining it, and commencing an attack themselves. One of the most important points in "Soccer" is to keep the ball on the ground as much as possible. Directly the ball is lifted it becomes far more difficult to control, with the result that an element of luck comes into the game to the exclusion of science.

Of course, on the less cultivated playing surfaces of North America there was often a good reason to elevate the ball, particularly if a lack of finesse could be overcome by greater exertion. Britain's expansive pitches did not exist within the confines of baseball parks or gridirons; in American soccer, there was often a lot less ground to cover, with or without the ball.

The two matches the Pilgrims played in Chicago illustrate this point graphically. The first, against a local all-star team, took place at a cricket ground. The Pilgrims won easily—and impressively; the *Chicago Tribune* claimed their 6–0 win had been "the greatest game Chicago has ever seen, and cleanly fought from start to finish." According to the paper, the cricket pitch, "lightning fast and thoroughly level, was admirably suited to their scientific work." The same may not have been true of other provisions. "The papers seemed quite 'tickled' because we ordered tea for refreshments at half time instead of wine, which is their custom," Milnes noted. "We were evidently giving a Temperance lesson, in addition to football, but all the same[,] the two go together."

When play moved the next day to a baseball park—the home of the White Sox—it was with dramatically different consequences. Except for a new right-back, Chicago was unchanged but their loins were girded; according to the *Tribune*, they "went after their opponents from the first whistle, rushing them off their feet, and, by aggressive playing, offset the advantage the Britons had by their slightly superior team work and combination plays." Yet they had also benefited from the "rougher ground" that had "favored [their] style of play." Within six minutes they'd taken the lead; midway through the second half, they scored again. All the English managed was a goal awarded after the Chicago goalkeeper fell into the net with the ball in his hands. Milnes claimed his team monopolized the second half with the exception of one counter-attack. But endeavor had triumphed over science, and before a sizeable crowd: according to the *Tribune*, "the attendance was the largest ever drawn out to a local association game, between 4,000 and 5,000 people being in the stands."*

From there, the Pilgrims would play three matches in Philadelphia on consecutive days. They won them all convincingly; their greatest foe seemed to be the unseasonably warm weather, which was "no joke, though the players be jokers." In winning 5–0 against the local Thistle club, the perspiring guests readily consented to shortening the second half to 30 minutes, doubtless to the relief of their overmatched hosts. The third game was played in Manheim, where an overflow crowd of perhaps 10,000 saw them trounce an all-Philadelphia selection, 5–0. "Such a crowd has not been seen at Manheim since the famous Penn–Princeton 6 to 4 game," claimed one report, referring to a gridiron contest staged there in 1892. Again, the true attendance is unknown; Milnes claimed it was 15,000, "twice the size" of a Penn–Swarthmore football game taking place the same day and something that "evidently proved that our game had 'won favour.'"

---

* Attendance estimates for matches from this era varied wildly. One newspaper reported that 16,400 had witnessed Chicago's victory.

But with whom? The arrival of the English gentlemen may have served as more of a social function than a sporting exhibition, with the city's butterflies drawn particularly to the baronet between the goalposts. Milnes noted:

> We were anxious to see how the games were reported by the press. Credit is due to most of the reporters, but one paper had evidently commissioned an inexperienced man to take notes; he devoted two columns to the Pilgrims v[ersus] "All Philadelphia" match but only about three inches alluded to the actual game. The remaining space was taken up in adequately describing the celebrities present and the lovely dresses worn. I wonder whether this man had been sent to the Lord Mayor's Ball, and had by accident wandered to the football match?

The next game could scarcely have offered more of a contrast. That Fall River, Massachusetts, a factory town of textile spindles and immigrant labor, featured at all on the Pilgrims' schedule instead of much bigger cities like Cleveland or Buffalo indicates just how popular soccer had become in what was then the country's thirty-third-largest city. None of the Northeastern metropolises left off the itinerary would likely have attracted anywhere near the 7,000 who squeezed into the cramped Fall River athletic ground, the "largest number that ever gathered on the local field." But, as Milnes noted, the occasion did not stand on ceremony:

> The reception committee to meet us was composed of one man, a real good fellow whose excitement simply bubbled over, and in consequence we had to do the best we could, but thank goodness, we did not have to stay all night. We got something to eat and then wended our way to the ground. It was certainly about the worst ground we struck throughout our travels, practically hard clay, with no grass except for a few "blades" at one end . . . at one end a big piece of rock or stone stood up, as if to say "A quarry once was here, and I'm the sole survivor." A funny—yet jolly—sort of individual informed us he was the referee, and half-way through the game he introduced himself as Mr. Pickup. He was most enthusiastic, and when at the start he found we were not in favour of goal judges, he simply revelled in the thought of "sole control of the game."

"Goal judges," stationed near the posts, were a recurring feature of early American soccer. Nets were not yet universal, but even once they were, many regarded the game as too fast for a referee and two linesmen. Against an all-Fall River eleven, the Pilgrims may have discovered how frenetic things could get: what Milnes extolled as a "ding-dong game" wasn't settled until five minutes from time, his side claiming a 4–3 victory. Hastily, the Pilgrims returned to Boston that evening "having sore feet, due to playing on the hard ground."

While the overflow crowd at Fall River was perhaps no surprise, even in less sympathetic parts of the country the English visitors also proved quite an attraction: few major-league baseball teams averaged more than 5,000 fans a game in 1905. Suddenly, soccer—or "socker," as it tended to be written—had become a focal point for the newspapers. The *New York Times* devoted half a page to the Pilgrims—and specifically to the aristocrat within their ranks ("Sir Charles Kirkpatrick is a type of the pure English country gentleman, passionately devoted to all branches of sport for sport's sake") and his wife (who regarded American football as "more of an exhibition of brute force than of genuine scientific skill"). Yet toward the sport itself the paper was less sanguine. "College coaches naturally give the American game the preference over English Association," it noted. "While admitting the many advantages of the Association game, they do not seriously consider the possibility of a displacement of the present college game." But football's advocates, it insisted, were not seeking to banish soccer; the sport "will serve a purpose entirely of its own."

Claims have been made that the Pilgrims met with President Roosevelt during their tour, and even that he'd helped to bring them across as a response to his concerns about football. Milnes and Woodward did travel to Washington with a view to being invited to the White House—so keen were they for Roosevelt to see one of their matches that they even considered organizing one in the capital—but the two parties did not meet. The president was busy preparing for a trip to the South and was only seeing those visitors with "urgent official business." Another popular assertion—that Roosevelt somehow had a hand in selecting the Pilgrim team—defies belief.*

---

* Many newspapers also reported that Milnes met President Eliot of Harvard, although the Pilgrims' captain makes no reference to this in his book and in fact writes that the team "went round Harvard University, with a guide called Purcell" but "never got inside, owing to some bungling on the part of our guide." While the campus was pleasant enough, according to Milnes, "the disappointment of not meeting the friends we were told we should meet, took a lot of the pleasure away."

So it was back to New England—this time to Boston, where, according to Milnes, they would face the "best football we had against us while abroad," a week ahead of their two games in New York. "On paper it looked a real Scotch eleven," he noted of the all-star opposition, "consisting as it did of six 'Mac's,' while the other five were thorough Scottish names, and their centre forward was none other than the famous J. W. Gillespie, late of Manchester City, the team that won the English Cup the previous year." Though the irrepressible Woodward scored almost from the kick-off, the "Greater Boston" eleven dominated much of the rest of the first half, conceding its other four goals only as it fell away in the second. "It was expected that the local aggregation would make a better showing than it did," read one report, "but the light New England players, although very speedy and abreast of their opponents in individual play, proved no match for the stalwart Englishmen, with their well-nigh perfect teamwork."

Nothing, though, stirred the sporting emotions of Bostonians quite like the football team at Harvard, and it proved especially true that autumn. While the Crimson had won its first five games, holding opponents scoreless in four of them, censure of the sport was reaching fever pitch. On October 18, the *Harvard Bulletin* published an article reflecting the views of certain exasperated alumni:

> Something is the matter with a game which grows more and more uninteresting every year, which takes the time and attention, not only of the player, but also of the undergraduates as a body until for weeks they talk and think about nothing but football, which requires the constant attention of skilled surgeons who conduct on the field what one of the most eminent has called a hospital clinic, which injures men so that they are crippled for weeks and in some cases permanently unfit for athletic exercise. . . . We do not want . . . ladylike games or to give up any form of athletics because it may cause injuries. Rowing, baseball, lacrosse, and association football are strenuous enough, and have a moderate risk of injury, but no one objects to them. When, however, a game becomes so dangerous that several players are sure to be hurt in every contest between two teams it is time to admit that something is wrong.

Something was indeed wrong. But it would take two tragic incidents, both on the last day of the season, to shake the game out of its complacency.

It was probably just coincidence that the *Bulletin*'s polemic appeared just days before the Pilgrims were to play in New York. Yet its appearance in many of the city's newspapers did nothing to dispel the notion of soccer as a potential alternative to the gridiron. In its report of the Pilgrims' 7–1 victory over an all–New York eleven, the *New York Times* noted:

> It was a clean, well-played contest, bristling with clever passing, intricate dribbling, capital dodging, and exceptionally hard kicking. Unlike the American college game, no time was lost in tending the injured, and not an unpleasant incident marred the display. It was a gratifying introduction of the English game to the New York public, and judged by the expressions, during and after the match, it is destined to occupy a high place in American sports.

Not all those present agreed. One of them was Bozeman Bulger of the *New York World*:

> Association football as it is played in England will never endanger the popularity of baseball or American football in the United States. It sounds nice and magnanimous to say encouraging things about the missionary trip of the English team in this country, but you can't fool the American sport lover, who likes science and excitement. You've got to satisfy his tastes, and the Pilgrims didn't do it. "Socker" football affords a very quiet afternoon's entertainment, but it seems more enjoyable to the player than to the spectator. There was a large crowd of Englishmen out in the Polo Grounds who enjoyed seeing a sport that reminded them of home, but the knowledge seeking New Yorkers failed to enthuse. I took occasion to question twelve American spectators. Seven of that number said they would take a game of baseball or college football for theirs.

Before 3,000 at the Polo Grounds, the home all-stars—as rife with Scottish surnames as Boston's—had given a "good exhibition" and "at no time were disgraced." But they had been outclassed: James Raine, the Pilgrims' diminutive outside-right, scored three goals, and Woodward, who added two of his own, produced "the cleverest exhibition of 'socker' play the critics had ever seen."

The tour was nearly at an end—the Pilgrims would spend part of the next day visiting a fire station in Brooklyn "to see some of the wonders of electricity"—but there was still an important match to play. For soccer to make any real imprint on America, it needed to connect with the college campuses, yet the dearth of college teams made this difficult to achieve. The Pilgrims would have to make do with a collection of past and present students who constituted a nominal University of Pennsylvania eleven—and whom they overwhelmed 10–0. Though a sizeable crowd had assembled on the Franklin Field gridiron for the occasion, they were, according to the *New York Times,* far from won over:

> A crowd of 5,000 persons, mostly devotees of the intercollegiate football game, were in the north and south stands, eager to note a comparison between the Red and Blue team and the British players. It was a hypercritical crowd, too, as it evidently looked upon the imported game as an invader. The student body of Pennsylvania, which completely filled two sections of the south stand, were derisive in their cheering. This was not aimed at the visitors, but at the sorry showing of Penn's team.

Or perhaps the sport itself. The perception of soccer as an invader was understandable, and while only the most partisan dared give serious thought to substituting football with an "import," the deeper it fell into disrepute, the less ridiculous the notion became.

The conclusion to the 1905 season did little to improve football's standing. Critics heaped scorn on a number of violent episodes, the most conspicuous of which occurred at the Harvard–Yale game on the last day of the season. A Yale player racing toward an opponent who was attempting to fair-catch a punt was seen to punch him full in the face. The official closest to the incident—who also happened to be chairman of the rules committee—not only failed to throw the assailant out of the game but did not call a penalty. As blood poured from the stricken player's nose, Harvard's coaching staff and fans reacted with outrage. One prominent alumnus passed a note to the Crimson bench demanding that the team be removed from the field.

That same day, an even more tragic event—and one with more lasting significance—took place in New York City. In attempting a tackle, a player from Union College of New York was struck on the head and died a few hours later from a brain hemorrhage. The chancellor of the opposing school, New York University, reacted to the episode with horror. Determined to take action but frustrated in his attempts to do so through conventional channels, he convened a number of football-playing colleges with a view toward either reforming or abandoning the game.

By then, some had already reached their decision. Columbia, the largest university in the country at the time, dropped the sport over Thanksgiving break, not long after police had stepped in to break up a melee in its game with Wesleyan. The trouble had begun when a Wesleyan defender was seen to kick Columbia's ball carrier in the stomach; matters hadn't been helped by the Lions' own coach running onto the field and taking aim at the assailant.

Faculty at other colleges were more ambiguous, though the voice of the student body was not. In the Midwest, one of the more visible opponents was Frederick Jackson Turner of the University of Wisconsin, who came close to persuading the school to drop football. John Sayle Watterson, in his book *College Football: History, Spectacle, Controversy*, describes the students' fevered response:

> On the night of March 27 students gathered on campus armed with rifles and revolvers and began to march toward faculty residences shouting "death to the faculty." When the arch foe of football appeared on his front porch, voices cried out, "When can we have football?" to which Turner quickly replied, "When you can have a clean game." Unwilling to back down, Turner shouted above the din, "It's been so rotten for the last ten years that it is impossible to purge it." His words were then lost in the hisses and calls of "Put him in the lake." Luckily for Turner, the students lost interest and moved on to other houses before disbanding. Still, his was one of three faculty members' effigies burned before the morning.

There would be football at Wisconsin in 1906, if rather less of it; the team played five fewer games than in 1905. But a number of other colleges, including Arizona, Baylor, Nevada, Northwestern, South Carolina, and Temple, gave it up altogether. Most conspicuously, California and Stanford replaced it with rugby and would not reintroduce it until the 1910s.

Was football's existence genuinely under threat? Certainly, it seemed unlikely to survive in its existing guise, regardless of the intransigence of Camp and his allies. Rule changes introduced during the winter of 1905–1906, which included the provision of a forward pass, did help, but the hazardous pushing and pulling of mass plays remained. While most of the schools that dropped football reintroduced it over the next few years, critics remained wary—and it did not take coaches long to discover new ways to exploit advantages in size and weight. Many of them did not care to throw the ball forward or spread out play.

Soccer's gains on campuses during this period were modest. Some, like the formation of an Intercollegiate Association Football League, had been in hand before the Pilgrims' visit. Milnes donated a trophy that for a number of years was awarded to the champion. The league, consisting of Columbia, Cornell, Harvard, Haverford, Penn, and Princeton, put together its first schedule in February 1906 (though many teams played practice matches before then). In the final game of a brief U.S. tour in December 1905, the University of Toronto faced Penn in Philadelphia; though winning 5–1, the Canadians had been "delighted and surprised at the good game played by the Red and Blue." Princeton withdrew from this league before the season began—they'd been forbidden from playing away from home—but other schools, including Yale, soon joined.

In the Midwest, the University of Chicago flirted with soccer. Under an English-born tutor, it staged exhibition matches ahead of the football team's games with Illinois and Michigan in 1905. Harvard even expressed an interest in meeting the Maroons over Easter. But Chicago's athletic director, for reasons that aren't clear, refused to sanction a varsity program and even repudiated the team that had represented the school. Not until 1906 did the Midwest stage a sanctioned intercollegiate soccer match, and then between the less conspicuous representatives of Elmhurst and Knox. Other schools that formed teams had to make do with playing in local leagues or inter-class tournaments.

Alongside the hundreds of institutions that continued to play football, such progress was barely perceptible. But it was encouraging, as were developments away from the universities. In the nation's largest city, one paper noted that, although there was a soccer league, "the general public paid no heed to the sport until the advent of the Pilgrims team." Another claimed that, "owing to the great interest aroused in 'socker' football by recent visit of the Pilgrim team," eastern clubs were "agitating a movement to have intercity matches arranged between the best players of the leagues of New York and Philadelphia." Proposals had also been put forward "to form a national organization of association football interests, and to affiliate with the Amateur Athletic Union." In Chicago, a Western Association Football League was being mooted with the intention "to arrange a series of matches to decide the western championship."

There was also more tangible progress, as the historian Gabe Logan notes:

> Following the Pilgrims' visit Chicago soccer saw significant growth in the adult leagues and nascent development in academic sponsored soccer. The Chicago Football Association grew from six first division clubs in the fall to 15 the following spring. The University of Chicago, Elmhurst College and Englewood High School commenced playing friendlies around the city. Likewise, Northwestern University invited the Chicago Football Association's Hyde Park Blues and Calumet Reds to demonstrate soccer at their Evanston athletic fields.

If this was a rather restrained advance, at least the game ran no risk of burning out as a fad. But any notion that soccer would overtake gridiron remained dubious—indeed, no sport, however manly, "scientific," or otherwise desirable, stood much of a chance. This became blindingly apparent in November 1905, when Harvard, doubtless induced by the lamentations of the *Bulletin* a few weeks earlier, took the unusual step of staging an exhibition of rugby between two Canadian teams. "Five years ago," wrote the *New York Times,* "any suggestion that the alumni and undergraduate body at Harvard would consider a substitute for the present game would have been ridiculed." But even the brawn and ferocity of this code carried little favor. The contest, which ended in a 3–3 tie, "fell flat," according to the paper, and "in the opinion of the undergraduate is 'tame.'" Rugby football, the *Times* concluded, "lacks the vim and dash and spirit of the American game, and in no way appeals to the college man who is used to an entirely different style of play. . . . If the students exert any influence the game will never be heard of again." That same day, Harvard's football team lost 12–6 at Penn, a defeat attributed in no small measure to the fact that the hosts had watered the field just before kickoff so they could wear longer cleats than their foes'. The Crimson's center was also disqualified for punching his opposite number in the face, having apparently grown tired of being kneed by him in the groin.

If rugby was not rugged enough for the gridiron, what chance did soccer have? Writing in October 1905, the *Washington Post* asserted that "Herculean efforts to make socker football popular in the East have thus far failed to create more than an impression" and, while accepting the game was a safer alternative, noted "a difference of opinion as to the interest it can arouse among the enthusiasts."

Some were not aroused in the slightest. A few even took Milnes to task over his blithe predictions of the gridiron game's demise (he'd claimed there was "little doubt that the outcome of our tour will be the adoption of the British style of play in the States"). The *Oakland Tribune* rejected soccer out of hand:

> A few teams may have been formed to play soccer exclusively, but Captain Milne [*sic*] has another think coming when he says that socker will entirely supersede the game as now played. Football has received some pretty hard knocks the present year, and it may be that the pressure brought to bear by President Eliot of Harvard, and a few others, will have the effect of causing the introduction of modification of the rules and possibly the discontinuation of the sport at the Cambridge institution, but it is a certainty that the dull and uninteresting socker will never take its place.

The oddly Darwinian reaction of the University of Chicago's Amos Alonzo Stagg carried a familiar air of complacency:

> The English association football game cannot be used in this country to displace the present game because American colleges have chosen the style of play that is in vogue here. Natural selection determines the form of sport or game followed in every community. . . . I should not consider seriously the proposal to try to substitute the association game of football for the game now followed in this country. Whatever dangers and brutality there may be in the game here is an accepted part of it. The players enter into and the spectators watch the contests with the understanding that they are to take the dangers with the fascinations.

Yet Stagg was certainly not anti-soccer and even backed a movement to bring intercollegiate play to the Midwest. The game could also lay claim to one or two converts from the gridiron. Jake Stahl, a major-league first baseman who had captained the football team at Illinois, valiantly asserted that "this English soccer game will take place of the present college game. . . . [I]t is fully as spectacular and not half so dangerous as the old rugby style."

The debate certainly did not end once the Pilgrims returned to England; in some ways it had only begun. Before the first intercollegiate league season had finished in the spring of 1906, the Corinthians revived their interest in visiting North America. With the financial support of the *People,* a British newspaper, they arrived in August for a seventeen-game tour.

Much like the Pilgrims, the Corinthians were a group of well-to-do amateurs who could pursue the game as an avocation ("There is no fixed rule defining a member's qualifications, but there is an unwritten law confining election to Old Public School Boys or members of a university, playing merit, of course, being essential"). But unlike the Pilgrims, they were a permanent entity, formed in 1882 partly as a response to England's repeated losses to Scotland in the annual international match. So swift was the club's rise to prominence that in 1884 they handed an 8–1 loss to Blackburn Rovers, the English cup holders and one of the strongest teams in the country.

By the turn of the century, though, victories against top teams, let alone anything lopsided, proved harder to come by, and the Corinthians turned their attention to other parts of the world. They visited South Africa in 1897 and 1903 and Central Europe and Scandinavia in 1904; four months before heading to North America, they went to the Netherlands and Germany. While the team that sailed from Liverpool in August 1906 may not have been the strongest the club had known, Rob Cavallini's chronology *Play Up Corinth* maintains that it was "probably the finest Corinthian team to ever leave the British Isles." The American press treated it with reverence. "Their style has always been unique and has never been absent, even in the club's worst years," one report claimed. "There is plenty of life and go, and the team gives the most finished exhibition of association football of any organization in the world."

The team's first five matches were played in Canada, with only the Huron club of Seaforth offering much resistance. One of the touring players recalled:

> It was the irony of fate that on the hottest day in the Canadian summer, the Corinthians should have to meet Seaforth, the champion team of Canada; add to this a narrow ground, an early kick-off in the heat of the day, an offside goal allowed; and there is some excuse for the result, a draw of one goal-all. . . . The Corinthian forwards were very much hampered by the small ground and could not open out the game as they usually do.

The first American match came three days later, on the campus of the University of Chicago. The local all-star opposition bore a strong resemblance to the all-Chicago team that had beaten the Pilgrims the year before. But on the broad, even surface of Marshall Field the guests made themselves at home and won, 5–2.

Curiously, there was no venture into St. Louis; instead, the club traveled east to Cincinnati. Unfazed by having lost all their luggage en route, and playing in unfamiliar togs, they won 19–0 against the local Shamrock club. An 8–0 win in Cleveland and three similarly lopsided victories in Philadelphia followed. ("There seems to be no limit to what the Britons can do," one reporter gasped. "The harder they have to work, the better they can do it.") At Manheim, the Albion club of Philadelphia was "content to rest mainly on the defensive and pack their goal" and limited the damage to nine unanswered goals; a more daring all-Philadelphia eleven lost 12–0.

While all this suggests the Corinthians may have been a stronger team than the Pilgrims—or at least a less merciful one—with no baronet in their ranks they received much less newspaper attention than their predecessors. On reaching New York there was no half-page write-up waiting for them in the *New York Times,* and they played not at the Polo Grounds but at the less familiar Staten Island Cricket and Tennis Club. In the first of two matches there, a team of "the best university players in America and England" and captained by an American studying overseas at Cambridge lost 11–1. Yet the match may not have been the centerpiece of the occasion: the half-time interval stretched to eighteen minutes to allow the teams to take tea in the ladies' pavilion, and the British ambassador was on hand to exchange pleasantries (he apparently "saw no reason why Association football should not flourish in this country along with the American football, as he did not think it would ever supplant the latter").

By the *New York Times*'s reckoning, though, this contest was merely a curtain raiser to the one that would take place at the same venue two days later. The pairing of the Corinthians with an all-star team from the New York state association was "the most important of the Britishers' tour, as they will be opposed by one of the strongest 'soccer' organizations in the United States." So seriously did the state association treat this contest that it held a series of trial matches to help pick the team, one that then warmed up with a 3–0 win over the collegians.

The showdown with the Corinthians drew 5,000—considerably more than had seen the Pilgrims at the Polo Grounds—but it was hardly the feast of competition the *Times* had anticipated. In the first half, the visitors ran up a 5–0 lead; in the second, they scored thirteen times more as the New Yorkers displayed "signs of lack of condition," according to the *Sportsman.* More likely they had exhausted themselves in futile pursuit of the ball; the paper claimed that the pitch had been made ten yards wider from the previous match and that the margin of victory was "in no small way due to the widened ground."

For the *Times,* the lopsided score had not spoiled the occasion; rather, it had been "a remarkable illustration of the scientific points of the 'soccer' game." But converts were few; the audience was "mainly composed of Britishers, who cheered the British team as goal after goal was scored with painful regularity to the home eleven."

For a recently organized team from Newark—beaten 7–1—the agony proved almost as excruciating; the home eleven "appeared to have a case of stage fright, the fast, and dazzling field work of the visitors completely nonplusing them." Three of the Corinthians then returned home—and the twelve who remained struggled through the final two games, apparently sapped by the alien summer heat. "Had this weather been cold, we would have been able to continue almost indefinitely," claimed the club's captain, Charles Wreford-Brown.* Now, though, came a match in Fall River, on the same narrow patch of hard ground the Pilgrims had found so unsatisfactory, and with no sign of any autumn chill. That the local eleven managed to win was not altogether surprising, though few could have expected the 3–0 score line. The *Sportsman* stood ready with excuses, including the assertion that the local referee was "not sufficiently accustomed to the rules of the game."

Plenty had been prepared to at least bend the rules. Having grasped that the English were easier to contain on a narrow pitch, Boston's Fore River Rovers had prepared their Locust Street ground accordingly. It left the Corinthians, as one player recounted, with little choice but to compromise their tactics:

> A wretched ground had been chosen for the match, and what was more curious it had actually been reduced in width for the game from 66 yards to 56, which was hardly a sportsmanlike action. Decent football was out of the question on such a rough, narrow patch. The game, which ended in a draw of one all, consisted throughout in a high kick and rush business. The Corinthians started by trying their ordinary game of short passing and keeping the ball low, but at length relinquished it for the only style of game which promised success.

---

* Some sources credit Wreford-Brown for coining the term "soccer"—the association code's equivalent to "rugger" for rugby.

The team's manager had few happy memories of the occasion:

> They had evidently learned at Boston that the Corinthians had
> lost the game at Seaforth because the grounds were so small, and
> there was every indication at Boston that the ground had been
> deliberately shortened in order to embarrass the Corinthians, and
> we have made a complaint upon that score, which is now being
> investigated. In fact, all the Corinthians felt sore at the way they
> have been treated in Boston. While everywhere in Canada and at
> most places in the United States we were splendidly received, at
> Boston not the slightest effort was made in any quarter to look
> after the team. This was the more surprising because our men
> included the best Oxford and Cambridge players, who would nat-
> urally expect some welcome from the great American university
> town, the more so after the magnificent reception given the Har-
> vard men at Cambridge.

The tour was at an end—and financially it had flopped. While the *People*
had expressed an intention to "devote any profits to presentation of cups
for competition in Canada and America," it had been foiled by "indifferent" attendance. But the game appeared to be catching on. Wreford-
Brown claimed that in the fourteen years since he had last visited the
country, interest had developed from where soccer was little known to
where the Corinthians had found themselves up against "really good
teams." Not that British supremacy was under any sort of threat. "We do
not wish to offer any excuses for our defeat at Fall River . . . for the showing made by our team on the following day," he insisted, "but it is surprising to me how the members of the team stood the weather the way
they did. It has been excessively hot, and we are really not used to such
weather. We played too many games, and are all tired out."

A less guarded assessment from one of the players appeared in the
Sportsman a few weeks later:

> Seaforth, Fore and Fall River, with their style of play peculiarly
> adapted to the style of ground, would always be difficult sides to
> beat, but it is to be hoped that Canadian and American football will
> not develop on those lines. And thus it is open to question whether
> the tour has been altogether successful in the objects which were
> in view. From an educational and spectacular standpoint, the game
> suffered in most places from these unfavourable conditions. It is

certain that if Association football is to flourish alongside of American football—for supplant it it never can—at any rate in the colleges more attention must be paid to the ground question, so that the game has every chance of developing as an exposition of scientific combination and not as a kick-and-rush business.

Scant attention would be paid to "the ground question" for a long time to come. But those disposed toward soccer could be forgiven for thinking the two sets of British visitors had helped the game to pass some sort of landmark. "Association football has won thousands of admirers on the strength of the brilliant exhibition of the favorite English game by the Corinthians," the *Washington Post* claimed. "Apart from the many objections urged on all sides against the American college game, there is abundant room for a game which can be played all through the winter, and which appeals to every youth of normal physical powers. There is, in fact, no need to compare association football with other games. It has many merits which are all its own."

But who was interested in acquainting themselves with them? Certainly not the press, who preferred the familiarity of the gridiron. Soccer manifestly lacked football's sense of occasion, particularly on campus, where the few collegiate contests it could muster were utterly overshadowed by the gridiron equivalents. Hopes that the Pilgrims would raise the game's profile with a second tour—just weeks after the Corinthians' visit—were dashed when the team backed out, apparently owing to "the illness of the promoter on this side of the pond." Wreford-Brown had vowed to bring across a combined Oxford and Cambridge team in 1907 but never did. Nor did anything come of plans to send an "All-American" college selection to London in April 1907 (the week before the FA Cup final). In the meantime, the six Intercollegiate League schools met with a "short season of disaster," according to the *New York Times.* "It was not that the game has not a strong support at Yale, Harvard, Princeton, Pennsylvania, Columbia, Cornell and other colleges," the paper claimed, "but lack of experience on the part of the officials, absence of proper support by the athletic authorities, and the breaking up of athletic relations between colleges were the contributory causes." Penn had decided not to play Harvard at any sport in the wake of the gridiron field-soaking incident and questions over the eligibility of a number of players at Columbia had led to soccer being dropped for the year.

If the British visits had lit a torch for soccer, many seemed content to let it burn out. Cornell's plans to tour Brazil in the summer of 1908 were scrapped after several key players (all of them foreign-born) were refused permission to travel because "they were behind in their schoolwork." Columbia announced an intention set to send its team on a tour of English colleges but never did; plans for Haverford to tour the Midwest were abandoned; and Harvard is still to play its first soccer match against the University of Chicago. "Football of the soccer variety could be made an entirely popular sport in this country were it managed right," sighed one writer, hardly the last to make such a claim.

Yet the fire flickered. The National Association Foot Ball League, a semiprofessional circuit centered in New Jersey, had disappeared amid the economic crisis of 1898 but returned in 1906 with a record number of teams. By 1907, St. Louis was operating no fewer than nine separate leagues, and around thirty teams were playing in Chicago, some in a circuit popular enough to charge admission. A match between teams from New York and Philadelphia on the first day of 1906 attracted 6,000 to Manhattan's Equitable Park, reportedly "one of the biggest crowds ever seen at a contest of this character." As far away as Seattle, the formation of a Pacific Coast Association Football League had generated proposals to stage games "between picked teams from Portland, Tacoma, Seattle, Vancouver, Victoria and possibly Nanaimo and Ladysmith, and a picked eleven from the California Football Association." Even in the most unlikely places—Butte, Montana, for instance—soccer found itself with "many devotees," and teams were "found practicing almost every night." One widely circulated report claimed that James Sullivan, the august secretary-treasurer of the Amateur Athletic Union, had "made the prediction that in the course of a few years there would be more soccer than intercollegiate football teams in this country." This would have belied his earlier view that colleges would not "adopt it for our game" and that rugby was a more likely gridiron substitute.

But many believed that college football had put its house in order after its troubled 1905 season, having at last agreed to meaningful revisions in its rules. The next three seasons passed without a catastrophe—and the six biggest contests of 1907 were said to have generated $300,000 in gate receipts. All the same, the game still consisted of frequent displays of brute force and the treacherous pushing and pulling of mass plays. There was nothing to prevent a team from spending most of the afternoon collectively forcing the ball carrier across the line of scrimmage or repeatedly directing an attack at a vulnerable defender.

In 1909, tragedy threw the sport into crisis once again. In a game at West Point, an Army tackle, targeted all afternoon as the weak link in the defensive line (and, according to one account, "virtually dead on his feet" after Army's coach refused to substitute him) ended up with a dislocated vertebrae. Unconscious when removed from the field, he died in hospital the next morning. Two weeks later in Washington, D.C., a ball carrier from the University of Virginia collapsed in a pile-up and died of a brain hemorrhage. Army and Virginia canceled the rest of their schedules; so did Georgetown, Virginia's opponent that day, and North Carolina, who would have played them the following week. Harvard, the opposition on Army's fateful day, did not.

Enough was enough for some. "So-called 'intercollegiate football' has been killed beyond the possibility of a resurrection by its own most ardent votaries," claimed one writer, who thought that soccer would "undoubtedly be the football sport of the future all over the country as soon as the people ha[d] passed through a term of education and underst[ood] it." This kind of rhetoric may have been aimed more at discrediting gridiron than promoting an alternative. But the college game had again been sent hurriedly into conference.

It had only been a few weeks before the start of the 1909 college season that the Pilgrims, having accepted a $10,000 offer from a consortium in St. Louis, returned for a second tour. (Their "amateur" status did not preclude them from accepting 25 percent of the tour's gate receipts or a £200 guarantee.) There were to be no matches in Canada, just twenty-two in the United States, spread across just forty-five days. Milnes returned to captain the side but with an entirely new set of players. There was no Woodward, who'd left Tottenham to focus on his architectural practice (though he'd sign for Chelsea before the year was out). But Tom Fitchie, expected to partner him on the 1905 tour, did make the trip this time. Like Milnes, the Edinburgh-born Fitchie was something of a freelance amateur, joining and leaving teams with dizzying frequency.

Milnes prepared for a sterner test from his American foes:

Four years ago we came to this country as missionaries in what we sincerely believe to be a good cause and we have been more than pleased over the satisfactory reports of the steady advance of your players since then. . . . Who knows but we may have something to learn from our trans-Atlantic cousins? If so we shall be apt pupils and ready to face defeat like good sportsmen. But I have been favoured by the co-operation of some very clever talent. The team that accompanied me is in every respect a strong one and will take a lot of beating.

They did indeed take a lot of beating: the first five opponents fell by a combined score of 47–0. But on unsympathetic playing fields, against teams that perfected the "kick-and-rush business," outcomes were less certain. At a baseball park in Trenton, New Jersey, a local all-star team only lost 2–1 despite playing much of the first half with just ten men. The *Trenton Evening Times,* exalting the Pilgrims as "unquestionably the greatest aggregation of soccer-football players ever gotten together on one club," claimed that the local team had narrowly missed out on a $100 award the tourists had offered to the first team that could beat them and that the local outside-left was entitled to $25 for scoring a goal against them. Other reports claimed the Pilgrims had offered a trip to England to the first team they lost to, though talk of such prizes seems to have been limited to the more provincial press.

One week later, an eleven from Gillespie, Illinois, forty miles east of St. Louis, ran the tourists even closer. The local Thistle club was said to have benefited from the presence of two "former stars of the soccer game from England" and other British migrants employed in the coalmines. The account in Spalding's 1910 *Guide* suggests the match was one of the most interesting of the tour:

> This was a terrific draw battle, each side scoring a single goal. It was played in a downpour of rain, which made the field heavy with mud. In spite of the bad condition of the field the men played great foot ball. It was a case of science and skill on the part of the Britishers and science and strength on the part of the rugged miners, who had practiced a month for the fray. The Americans tried hard to beat the Pilgrims, and in the last ten minutes of play, had Bayley [the Pilgrims' goalkeeper] on his back most of the time, with Captain Milnes playing the most wonderful game of the trip, protecting his own and Bayley's territory brilliantly, thus preventing a decisive score by the Gillespie coal miners.

The English were also held to a draw by a strong native-born aggregation from upstate Coal City, with the whole town more or less closing down for the day so it could take in the match.

It is a pity the Pilgrims evidently didn't publish an account of their 1909 tour, especially considering some of the places in which they played: not only hardscrabble mining-town lots but also one of the most pretentious arenas in the country. What Milnes and his cohorts would have made of the Cincinnati Reds' grandiloquent "Palace of the Fans," with its private boxes and hand-carved columns, one can only wonder; that the match there, a 9–0 drubbing of a local all-star team, took place under electric lights would have made it all the more remarkable.* Curiously, the *Cincinnati Post* gave only passing reference to the "huge success" of the event—apparently a sporting first for the city—and took only slightly more interest in the gridiron contest that followed it.

Success, of course, was relative. None of the Pilgrims' matches had drawn an especially large crowd, and for the St. Louis-based promoters, the turnout for the four games they had arranged for their own city must have been bitterly disappointing. Granted, there hadn't been any baseball games to latch on to (the season was over), but fewer than 9,000 in total stumped up for tickets. With the Pilgrims outscoring the locals 31–2, fans were given little to cheer about, though the ball artistry of Fitchie, who scored seven times, left the local press spellbound. "He does with the soccer ball pretty nearly what he pleases," observed the *St. Louis Globe-Democrat*. "He seems to have magnets in his shoes which attract the ball and make it dance and jump about his shins as he dashes down the field. To see him play is to see the perfection in soccer football."

Only 1,600 had paid to watch the first match, despite the preliminary attraction of a football game ("Barnes playing the Osteopaths"). But with Fitchie's two goals inspiring a 5–0 defeat of the local Blue Bells, the paper made its allegiances clear. "The college game was slow and wearisome compared to the soccer," it wrote. "Much of the time in Rugby is consumed in arguments with the officials."

The very next day the Pilgrims took on St. Teresa, who had finished second in the city's professional league and were expected to provide a much sterner test. But short on technical ability—and hopelessly out of condition—they were left to chase shadows. The *Globe-Democrat* wrote of their 10–1 collapse:

It was distressing and almost pathetic to see the British players break down the locals' attack and rip up their defense. From the kick-off until the whistle announced the cessation of hostilities the Pilgrims bombarded the local goal almost incessantly. . . . Early in the first half the spectators realized that the contest had resolved itself into a mere exhibition for the players from England. When

---

* As early as 1885, a soccer match between teams from New York and Canada was played under lights. The Reds were the first team to host a night game in major-league baseball, but it didn't take place until 1935.

the Pilgrim backs delivered the ball to their great forwards the crowd in the ground would jump from their seats and yell: "Here they come!"

The afternoon proved particularly unsuccessful for St. Teresa's left-back, Dr. C. H. Jameson, who was credited with scoring three own-goals. "Dr. Jameson has not played a great deal of football of late," the paper noted, "and was very much distressed at the serious manner in which the Englishmen set about their task. One of [his] friends, who owns an uncommonly strong pair of lungs, advised him early in the game that he was 'behaving like a windmill.'"

By now the Pilgrims had suddenly become "amateur champions of England" in the *Globe-Democrat,* which seemed as distressed as its readers by the naked inferiority of the local opposition. Even St. Leo, winners of the professional league in each of the past four seasons (and "champions of the western states," according to Spalding's *Guide*) were made to look foolish. Though ahead only 2–0 at halftime, the Pilgrims "ran like deers and dribbled the ball like only imported players can," scoring without mercy in the second half. Whether the firmer, drier pitch suited their game or whether they took offense to St. Leo's overly physical approach, they walked off the field 12–1 winners.

No one could doubt their superiority, but as with the Corinthians, playing three and even four times a week took its toll. The Pilgrims left St. Louis with just twelve fit players—and with football under such scrutiny, it was inevitable that the injuries they'd suffered in St. Louis would attract attention. When outside-right Hector Eastwood was removed from the field during a 4–0 win over an "all-Western" eleven (one that looked remarkably similar to the one that played as St. Teresa), newspapers speculated that he might "lose the sight of that member"; little mention was made when he returned to the lineup two weeks later evidently intact.

But the Pilgrims were considerably weakened for their three games in Philadelphia—and in the first of them, a 3–0 victory over a cricket league all-star team, Fitchie broke his ankle. Two days later, having been obliged to "play on the defensive during the greater part of the game," they lost 1–0 to the Hibernian club of Kensington. No mention was made of any free trips across the Atlantic for the winners, though one account claimed, "Kensington never saw such a celebration as occurred that night within the memory of the oldest inhabitant."

Another defeat followed nine days later; not surprisingly, it took place in Fall River. Spalding's *Guide* regarded the 2–1 score line as an outcome "of which the Pilgrims can say nothing by way of specific excuse" and pointed out that the Rovers had played almost the whole second half with ten men. It had been the second of two encounters in the city—the first ended 1–1—and for both of them supporters had turned out in force. "Not only was every point of vantage taken, including the tops of all the fences and the bill sign," one account claimed, "but many must have been unable to catch more than fleeting glimpses of the play."

The enthusiasm proved more muted in Brooklyn, where the tour ended; just 450 turned up at Bay Ridge to watch the Crescent Athletic Club fall, 6–1. Two days earlier, at a minor-league baseball park, the Pilgrims had scraped a 2–2 tie with an amateur all-star team; they were "well-nigh tired out," with "several of their men scarcely fit to go on the field." Yet they could still put on a show: in the final match they had "toyed with the ball and showed a collection of clever tricks that had the Crescents bewildered."

Exhausted or not, British visitors had again provided a prodigious demonstration of soccer's appeal. To the ever optimistic Spalding *Guide,* the 1909 tour had been "the most successful of the series," attracting "far greater interest than any of the previous invasions." This was disingenuous, though, and the *Guide*'s insistence that attendance "exceeded those of former years greatly" was patently untrue: no mention was made of the fact that the promoters had lost money.

But over-enthusiasm was excusable. Not long after the Pilgrims had headed home, one of the St. Louis promoters predicted an organized league of teams "on the same line that professional baseball is conducted." Schools across the country dabbled with the game, if largely out of fear over football. Many colleges claimed to be considering a similar course of action, though most preferred to advance soccer for its own sake. Most conspicuously, plans for intercollegiate play among the major schools in the upper Midwest, encouraged by the likes of Amos Alonzo Stagg, reached their fruition in 1910. But of the major colleges, only Illinois, Chicago, and Purdue appear to have staged matches, the latter two as a curtain raiser to football. They gave up not long after that. Progress farther west was no less frustrating: one wonders how long it was before the Thanksgiving Day match between seniors and faculty at the University of Nevada, reported in 1910 as an "annual event," was discontinued.

Could it have turned out differently? For soccer to make an impression on the American sporting landscape—however tall an order—the colleges needed to respond with enthusiasm. Yet neither the Pilgrims nor the Corinthians faced a proper collegiate eleven, and they were able to appear on very few campuses. Moreover, the game in America badly lacked willful leadership; it certainly had no equivalent to the oligarchic rule of Walter Camp. Plenty of athletic departments and administrators may have thought soccer was vaguely a good thing, yet none seemed to possess the eagerness and ambition to lift it to greater prominence. Harvard and Yale's ambivalence was particularly crucial. Had matches between these two institutions been more conspicuous—and had the British tourists parlayed their skills on their respective fields—other schools might have more readily embraced the game. A logical next step would have been a league of the major athletic powers of the Midwest, but that proved excruciatingly slow to come. Not until 1991 did the Big Ten instigate a soccer championship, and then among only six of its schools.

Though all sorts of reasons have been advanced for the colleges' indifference to soccer, many of them seem to be encapsulated by a peculiar 1910 wire-service story purporting to note the reaction to a match at Penn of a "dashing girl with good rich American blood coursing through her heart":

> It is so idiotic. Now they just kick the ball right up to the point of doing something, along comes a fellow and with one foot he undoes all their labor or the fellow that stands in that hoopskirt net kicks, and someone bawls, "Well played, sir." Permit me to remark that in football it's different. Let Bill Hollenback or Danny Hutchinson get the ball on the one-yard line, third down and a yard to go, and if they don't take it across there will be half a dozen hurt. Let's go home.

Though the winter of 1909–1910 proved to be an anxious one for college football, very few schools ended up barring the sport for long. Most had been persuaded by a new series of rule changes, more measured than those of 1906, that lent greater encouragement to the forward pass and finally outlawed mass plays. As a result, speed and deception became more essential constituents of football, and the number of deaths and serious injuries fell away. By the time of Notre Dame's celebrated victory over Army in 1913, in which it deployed the forward pass to devastating effect, few expressed any doubts over the game's future.

The Corinthians made a second North American tour in 1911 and returned again in 1924.* The Pilgrims, though, were through with touring and appear to have disbanded for good after 1909. While the game in the United States may owe much to these two teams, it is tempting to read too much into their efforts. The restoration of the gridiron did not really occur at soccer's expense; even at its lowest ebb, football never faced a serious rival. Soccer would remain poorly organized, and its leaders— such as they were—lacked the sort of controlled ruthlessness that had propelled professional baseball and college football to prominence. The legacy of the Pilgrims and Corinthians is not in some forlorn attempt to oust football, or even to establish soccer as an American pastime, but merely in bringing the game to its feet.

In other parts of the world, touring British teams would make much more of an impact (one of the most popular clubs in Brazil, founded in 1910, bears the Corinthians' name). But America's sporting terrain proved rather more challenging. For most of the twentieth century, soccer's appeal would reside largely with hyphenated Americans—of the sort Theodore Roosevelt and his ilk so virulently denounced. One can only wonder what the nation's twenty-sixth president would have made of a photo that appeared in many of the country's newspapers in 1934. It was of his grandson, Theodore III, a student at Harvard, dressed not for the gridiron but for the freshman soccer team.

---

* The 1924 team was decidedly weak and did not even include a recognized goalkeeper. It played only five matches in the United States (four of them in Philadelphia), winning three and drawing two against professional teams from the American Soccer League.

2

Foreign Bodies and Freezing Fans

The Births of the USFA and the National Challenge Cup

It has been a rather strange condition that this country, excelling in almost every other branch of sport, as demonstrated at the last Olympic games, has never been much interested in soccer. This lack of interest is due chiefly to the fact that no cooperative organization has ever been effected in the sport and it has never been developed to a point where the public could be made to take a general interest in it. As a game it is acknowledged to be on a par with the best of American sports.

—*New York Sun*, November 22, 1913

A S THEY RETURNED HOME in 1911 from their second North American tour, the Corinthians had little idea of the commotion they had left behind. Their presence in the United States had been fleeting; all but five of the twenty-one matches had been played in Canada, and the likes of St. Louis and Fall River were left off the final itinerary. The team won handily its two matches in Chicago, though under the electric lights at White Sox Park the players struggled to pick out the ball against the night sky. In New York, they attracted several thousand to the Polo Grounds to see them defeat a local all-star team; they made a "pretty display" in trouncing the Newark Football Club, 6–2; and they ended with an anticlimactic 19–0 romp over members of the Philadelphia cricket club league. But the legacy of the Corinthians' visit, a far more controversial affair than the first, had little to do with the outcome of their matches—or, for that matter, with anything that had taken place on the field. It instead had served as the catalyst for a reorganization of soccer in the United States. Out of it would emerge a new, more ambitious governing body, as well as what ranks today as one of the oldest prizes in American sports.

The competition, which began life as the National Challenge Cup and is now known as the U.S. Open Cup, was instigated in 1913 as the country's national soccer championship. Few would claim such a lofty designation for it these days, though, and if it no longer produces America's champion, it would be difficult to identify precisely when it last did. No one even seems to know when or why the name of the competition was changed. Annual reports issued by the United States Soccer Football Association (USSFA) in the late 1940s and early 1950s use the two titles interchangeably; well into the 1970s, the *New York Times* referred to it as the Challenge Cup.

In particular, two of the Corinthians matches in 1911—in Newark and New York City—can lay claim to altering the course of American soccer. That they went ahead at all brought sharply into focus a lack of autonomy and ambition on the part of organizers in the United States. The reasons for this necessitate a brief detour.

Almost from its earliest days, soccer in the United States had made gestures toward a national governing body, of the type England had established in 1863 as the Football Association. At first glance, the formation of an American Football Association (AFA) twenty-one years later seems a momentous occasion, but this proved to be little more than an attempt to capitalize on the popularity of the game in selected parts of the Northeast. Formed by British expatriates on the premises of the Clark Thread Mills in Newark, New Jersey, the AFA led a fragile existence. From 1899 to 1905, it didn't even operate, and even at the height of its authority it ventured little farther than a hundred miles from its front door. That its officials were transplanted Britons was hardly surprising—that was true in many parts of the world—but the links they established with the mother country were intimate. Each year, the AFA paid a subscription to the Football Association and, operating almost as a subsidiary, took much of its direction from London.

For a while, this didn't seem to matter. But by the start of the twentieth century, the landscape was changing. The formation of FIFA in 1904 (which, initially, the English and other British associations refused to join) was an obvious manifestation of interest beyond the British Isles; by 1911, membership had grown from seven countries to nineteen. At the same time, soccer leagues were forming in most major American cities—even in places like Atlanta and Salt Lake City—and the game started to encroach on a few college campuses. Tours by the Pilgrims and Corinthians had helped to accelerate this interest. They also instilled a greater spirit of self-determination: in a country steadfastly charting its own sporting course, encumbering allegiances with the mother country carried little favor. After the Pilgrims completed their second tour in 1909, one commentator insisted the Americans had shown "that the need of soccer missions has passed away and that the Englishmen had better prepare to beat America's best on their next trip, rather than bring over teams organized for purposes of instruction." Attention, he argued, was better focused on the administration of the game. "Strict government of players, clubs and leagues by one big national body of men of standing should advance the game a great deal," he wrote. "Its only drawback just now seems to be lack of effective national organization."

The implication was clear enough: the AFA was not up to the task. Shortcomings aside, though, it had devised a profitable competition, one organized along predictably British lines: a single-elimination tournament in the manner of England's FA Cup (which began in 1871–1872) and Scotland's equivalent (1873–1874). At the time the Our New Thread eleven of Kearny, New Jersey, won the first of them, in 1885, the concept of league soccer had still to be introduced, in America, Britain, or anywhere else. As the British writer Simon Inglis has noted, "The idea of a group of teams playing a pre-arranged schedule of games against each other, home and away, seems so natural to us today that it's rather hard to imagine why it took the Victorians so long to stumble upon it." Stumble they finally did in 1888, well behind their counterparts in cricket and, less consciously, American baseball. By then, possession of the AFA Cup had become a considerable source of pride. When the Rovers of Fall River claimed the 1888 title, they were welcomed home with a procession from the train station, a brass band, and banners proclaiming them champions of America.

Not everyone blew their horn. The following year, the *New York Times* asserted that the AFA was "in danger of going to pieces," with many clubs objecting to the basis on which the trophy was contested. "They did not like the idea that, when they had been defeated in one match, they were debarred from participating any longer in the championship series," it wrote, noting that "the Trenton Football Club was defeated in the first round, and, although they had trained hard and were good and enthusiastic players, they were not permitted to play in any of the other rounds."

In the same article, the *Times* also reported that a league was being formed in New York and that "a schedule of championship games will be played similar to the schedule of the baseball league." But the advent of league play did not extinguish the excitement of what some Americans had taken to calling a "Cup tie competition."* The 1908 final between West Hudson and the True Blues of Paterson—teams not a dozen miles apart from each other—attracted around 10,000 fans to Newark's Morris Park. It was this sort of occasion that kept the AFA going.

Yet because it remained manifestly self-contained, the association attracted criticism over its failure to harness soccer's emerging popularity. The AFA had not been responsible for bringing across the Pilgrims and Corinthians; it wasn't particularly interested in amateur soccer; it could do little to cultivate the sport in schools and colleges; and it made little attempt to support the myriad leagues and competitions sprouting up beyond its familiar reach. The men from Newark seemed happy merely to feed off the proceeds of the game in places where its existence was well established.

The seeds of the AFA's downfall had been sewn in London in 1907, when the Corinthians and a number of other English amateur clubs withdrew from the Football Association in a dispute over professional clubs' being admitted to county associations. The split prevented the Corinthians from engaging with most of England's top teams and helps to explain why the club had spent so much time overseas (it had visited Bohemia and Switzerland in 1909, Brazil in 1910, and Spain early in 1911). The club's North American tour in 1906 had hardly been a financial success—one source claimed that it finished $2,000 in the hole—but it had been well enough received.

The timing of the Corinthians' second visit could scarcely have been more opportune. A New York publication claimed that "so many things of outstanding importance have been compressed into the [1910–1911 soccer] season that it will long be recognized as marking a new epoch in the now popular winter pastime." Twenty-eight teams had entered the AFA Cup—a record—and money-spinning crowds of around 5,000 watched both the deadlocked 1911 final and the rematch two weeks later. The National League, a popular semiprofessional circuit, had completed its fifth season since its resurrection alongside the AFA, while an ambitious Eastern Professional League had brought together teams from New England, Philadelphia, and New Jersey for the first time before collapsing under a harsh winter. Edward Duffy of the *Newark Evening Star* claimed that the AFA had "the opportunity of a lifetime before it now"; he urged it to look beyond its familiar milieu and "weld together the great soccer

---

* In British sporting parlance, a "tie" generally refers to a match at any stage of a tournament in which the losers are eliminated.

country in the Middle West with the East under a national body that would resemble the National Commission of baseball. . . . The government of the game is now too provincial."

Provincial but not toothless—and in attempting to schedule games against AFA-affiliated teams, the Corinthians discovered that the association was prepared to bite. Under orders from London, the AFA forbade its members from playing against the English renegades. To the New Jersey-born Duffy, such high-handedness begged the question of who actually governed the game in the United States:

> As a free American who does not in any way depend on England for aid or advice in soccer, the writer fails to see where the "F.A." has any strong ground to stand on in forbidding the American Football Association teams to play the Corinthians. Theirs is a fight that doesn't concern us and there is no reason that it should. . . . There are some independents among the eastern soccerites who are independent enough to be Americans, among them the New York Amateur State League officials, who, though "A.F.A." cup competitors, openly defy the order from England and will pick a team from the league to play the Corinthians on the Polo Grounds September 18. This is as it should be. There is no reason why England should control soccer in this country now or in the future. We can take care of ourselves.

A headline to one of Duffy's columns even asserted that AFA-affiliated clubs such as Newark FC, who had agreed to play the Corinthians, were being "ruled by a foreign body." This was a view shared by many. The short-lived *Association Football News* of Harrisburg, Pennsylvania, featured a lively exchange of letters, including one from a reader identified as "True American":

> The American Football Association, officered and composed, as I understand, of men born across the water and apparently filled with the idea that those on the other side should in a measure control the destinies of the game in this country, fails to take into consideration that the average American enthusiast cares not at all about the squabble which "outlawed" the Corinthians, and is desirous of seeing the visitors play for many reasons. . . . The average American regards the game as a foreign game played by foreigners, and the action of the A.F.A. will tend to increase this opinion and lessen his idea that it is played by Americans to any

extent. . . . No sport will ever succeed here which is directed across the water, and until the American Association show its independence of foreign domination, Soccer will always be regarded as a sport peculiar to Britons in America—the idea which most people here have now.

Another reader disagreed:

> It is a universal admission that Great Britain is at present superior to us at soccer and why shouldn't it be? Soccer has been the national game over there for nearly half a century, whilst it is only during the past few years that we have begun to take the game seriously and have yet a lot to learn about its fine points. Where are we going to learn these fine points except from the best exponents?

On the whole, though, most of the letter writers sided with the likes of "Get Together," who disparaged the AFA:

> For your information, and others who may not know, I will state that during the 26 years that they claim to be in existence, that not once has an American born held the office of President, nor is [there] any likelihood of ever doing so under the present regime. I will also ask you the question or anyone connected with the A.F.A., What have they done to advance soccer in the United States?

But perhaps the most damning indictment of the association had appeared in an earlier edition of the *News* in a report on the AFA's annual meeting:

> The Auditing Committee's report was read and showed the organization to be in a healthy condition there being $689.00 in the treasury. The delegates voted unanimously to give Mr. A. N. Beveridge, Secretary of the Association, $250.00 for his services, $75.00 was voted to Harry Craig, the Treasurer. Duncan Carswell, the financial secretary[,] was granted $50.00 for his work. To John Watt[,] the president, the delegates voted $100.00. John Love, the vice president, was awarded a gold medal. There was some disposition shown to "blow in" a portion of the balance of the funds. . . . Mr. Grundy of the Jersey A.C. made the good suggestion that a sinking fund be established for the ultimate purpose of buying suitable grounds to be controlled by the AFA. Nothing definite was decided upon.

"Get Together" claimed the AFA had also authorized $100 for "a general outing and good time for a selected few to take the [AFA] Cup to Pawtucket and present it to the winners"; he thought it "clearly evident that the sole purpose of running this Association is not for the good of Soccer, but to furnish good times and funds for those fortunate enough to be holding office."

Secretary Beveridge wrote a letter of his own to the *News,* stressing that membership in the FA kept it "in touch with all that is going on in the football world" and making various largely irrelevant accusations toward the promoters of the Corinthians' tour. He denounced the team as substandard—which, too, was beside the point—and promised, in vain, that a high-flying, officially sanctioned club would tour the United States "by the spring of 1912." But the mood for change was hardening. Duffy expected the AFA to "die the slow death its antiquated methods are preparing for it" and fearlessly claimed that "in ten years the baseball men will control the game."

The AFA largely succeeded in keeping its members away from the British outlaws. Newark was the only club to break ranks; its president thought it was "for the good of the sport that the Corinthians show in this city," and his club was "willing to take the punishment meted out to us by the AFA." On September 18, a crowd of around 2,000 saw the English win, 6–2—and a few days later, the AFA threw Newark out of the National League. In addition, it suspended indefinitely several players who had faced the Corinthians as part of a New York all-star team and had also been "entered as members of the teams that have been booked for the [AFA's] cup tie contests."

For the Southern New York State association, one of the largest and most ambitious of the affiliated bodies, this was the last straw. It not only withdrew from the AFA but, within a matter of months, effectively declared that it had become a national governing body in its own right: the American Amateur Football Association (AAFA). One of its representatives, Thomas Bagnall, explained:

> The AFA assumed control of soccer in the United States and professed to exercise it by virtue of an affiliation with the Football Association Limited, the governing body in England. For 26 years it has claimed this control, and in those 26 years it has done nothing to advance the game. . . . As members of the AFA we tried earnestly and consistently to broaden its view and to urge it to try to make its influence national in fact as well as in name. We pointed

out that the United States, because of its size and its very proper feeling of national pride could not be considered as being under vassalage of an English organization, in football any more than it could in any other sporting or business enterprise.

Paradoxically, several of the AAFA's officers were British-born, including Bagnall, who worked for the British Ministry of Munitions—and whose pronouncements about the need for greater independence proved ironic in the wake of his fate as a soccer official. In 1918, he would be forced from office after refusing to become an American citizen, having dismissed the precondition as "mere pieces of paper."

Not that the AAFA was cut from the AFA's cloth. Its New York-born, St. Louis-bred secretary, Thomas Cahill, was particularly determined to shake the game free from the clutches of the old country. Duffy, too, joined the organization as a delegate-at-large and used his newspaper column to push for more independent thinking. As its president, the association elected Dr. "Guss" Randolph Manning, an English surgeon who had emigrated to the United States in 1910 and would serve his adopted country during World War I. Manning had spent several years in Germany as a medical student and, as secretary of the Verband Süddeutscher Fussballvereine (the Federation of South German Football Clubs), helped to form Germany's national association in 1900.

Though it may have had loftier pretensions, the AAFA's stated aim was national governance of amateur soccer. This was an area the AFA had largely ignored—and it offered the greatest opportunity to develop the sport. The AAFA was also keen to expand its authority beyond New York State and in a matter of months had signed up leagues from Michigan, Pittsburgh, St. Louis, and Utah. It wasted little time in organizing its own cup competition, which it touted as a national championship even though twenty-three of the twenty-seven entrants came from New York.*

The AAFA's cup competition ran for two years and proved only a modest success: a rainy 1913 final between two teams from Yonkers attracted a paid attendance of just 547. By then, though, the association had set its eyes on the wider world. A year earlier, at FIFA's annual congress in Stockholm, it had pushed for international recognition as the country's sole governing body. Cahill had even argued its case in person,

---

* One of the four out-of-state teams was the outcast Newark FC, who reached the final that season and also claimed the New York and District Amateur League title. The following year, though, the club rejoined the AFA.

having offered to pay his own way to Sweden if the association would contribute $100 toward his expenses. The AFA, too, was given the chance to speak, though it hadn't sent an envoy of its own; its interests were represented by the secretary of England's Football Association, Frederick Wall. The two men met in London and traveled to Stockholm together. "[Wall] made the statement to me that he did nothing on behalf of the AFA and that he wanted it to be known that he was in favor of a National body governing soccer in the United States," Cahill reported, "and under no circumstances would he stand for the Federation being used as a clearance house for quarreling factions, either in the United States or elsewhere."

In addressing the congress on June 30, Cahill claimed to have "made a most complete statement of what we had done for the game in the States, and what we expected to do if given recognition." FIFA's own minutes reveal the level of his association's paranoia:

> The representative of the A.A.F.A. [Cahill] gave a review of association football in the United States. It is badly lacking organisation. He expressed his opinion that a delay in recognising the A.A.F.A. would be dangerous, it stands for honesty in sport and will lift up the game. It is doing missionary work in public schools and in educational institutes. He strongly urged that if the recognition could not be given at once, it should be given for one year. The A.A.F.A. knew what was expected from them and their earnestness was shown by sending a delegate to the congress.

According to Cahill, Wall then "took up the AFA application, and held the floor for about thirty minutes." But in Cahill's view, the pivotal speech had come from a German delegate, Robert Hefner. "Professor Hefner spoke for fully forty minutes on our behalf, and made a great impression with those present," he claimed. "In fact, I feel confident that only [but] for Professor Hefner's efforts, the AFA would have secured the desired recognition." FIFA's minutes show that Austria proposed to accept the AAFA provisionally for one year and that Germany "strongly recommended to accept the AAFA as full members." This enthusiasm, though, was tempered by the English:

> England reminded the Congress that the Federation had received two applications from America asking for recognition, one from the American F.A., which was a body established 16 years ago, and

claimed to control both amateur and professional football, the other from the American Amateur F.A., a newly formed body, and that the Congress had no information before it as to the constitution of either association. England therefore expressed its opinion that it would be a blunder to admit one of the two American Associations applying for membership, that it might be possible to bring them together.

Wall's proposal to refer the matter to the emergency committee—who seem to have kicked the whole issue into touch—was accepted by fifty-five votes to twenty-five. It left Cahill to reflect on the reservations about the AAFA's bid:

> Mr. Wall gave me to understand that he could not support our organization in its present form, namely until its constitution was changed, so as to take care of the professionals as well as the Amateurs. I told him that we had under consideration, just such a plan, but did not consider the time ripe for such a change, but it was our idea when the time required us to take care of the professionals, we would be in a position to do so. His other objection was that our title was wrong, for a National body, in other words, we should select a name, such as the United States Football Association or the National Association Football Union of the United States, or in other words any name which would indicate a National body.

In the months that followed, the AAFA and AFA turned more conciliatory, forming separate peace committees in a search for common ground. But the enmity continued to fester. In December 1912, just when a resolution seemed at hand, the AFA decided against merging and backed out. Within a few months, though, the influential Allied American Association of Philadelphia jumped sides and lined itself up behind the AAFA. Sensing it now had the upper hand, the new association pressed home its advantage. On April 5, 1913, it instigated a "national soccer congress" at Astor House in New York City, hoping to gain sufficient consent to form a united national body. The meeting attracted representatives of most of the country's major soccer organizations, including the rather recalcitrant president of the AFA, Andrew Brown. "My position is somewhat antagonistic," he admitted. "The [AFA] has felt that football up to a few years ago had made no progress, but about three years ago things became active, and we were just at a point where great progress was being made when the New York State League split from the ranks."

But most of the delegates believed the AFA had lost its chance. A resolution that a "national organization be established at this Congress and under this date, and be given the name United States Football Association" carried the day; against the objections of at least one AFA delegate, it even included the provision "that a copy of the minutes of this Congress be sent to the Secretary of the Federation Internationale de Football Association with a plea for admission to membership in that body." Manning would travel to FIFA's congress in Norway that summer to support the application.

The framework for the United States Football Association (USFA) took shape over the summer—and so, alas, did the political infighting and grudge bearing that would become the group's unwitting hallmark. The AFA refused to disband and voted against joining the new body, changing its mind only after the USFA received notice from FIFA that it been granted provisional membership. Manning was elected president and Cahill, secretary; the AFA could muster only the third vice-president's chair. The election of officers did little to end the AFA's intransigence, or its existence. Gamely, it continued to operate until 1924, if only as a peculiar subordinate.

The USFA wasted little time in devising a cup competition of its own. Though at the 1913 national congress the likes of Andrew Brown pleaded for it not to do so (he wanted the association to "attend to work that has long been neglected, which you only can do"), the USFA ignored him; it had seen the crowds that cup soccer could attract. While allowing the AFA to continue with its tournament, it declared that its own National Challenge Cup would take precedence over it and all other play. In London the previous summer, Cahill had met Thomas Dewar and discovered that the Scottish whisky distiller's celebrated sporting philanthropy extended to the provision of a sterling-silver trophy for an American soccer champion.* Though the thirty-two-inch-high prize, fashioned by the Reed and Barton Company of New York, was first awarded to the winner of the AAFA Cup in 1912, that competition had been disbanded with the formation of the USFA. The trophy would now be put to more lasting use.

---

* "I hope this will be the means of yet further stimulating the interest in the game and may it enthuse the inhabitants from New York to the Pacific Coast," proclaimed Dewar, "and I trust that one day foot ball will be found a formidable rival of that great national game, base ball, a game for which I also have a great respect, having been in fact for several years president of the Base Ball Association in England."

Every year since 1913—through world wars, hard times, and long stretches of indifference—teams have competed for the Challenge Cup, if not always for Dewar's offering; the trophy was retired in 1979 (though the 1997 and 1998 winners were also presented with it). For what it's worth, it is the longest continually contested team competition in the country, even if it appears only as a pinprick on the American sporting map. In 1913, though, 120,000 had attended the English FA Cup final between Aston Villa and Sunderland, and there were many who believed America would soon work up a similar enthusiasm for its own equivalent. Ironically, though, the association that had so palpably objected to Britain's influence on the governance of American soccer had settled on a decidedly British means of picking a winner.

Manning thought the cup valuable in other ways, as well:

> The competition will also enable the officers and members of the council to look over the material that presents itself on the fields in the cup ties for the purpose of selecting representative teams in inter-state games as well as national representative matches. And there is no getting away from the fact that these games in time will prove a great attraction, as they have done in other countries: the public will become more intimately acquainted with the game and the increasing crowds will strengthen the clubs and leagues financially.

But the competition also brought into focus many of the barriers soccer in America would face in its bid for mass appeal: distances between major centers that made travel cost-prohibitive; the utter folly of playing in the winter months; and uncontrolled antagonism from participants on and off the field.

Some gave the cup a wide berth. The absence of clubs from St. Louis, which all but proclaimed itself the home of American soccer, was disappointing, if not too surprising. In such a distant outpost, the USFA had managed to establish little more than a toehold; moreover, the city played the game largely as it saw fit, unconstrained by British precedent. The view of the *St. Louis Globe-Democrat* was typical:

> Some day and possibly not in the so distant future there will be a more satisfactory way of settling the soccer championship of this country and then St. Louis should rank high. . . . What is needed is a system whereby championships of growing importance will be played for until a national championship is reached. The first

thing that should be played for is city titles and then state titles. This will lead up to interstate titles without forcing teams to travel inconvenient distances. After this will come sectional titles and these can also be arranged conveniently for the contending teams. Clubs getting into the national championship played in this way can afford to make some sacrifices and will undoubtedly do so. And when a championship is arranged those back of it should see that the cup awarded is something besides an advertisement for a Scotch whisky.

Another notable absentee was Fall River, a city that would give the USFA no end of trouble in the years to come. Before the season was through, the association would suspend the Rovers club for playing unaffiliated St. Louis teams on a Midwestern tour. Some press reports, noting the resentment of some southern New England soccer officials toward the USFA, suggested the Rovers had made the trip partly to undermine the association's fragile authority.*

But the most significant omissions were probably those of the National League. Eleven of its twelve clubs had refused to take part, doubtless out of loyalty to the marginalized AFA. Oddly enough, the team that did play, the Brooklyn Field Club, ended up with the trophy. Its participation might have come down to the fact that Manning was a member of the club, though this may have been only a ceremonial association: the USFA had insisted that all of its officers be members of an affiliated team. (Remarkably, the other Challenge Cup finalist had chosen Cahill as its honorary president.)

The Field Club's rise to supremacy was astoundingly quick. As an amateur side in 1912–1913, it finished at the bottom of the National League, then abandoned its pretensions and began to sign professional players. Many were British migrants, and the best of them was inside-forward Bob Millar, once the property of Scottish League side St. Mirren. Millar had joined Brooklyn from the Tacony club of Pennsylvania, though he never stayed long in one place; over his career he would be associated with at least fifteen other clubs. Centre-half Neil Clarke, once of Celtic, had been a classmate of Millar's; goalkeeper Archie Pennell, "well-known throughout Scotland and England," had joined from Burnley, and forward James Black arrived from Newcastle United—though none had played a league match for those clubs. The Field Club's lineup

* The Rovers were readmitted the following year—and in 1916, they reached the Challenge Cup final.

also featured the native tandem of outside-right James Ford and inside-right George Knowles, regarded by at least one source as "the strongest American-born right wing in the country."

While there's no reason to believe that this transatlantic collective wasn't worthy of the national crown, to claim it they had to play only six matches—rather fewer than the 152 games required of a World Series participant or the thirty-eight times clubs in England's Football League faced each other. Admittedly, the demands of league play in American soccer were not particularly taxing—the National League of New Jersey set out a modest eighteen-game schedule in 1913—but the USFA's creation was an even less convincing approximation of a championship.

The inaugural draw for the National Challenge Cup included forty entries from seven states; it took place at New York's Broadway Central Hotel on October 11, 1913. Twenty-four clubs were given byes into the second round, meaning that with a little luck, the Field Club would have had to play only five times to lift the trophy. As it was, they traveled to Hedley Field in Queens for a first-round match with the Interborough Rapid Transport Strollers. Their 3-0 victory was achieved with a team rather different from the one that would lift the cup six months later: neither Millar nor Clarke featured in the match, and three others who did would leave the club in mid-season.

Amid the seven other first-round matches, an eleven from Harrison, New Jersey, known as the Alley Boys streaked to a 7-0 halftime lead against the Jersey City Blues and won 8-5 in what one reporter regarded as "a game full of vicissitudes." In Bayonne, the works team of the boiler manufacturer Babcock and Wilcox claimed a 2-0 victory over the Cowboy Club of Jersey City. Bethlehem FC, yet to join forces with the city's mighty steel company, rolled over Disston of Tacony, 7-0, and at the Columbia Oval, on the corner of Gun Hill Road and Jerome Avenue in the Bronx, the economically named German FC eliminated Cameron FC, 5-0. At this stage of the game's development, clubs of continental European designation were rare, although how "German" the team in question actually was is unclear. One paper reported that "after the game the winners were taken to the Cafe Bismarck, where a reception was given them and each member of the team was presented with a silver medal by W. S. Ealing, one of the officers of the German football club."

One first-round match was never played. Tacony FC, runners-up in the AFA Cup the previous season, forfeited their game against Kensington of Philadelphia so they could take part in a rearranged AFA Cup contest with the Hibernian club of Trenton. How the USFA responded to the apparent breach of its us-first policy is unclear, but Tacony's progress in the AFA Cup that season probably negated any penalties levied against them. Fifteen thousand were said to have watched them take on Bethlehem in the final, which they lost after a replay.

If such cold-shouldering suggested the USFA had only a tenuous grasp on the game, the association could take comfort in the much broader footprint of its own competition, the first to link cities in the Midwest with those in the Northeast. (For a time the Michigan State League had been affiliated to the AFA, but its teams never entered the AFA Cup.) Four clubs from Chicago and two from Detroit had entered the Challenge Cup, and all were given byes into the second round. But by the time they were called into action, winter had made a forceful intervention. Second-round matches were meant to be completed by December 6, but some were pushed back almost to Christmas, and even those that went ahead did so under forbidding conditions.

The corner of 52nd Avenue and West Madison Street in Chicago was no place for the casual fan the day Pullman FC defeated the Campbell Rovers, 3–0. "A biting breeze from the north swept the field, which was frozen hard but had little snow on it," noted the *Chicago Tribune*. "Under the slippery and windy conditions combination play was difficult, and the best form of attack was to pull the ball as near the goal mouth as possible and take a shot at goal." Over at Aviation Field, on the corner of 16th Street and 48th Avenue, the Hyde Park Blues (a "high school eleven") defeated MacDuff, 2–0. To the *Tribune*'s shivering reporter, the match had been "a frigid proposition for the thinly-clad kickers," with two outfield players leaving the field in the second half "to escape turning into icicles."

In Detroit, a 2–2 draw between Roses FC and Packard FC at Maloney Park was a similarly icebound proposition—though for the neophyte correspondent of the *Detroit Free Press* it was not without its exotic charms:

> A crowd of over 500 persons braved the cold raw day to view the struggle and found plenty of excuses for rooting. This feature, by the way, was characteristic of the game. Instead of the yells familiar to baseball and rugby followers, was heard the jargon of soccer in the Scottish burr, the Irish brogue, and the typical English sporting lingo. . . . Anyone who has the impression that the game is gentle is far from the facts. On the contrary, the men are in constant danger of being kicked when they charge for the ball, while it is no joke to be spilled on a hard field in the light and airy costume of the sport.

The paper was not alone in its unfamiliarity with the sport, claiming that many in the crowd were witnessing their first soccer contest and, "as the ball traveled from end to end, and ever in view, it was apparent that it was being appreciated." The rematch at Packard Park—"one of the most up-to-date soccer grounds in the country"—went to extra time and was settled by an early Roses goal.

But however thrilling or novel these contests were, in the dead of winter only the most committed were likely to attend them—and if play wasn't blighted by snow and ice, there was usually rain and mud. One account of a decidedly aquatic second-round duel on Long Island between Yonkers FC of the New York State Amateur League and the Fulton Athletic Club noted that as the referee blew his whistle for halftime, "six players were trying to kick the ball out of a big puddle," and spectators, "armed with umbrellas and raincoats, stood around the field ankle deep in mud during the entire game." Though cities such as Chicago had already learned to shut down their leagues during the most gelid months, the USFA seemed oblivious to such discretion. Not until March 8—nearly two months after the intended date—did the Hyde Park Blues and Pullman contest their third-round encounter, the latter negotiating the mud more productively to win, 4–2.

For much of the country, soccer and bad weather would become almost inseparable; not until the 1970s would it come to be regarded as a summer game. But other maladies proved just as enduring, and the most conspicuous of them was fighting. In decades to come (and in common with nearly every other soccer competition in the country), the Challenge Cup would be riddled with everything from assaults on referees to riots in the stands. It seems to have acquired its first serious blemish at a third-round contest between New York Celtic and Yonkers FC. The *New York Press* chronicled it in detail:

> Refusal to leave the field when ordered to do so by the referee caused the forceful removal by the joint efforts of two policemen of J. Duffy, inside left for the New York Celtics, in the United States of America Football Association Cup tie game with Yonkers at Lenox Oval, yesterday afternoon. . . . Duffy fouled a Yonkers player who was on the ground. Duffy was ordered off the field but refused to leave. One of the Yonkers men started to wallop Duffy and he too was ordered off. Duffy continued to be stubborn, but finally went. Soon he was back and attacked [George] Caldicott, the referee. Thereupon the police took a hand and Duffy was removed.

Ten minutes later [James] Waters, right fullback for the Celtics, displayed a similar streak of stubbornness and upon his refusal to leave the grounds when directed to do so the referee called the game.

Duffy was banned for a year and Waters, for four weeks, with the beleaguered Mr. Caldicott even "censured for being lax in handling the trying situation."

Another predicament was the exacting distinction between amateur and professional players, an emotive issue most sports would wrestle with for some time to come. In the Challenge Cup, this led to a rather embarrassing dispute in the second-round contest between the Macnaughton Rangers of Rochester and the Niagara Falls Rangers. Niagara complained that a Macnaughton player had been registered as an amateur, though he was paid to coach a high-school team and was thus considered a professional. Initially, the USFA threw out the protest, but it ordered an investigation and a month later changed its mind, instructing that the match be replayed without him. (It also fined Macnaughton $15 for not charging the mandatory minimum admission of 25 cents and for what one paper described as "failure to make any attempt to repair breaches in the hedge which ran down one side of the field and which formed a free entry to many hundreds of spectators.") But the replay never happened; with "three men on the sick list and two men away from the city," Macnaughton withdrew.

Niagara's captain was none other than Fred Milnes, the well-to-do Englishman who had led the Pilgrims on their North American tours a decade earlier. Milnes had returned to the United States in 1912 "for the purpose of locating here permanently" and for a time played in New York City (he attended the Astor House congress in 1913). By the winter of 1913–1914, he'd become the driving force behind the Rangers' bid for the cup, even filling in as goalkeeper during the team's opening-round win over the Corinthians of Buffalo.

In December, Milnes and his team traveled to Detroit's Maloney Park for a third-round encounter with the Roses, yet another occasion the weather would spoil. "The ground was covered by a foot of snow, which made it very hard work for the players," the *Detroit Free Press* observed. "The Roses in the first half should have been at least three goals up but failed to take advantage of the opportunities, the deep snow being a great handicap." The visitors, it noted, "proved the better snow wallowers" and won, 2–0.

Paired at home to Pullman in the quarterfinals, Niagara needed to wait another two months for the weather to clear up and even then found themselves contending with a heavily waterlogged surface. The club attempted to get around the problem by covering its Aluminum Park pitch with "several loads of coke screenings" but could do little about the snow that fell during play. Once again, their sure-footedness helped propel them to victory, with Milnes opening the scoring in a 2–1 win.

The erstwhile Pilgrim was far from the only famous name christening the competition. Playing for the West Hudson Juniors team defeated by Harrison's Alley Boys in a second-round replay—and celebrating his sixteenth birthday that day—was Archie Stark, destined to become one of the country's most prolific strikers. There was also Pullman's Sheldon Govier, whose feted career at center-half (he was fifteen when he broke into the first team) was followed by an equally long tenure as a Chicago alderman. At the Pittsburgh Pirates' baseball park, Bethlehem's Tommy (Whitey) Fleming, one of the era's fleetest forwards, scored a hat-trick against the hometown Braddock club. His team would be eliminated in the next round by the eventual champions—in the wake of a penalty for hand-ball given against inside-right Edgar Lewis. Lewis, a Bethlehem Steel Corporation executive, was by no means a mainstay of the team and would soon hang up his boots, but his association with the game would prove momentous. In a few years, he would transform the club into Bethlehem Steel FC, the first genuinely professional soccer team in the country.

But the luminary of the first Challenge Cup proved to be Bob Millar, who scored four times in three matches and featured conspicuously in nearly every account of his team's play. One report noted how, in a quarterfinal victory against Yonkers, he "played the star game," scoring once and making "a brilliant stop" to set up another. Though not yet twenty-four, the striker, to one writer, was already the "best man in the country at that position"; to another, he was "easily the classiest player in the New York district."

Through to the semifinal, Millar's club was paired against one of two Massachusetts teams to have entered the competition. On the south coast, the whaling port of New Bedford had evolved into a major center of cotton manufacture, and a hub of British emigration. Soccer naturally was no stranger to the community, yet it had been confined largely to local factory leagues. But several enthusiasts were keen to advance the city's pedigree and formed an all-star "New Bedford FC" specifically for the competition. (This was perfectly within the rules; in fact, the Niagara

Falls Rangers appear to have augmented their Challenge Cup lineup with several members of the rival Wanderers club, which hadn't entered.) The made-to-order eleven had little difficulty in eliminating Farr Alpaca of Holyoke or Presbyterian FC of Bridgeport, Connecticut, and soon had local fans rallying to their cause. The *New Bedford Sunday Standard* reported that a crowd of 1,100—the largest paid attendance for soccer the city had seen—had attended the 3–0 victory over the Calvinist eleven, one which it claimed had secured the team the "championship of New England."

Drawn at home in the third round, New Bedford claimed a 2–0 win over West Philadelphia in a driving rainstorm that took its toll on the pitch. One account, noting that the visitors "changed their red sweaters for white shirts during the interval," maintained that the losers, "by reason of their having played together as a team for several seasons, displayed the prettier football, but made a mistake by not changing their style of play."

If Challenge Cup fever had struck anywhere that season, it was probably in this corner of the Bay State—and it came as a bitter disappointment for New Bedford to be drawn away from home in the quarterfinals. But for $225 and 10 percent of the gate, the Peabody club of Philadelphia agreed to forsake their own Washington Park ground (at 26th Street and Allegheny Avenue) for New Bedford's Athletic Park. While the USFA frowned on such inducements, it had not prohibited them, and with around 3,500 turning out for the match, it's not hard to see why. Peabody returned to Pennsylvania $400 richer, and New Bedford cantered to a 4–1 win.

Semifinal venues, though, were out of the competing clubs' hands; as in England, they were to be played at a neutral site (for the time being). All the same, the selection of Pawtucket, Rhode Island, for New Bedford's clash with the Brooklyn Field Club was rather handier for the former team than the latter. With Pawtucket's own fans also warming to the big event, nearly 5,000 filled the city's Lonsdale Avenue grounds. According to the *Providence Sunday Journal,* "Long before the hour set for play every car bound for the park was crowded, a number of specials being used during the rush hour to accommodate the gathering." It was the first Challenge Cup match played in the city that season—no team from Rhode Island had entered—and it ended in a 2–1 Brooklyn victory. Both sides finished with ten men in the wake of a first-half brawl, though Millar wrote most of the headlines. "Besides scoring both tallies for his team, the rangy forward twice bounded the ball off the crossbars of the opposing goal," the *Sunday Journal* noted, "and on several occasions, to the delight of the fans, carried the ball from his own goal mouth the entire length of the field. . . . [He] was the centre of attraction after the game, and his fellow players, overcome with joy, placed him on their shoulders and carried him from the field."

The other semifinal, between the Rangers of Niagara Falls and Celtic of Brooklyn—Rangers and Celtic, echoing the names of Scotland's two biggest clubs and notorious rivals—proved less of an attraction, which was surprising given the city in which it took place. Paterson, New Jersey, ordinarily teemed with soccer interest; it was home to no fewer than three teams in the National League. But none of them had entered the Challenge Cup, and on a rainy April Sunday, only around 1,000 thought it worth venturing into the city's baseball park. They didn't see much of a game. Celtic, an amateur eleven, jumped to a 5–0 lead and won 6–2, bolstered by a hat-trick from their center-forward, Roddy O'Halloran.

While the lack of interest in Paterson was disappointing, the USFA's share of the gate money from the two semifinals had exceeded that of all the previous rounds put together—and no one had complained about the size or enthusiasm of the crowd at Pawtucket. Four cities now submitted bids to stage the final, but the decision to return to Rhode Island came as little surprise. "Down in New York the people respond well, but they don't understand the fine points of the game like your crowd here," Cahill confided to a local reporter. "They are really football intelligent, if I may coin a term, and in staging the final here a week from Saturday we are not moved entirely by business reasons, but by sentiment as well." The association agreed to push the start of the match back to 3:45 P.M., giving fans from Massachusetts "ample time to make the trip by connecting with the 12:45 electric from Fall River."

The final put money in everyone's pocket. More than 4,100 tickets were sold, though the actual crowd was considerably larger. Photographs show the main stand filled to capacity, with hundreds sitting perilously close to the touchlines. Providence's *Sunday Tribune* noted:

> It was in many respects a sensational contest and the 6,000 spectators who journeyed to the grounds were well repaid for their interest. From all parts of the State and, indeed, from without its borders, the crowds thronged to the grounds and long before the captains met in the centre of the field and tossed a coin for choice of goals, every seat of vantage was occupied. Carriages and automobiles were a-plenty and were well filled and even the fence tops and the score board held their full quota of hardy and daring ones.

The match was evenly fought and fiercely contested. Doggedly, Charles Creighton, the referee, tried to keep everything under control: he was said to have warned Field Club's center-forward Percy Adamson about "rough playing" four times in the first five minutes. Aware of the threat posed by Adamson and Millar, Celtic rolled up their sleeves. One report claimed that Jack Robertson, the club's stocky left-back, was said to have given "one of the grandest performances of playing ever witnessed by soccer fans in this section" and had Millar "covered every minute"; another, that Dave Flanagan, "a diminutive but fearless back," was responsible for "blocking" Millar and Adamson "so hard time after time that they threatened to mix matters with him and had to be held back by their team mates."

For the likes of Creighton, it was all in a day's work. Good referees were aware that the game's proclivity for roughhousing often culminated in shameful bursts of temper. Millar, for all his talent, was encumbered by a short fuse; that season he'd left the field of play during an AFA Cup contest to exchange punches with an abusive fan. (Play was stopped, the heckler was removed, and Millar re-entered the game.) O'Halloran had been dismissed from the same competition that season after delivering "a stinging wallop on the jaw" of the referee.

In Pawtucket, both teams finished with all eleven players, and Creighton was criticized by some for his leniency. The *New Bedford Standard,* perhaps still smarting from the elimination of its local team, certainly didn't like what it had seen. "The Celts, knowing that the Field club played a game which included hacking, backheeling and hard body checking started in to do the same sort of stunts," it wrote. "The Celts were not so polished at this foul work as the Field club and consequently had more fouls called on them." All the same, the paper conceded the best team had won ("Of that there is no question").

They'd left it late. Only five minutes remained when, after a prolonged scramble in the Celtic penalty area, outside-right James Ford headed in what proved to be the winning goal. Millar, though not scoring himself, played his usual influential role: as early as the third minute he supplied the opening goal for Adamson, an English forward who had once "played with much success at Chorley in the Lancashire Combination." Celtic drew level twenty minutes later after O'Halloran was fouled in the penalty area, and Tommy Campion converted from the spot. But they spent much of the remainder of the game trying to get the ball out of their own half.

While the Field Club celebrated their hard-earned conquest—a triumph of professionals over amateurs—the broadest smiles may have belonged to the USFA, ably marshaled by its gumptious secretary. One local paper noted:

> [Tom] Cahill was not satisfied with having only the semi-final in New England. He demanded that the final be played in this section. He had to fight his way through strong opposition but the sagacity he has displayed through the season finally led the [USFA] to throw the entire responsibility on Cahill's shoulders and order him to stage the game. If it was a failure the blame would rest on his shoulders. If it was a success, naturally the entire association, the teams and the officials would grab a share of the honors. The game was a success from every standpoint. The crowds were well handled, there was no disorder, the grounds were policed properly and everything possible to make the contest a good one for the spectator was provided for by Mr. T. W. Cahill and his assistant.

Though the activities of Cahill and his colleagues could not be said to have attracted much interest from the national press, his association emerged from the competition and its first year with considerable credit. New organizations from as far away as Seattle joined the USFA; its provisional standing in FIFA was made permanent by a unanimous vote; and there was even a surplus of $779.18 in the treasury. The new body had certainly proved itself more ambitious than the AFA, while the Challenge Cup, according to Manning, "had been brought to a most successful termination, despite the lack of experience, novelty of the attempt and an unprecedented inclemency regarding weather conditions." The president now looked forward to the following year's Panama Pacific Exposition in San Francisco, which he maintained would "introduce association football for the first time officially to the public." Argentina's football association had even expressed an interest in playing an American representative team.

Over the next two years, the number of Challenge Cup entries would more than double, and close to 10,000 attended the 1916 final. But the USFA had its hands full. Manning fell out with Cahill over a seemingly trivial administrative issue and resigned the presidency in October 1914.*

---

* Though he never returned to office, Manning held sway on a number of USFA international committees and from 1948 until his death in 1953 was a member of FIFA's executive committee (the first American citizen to serve in such a capacity). His medical expertise in diseases of the stomach gained him a measure of celebrity in 1926 as part of the team that tried to stop a perforated ulcer from claiming the life of Rudolph Valentino.

The following year, the USFA suspended the New Jersey association in a dispute over the registration of professional players; Fred Milnes was "indefinitely suspended" for his "failure to satisfactorily account for the funds" of the Northwestern New York State Foot Ball Association and swiftly disappeared from view; and the possibility of disgruntled officials' forming a rival governing body was mooted in a few parts of the country. Soccer was not "introduced" or even played at the San Francisco exposition, and it would be another thirteen years before Argentina got around to facing an American eleven. By then, World War I had forced many strong teams into a hibernation that they did not survive. Brooklyn Field Club entered the 1916–1917 Challenge Cup but disbanded before its opening match; Brooklyn Celtic, who'd repeated as losing finalists in 1914, folded not long after winning the Southern New York Cup in the spring of 1917. All the same, the Challenge Cup's best years lay just ahead. During the 1920s, the competition generated annual receipts of as much as $112,000 for the USFA; paid attendance of 10,000 was not uncommon for finals.

Such success would prove fleeting. There were a number of reasons for this and, sadly, many of them were of the USFA's own making. The hyphenated Americans it elected and appointed to positions of authority had not necessarily come to the United States to make soccer part of the sporting landscape; many saw the association more as an opportunity for personal gain and prestige than a cause to fight for. Even for the best of them, pulling together the disparate and scattered strands of American soccer was a tall order—particularly once it was discovered that there might be money in the game. As the 1920s drew to a close, the antagonism between the professional clubs and the USFA's band of volunteers boiled over. Then came the Great Depression.

Over the next half-century, perhaps the most amazing thing about the cup was that it somehow managed to keep going, producing champions year after year even when hardly anyone was paying attention. This isn't to demean the success of clubs like Philadelphia's Ukrainian Nationals, who reached the final five years out of seven in the 1960s, or Maccabi of Los Angeles, four-time champions a decade later. But their achievements were witnessed by few and went all but unreported by the media. Even the governing body seemed to give up. As an almost random example, the 1979 final took place at Winnemac Park in Chicago before maybe 1,000 fans. The finalists were from Chicago and Brooklyn; the former called themselves Croatan, spelling their name without an "i" because their league had banned all ethnic team names; the latter were no less helpfully known as the Brooklyn Dodgers. Brooklyn won, 2–1, but scarcely a newspaper in the country printed a report of the match. "It's a complete shame how this competition has been tossed aside by the powers-that-be," *Soccer America* wrote. "They didn't even bother to send out an advance man to handle a little publicity. They couldn't even come up with a program for the press."

Things would take a more hopeful turn in 1996, with the inception of Major League Soccer and the decision of its clubs to participate. Attendance rose, if gently: gatherings of a few thousand instead of the usual few hundred, though the finals of 1998 and 2000 attracted crowds of around 19,000.

For better and for worse, the cup today looks remarkably different from the way it did in 1913. Matches take place from coast to coast, many of them in places still fairly new to the game. Where once there was ankle-deep mud, there is now FieldTurf; where subzero temperatures had kept fans at home, there is now an October final. All the same, the record attendance for the competition remains the 21,583 who watched the Hakoah All-Stars capture the 1929 title at Dexter Park in Brooklyn.*

The most obvious change, though, has been more cosmetic. Since 1999, the cup has been officially associated with Lamar Hunt, the late oil millionaire and self-confessed sports fanatic whose interest in soccer did much to advance the professional game. What began as the United States of America Football Association Challenge Cup is now officially the Lamar Hunt U.S. Open Cup. Few would begrudge the honor to one of the game's most generous patrons, but given that the professional teams Hunt operated for fourteen years never took part in the competition, it is a peculiar one.

In truth, if anyone's name deserves to be paired with the cup, it is that of Tom Cahill, who diligently nurtured the competition through its formative years and held sway over its most hopeful era. In the generations to come, though, the efforts of the game's most tireless protagonist would largely be forgotten—and much the same could be said about the man himself.

---

* The "record" is, inevitably, open to question. The USFA's annual report indicates that 12,640 tickets were sold for this match, and that the first game, in St. Louis, actually did better (13,937 tickets sold). On other occasions, cup matches have been played as the lesser half of a doubleheader. Maccabi's victory in the 1978 final, against Vasco da Gama of Bridgeport, Connecticut, took place before an NASL game between New York and Tampa Bay that attracted a crowd of 60,032.

3

Bullets

Thomas William Cahill, 1863–1951

I never had but one rule for my guidance in my association with its affairs, and that rule was that the welfare of the organization was above the personal hopes or ambitions of any one associated with it. This has brought me into conflict with many men who had been my friends, but these disputes were all threshed out in open meeting. I never avoided a discussion, never failed to meet in open debate any one who questioned the wisdom of my acts. . . . Even those who have most bitterly opposed me have never questioned my good faith, the honesty of my purpose, the unselfishness of my aspirations. And for this I am grateful.

—Tom Cahill

ON THE MORNING of November 15, 1921, James Scholefield, secretary of the United States Football Association, gave word that he was ill and would not be in attendance at the organization's offices in Manhattan that day. The new season was in full swing, and Scholefield, appointed to the position only six months earlier, was a busy man. Apart from his USFA duties, was also president of Connecticut's state soccer association and chief of staff of referees for the new American Soccer League (ASL). There was very little time for his wife and newborn son, so during the week he stayed with his sister-in-law and her husband in Weehawken, New Jersey, returning to the family home in Bristol, Connecticut, on weekends.

Born in England, Scholefield had emigrated to the United States in 1905, quickly establishing himself as a capable administrator and a first-class referee. In April 1921, he'd taken charge of the National Challenge Cup final. But after calling in sick, he disappeared—along with around $1,200 of the money the USFA had entrusted to him: Challenge Cup entry fees, registration fees of professional players, and proceeds from association-sanctioned matches. His anxious wife, Ruth, traveled down to

New York to look for him; the USFA, having advised its bonding company of his disappearance, formed a committee to investigate. But all trace of him seemed to be lost.

Newspapers picked up on the story. One recalled that Scholefield had gone missing before: in Methuen, Massachusetts, when he had worked there as a city councilor. "A few years ago he was charged with deserting his four children in Methuen and was arrested in Connecticut," it reported. "After being brought back here for trial, Selectman James W. Riley of Methuen successfully pleaded for him to be given another chance, which the court granted." Shortly afterward, Scholefield's wife committed suicide—which, naturally enough, ended her husband's career in local politics. He moved to Bristol and married Ruth in 1920.

The second Mrs. Scholefield would spend two-and-a-half years searching for her husband. Not until the spring of 1924 did she find him—600 miles away in Greensboro, North Carolina, working as an accountant for an automobile firm and using his middle name as his surname. The local press said he spent much of his time raising money for good causes. But he had also married a "Greensboro society woman" named Nina Fulton, which was now enough to put him in the county jail for bigamy.

Sentenced to ten years in the state penitentiary, Scholefield attempted to account for his disappearance. "I went to New York in connection with my business and got into fast company," he said. "I absented myself from my office for a considerable time and there was an interval of several days that I don't remember anything about. When I came to myself, I was stranded in Rhode Island." From there, he had worked his way to Virginia and North Carolina, raising funds for the Salvation Army and the Red Cross. On the day of his arrest, he was collecting pledges for the Greensboro community chest.

BASEBALL HAS Alexander Cartwright, Henry Chadwick, and Harry Wright; football has Walter Camp, George Halas, and Amos Alonzo Stagg. Soccer, the ugly stepchild of American sports, has no such father figures or grand old men—or, at least, no one the casual fan might recognize. That isn't to say it lacks people with similar measures of devotion and ambition. Yet most soccer fans are unlikely to identify an American soccer official older than Phil Woosnam—and all but the most serious of them have never heard of Tom Cahill.

Much of the reason for Cahill's anonymity can be ascribed to the depths to which the sport sank after his time in it—and to the breathtaking indifference of the USFA toward its own legacy. In 1939, the association renamed its national junior championship in Cahill's honor, etching his likeness onto a huge trophy. Not long after he died, though, it apparently changed his mind—and somewhere along the way, the Cahill Trophy disappeared. In 1975, the competition was renamed after someone else.

Where is his trophy now? During the game's most expectant years, no one in America worked harder to put soccer on solid footing, and nobody had a better grasp of how to do it. His efforts may have ended in failure—no line really connects the game of Cahill's era with the modern one—but it was not for any lack of endeavor or insight. "Years ago, we had a grand chance to put soccer over in a big way," he mused in 1946, five years before his death. "Now it's a bit late to start trying to build [it] up into a major American sport."

Putting the game over in a big way was something Cahill pursued for much of his life. Whether he would have succeeded with better luck is moot; there were obstacles even his tenacity and perseverance could not remove. But no life offers a more vivid illustration of American soccer's early promise, or its pitfalls.

By the time James Scholefield succeeded him as USFA secretary in 1921, Cahill had been associated with the game for four decades. He was born to Irish parents in Yonkers, New York, probably on Christmas Eve in 1863.* While he was still a child, his family moved to St. Louis, where the notorious "Kerry Patch" of Irish Americans would have toughened his already thick skin. In time, some St. Louis papers would refer to him as "Bullets"; according to one of them, it was because he bore "the scars of several gun fights" and "partly because he was quick on the draw."

But distance running, rather than marksmanship or beating people up, was his early forte. By his mid-twenties Cahill had been called the "pet of the St. Louis audiences, and one of the greatest runners the country has produced." In perhaps his most famous race, over five miles for the putative "western championship" in 1887, he defeated D. G. Trench, a teammate at the Chicago Amateur Athletic Club. "The only time Cahill was weak was at the end of three miles but he recovered quickly and appeared stronger than ever," noted the *Sporting News*. "As they came for the last lap, Tom let out and ran so fast that a yell of delight went up. He finished like a race horse."

---

* Many sources claim that Cahill was born in 1864, though on his passport applications his birthdate appears consistently as December 24, 1863. In a 1926 interview, a Fall River sportswriter gave this as the correct date, noting, "Mr. Cahill asked the writer to get the date right as it has been printed erroneously on many occasions."

Soccer had already come to his attention with the visit of a Canadian team to St. Louis in 1884. "It was curiosity that took me there," he later recalled, "just the desire to see what was behind all the ballyhoo that had been going on for a Christmas Day match. What I saw that day fascinated me so that I haven't been able to give up the sport since." The following year, he began playing; within two years he managed a team, and by 1890 the *Sporting News* had appointed him its "Foot Ball Editor." A club called the Shamrocks, which he simultaneously owned, managed, and kept goal for, was said to have "won the pennant over the West Ends" in 1899. Cahill even claimed responsibility for setting up the league they played in, one of several that rose and fell during the era.

Though by then he'd retired his singlet, Cahill maintained a variety of other sporting interests, particularly baseball. In St. Louis, he managed and owned minor-league clubs and was on friendly terms with the two major-league entities. More conspicuously, he helped to organize the semiprofessional Missouri–Illinois "Trolley League" and served as its secretary from 1903 to 1909. He was also keen on boxing, cited by one source to have been no less than a "personal friend of Bob Fitzsimmons, Jim Corbett and John L. Sullivan." The only sport he seemed turned against was gridiron football, which he continued to disparage even after the reforms of the early 1900s. As late as 1915, he wrote that "the way [football] is played and has been played is below the standards of gentle-manliness"; he could not believe that fans should "conscientiously want a game which entails so much loss of life and accidents."

By the turn of the century, the ambitious railway switchman had begun to make a name for himself as a sports promoter. This was particularly true in St. Louis, where his organizational and administrative talents contributed in no small measure to soccer's burgeoning popularity. When, in 1901, Charles Comiskey and other baseball owners announced their intention to create a professional soccer league in the Midwest, they named him as its secretary-treasurer. The league never materialized, but Cahill was unruffled: two years later, he was appointed secretary of the new Association Foot Ball League of St. Louis. He also formed a team called Spalding, which finished the season in a tie for first place. "They lost the first six games and then [Cahill] secured some new material," one account noted. "Thus strengthened, the Spaldings showed an unusual amount of speed and played by far the most consistent foot ball until the season closed."

The team's name is worthy of note. By 1902, Cahill, married with two daughters, had quit the railroad for a position at A. G. Spalding and

Brothers, which had just opened a store in the city. The relationship was almost fated. As the world's largest sporting goods company, Spalding cast a wide net, hawking everything from punching bags to rollerskates—and in the wake of the Pilgrims' 1905 tour, sales of soccer equipment would receive a noticeable boost.

Cahill was not alone in identifying this tour as a watershed in the establishment of the game in America. That five-figure crowds had turned out to watch the two matches in St. Louis—and that he had helped to arrange them—did nothing to discourage his view. But soccer was still scrambling for purchase in the city, and the St. Louis League, of which he'd become president, was keen to bring the Pilgrims back. It took years to raise the money; not until 1908 did Cahill sail to England to clinch the deal.

While the second Pilgrims' tour did not attract the same crowds as the first, it seemed to confirm that soccer was taking root in the country. This, of course, was an enticing commercial opportunity to Spalding—and to Cahill. In 1910, he was transferred to Newark, New Jersey; soon he would feature in the trade press as a "live-wire salesman who knows what he is talking about." As ever, he was not short of initiative. "My experience in the trade has always been that the careful, courteous, conscientious clerk never has any trouble to keep his job and with any initiative and executive ability, he sooner or later rises above the mere routine," he wrote. "Suggestions are always welcome by a first-class manager. . . . No one man knows it all, and it would be a short-sighted manager who would turn down a good idea because he did not originate it himself."

No one could claim Cahill lacked such enterprise; indeed, his next position with the firm may have been one he'd helped to create. In December 1911, Spalding announced that Cahill was to leave his position as a "traveler" in order to "devote his entire time to the interests of the Association game," something the company clearly placed great faith in. "Soccer seems to be more than holding its own and is gaining among the Schools and Colleges," it noted, "but owing to the fact that it is played to a very considerable extent by foreigners, many of whom are factory hands, it is not the easiest proposition for our stores to handle, whereby the benefit of the trade will accrue to A. G. Spalding & Bros." In Cahill, the company noted, it employed "one of the authorities of the country."

Just how Cahill "devoted" his time to these "interests" isn't clear—he was said to have worked in a "special department"—but it is surely no coincidence that with his arrival on the East Coast, the course of organized soccer in the United States began to change. Cahill's work for the

AAFA (Chapter 2) brought a degree of autonomous national control—and ambition—to the game. He also became editor of Spalding's annual *Official Soccer Football Guide*, a "voluminous compilation on the sport" the company had first produced in 1904. Much of his time, though, was spent in train carriages, banging the drum for the sport and his fledgling association. These trips, though sometimes taking him as far as Washington State, were said to have been undertaken "without a cent of cost to any football organization, to lay the necessity of a national body before football promoters throughout the United States"; a clue as to who was underwriting them is provided in the July 27, 1916, issue of *Spalding Store News*:

> The promotion policy of A. G. Spalding & Bros. is a broad one. We try to work for the best interests of the athletic sport as a whole, knowing that much of what we are doing will benefit in some degree concerns and individuals who are active competitors, whose interests are directly opposed to ours, and who we believe never neglect an opportunity to work against us. . . . It is about ten years ago now when after one of his periodical trips abroad, our President, Mr. J. W. Spalding, made the prediction that some day "Soccer" foot ball would take hold in this country. At that time it was played very little here, and most of the equipment used was imported from English concerns, with the prospect that as the game became more popular it would result in more balls, shoes, etc. coming in to supply the players who mainly, he believed, on account of the fact that most of them were of English, Scotch or Irish birth, seemed to prefer the foreign product to the equipment we offered them. The prospect was not very encouraging, but we got behind the movement to promote the game in the United States, and although year by year we saw more and more equipment coming in to supply the increasing army of soccer players, we persevered, convinced that eventually "quality" would win out—the same with "Soccer" players as with the players of every other athletic game in the United States.

Cahill's offer of all but paying his own way to FIFA's 1912 congress in Stockholm could surely not have been made without help from his employer, and Spalding surely would have been less disposed to send its man all the way to Sweden were the Olympic Games not taking place there at almost the same time. Cahill attended the soccer tournament—which sanctioned Spalding's twelve-piece ball as its official model—and doubtless lamented the lack of an entry from his own country. His employer, meanwhile, had become so interested in the game that when the USFA came to life the following year, it was given a home at Spalding's offices on Nassau Street in Manhattan.

By a unanimous vote, Cahill was elected the USFA's honorary secretary ("honorary" meaning that he drew no salary) and rewarded with a gold medal for his endeavors in Stockholm. Assiduous, knowledgeable, and enthusiastic—and with a voice conspicuously devoid of British inflection—he was the ideal spokesman for the American game. "Mr. Cahill is the most energetic bundle of soccer information I have ever met," one sports editor asserted. "No question pertaining to the great national game is [too] obtuse for him to answer offhand and his supply of facts and figures on the game here ranges from coast to coast."

Not everyone looked on him as favorably. Some alleged his interest in the game was only so he could further the commercial interests of his employer (though Cahill himself claimed never to have used his position to solicit for business). Hyphenated Americans might have bristled at his staunch patriotism; equally, his desire for the American game to accord with the rest of the world did not sit easily in a country determined to play by its own rules. He had a short temper and a formidable ego. But above all, he was bluntly candid—a "rough rider, undiplomatic, uncouth at times," one observer wrote, but "resolute, faithful and tireless." The man himself was unrepentant. "I have had much abuse at times in soccer," Cahill would reflect, "but I have always put the interest of the game itself ahead of all else and have been willing to sacrifice friendships when need be to serve the sport's broader advancement."

He would be given ample opportunity to do that. Because not everyone had rallied behind the USFA—and many even plotted against it—the association seemed to spend as much time guarding its rear as leading from the front. The pressure took its toll on Cahill, who by the spring of 1916 had "broken down under the unremitting strain of handling the duties of his office." He had traveled to St. Louis to sort out feuding organizations there; faced considerable abuse in trying to bring the New Jersey association into line over a wayward factory league; and, according to the USFA president, "very rarely [spent] a week without traveling to some section of the country in the interests of the game." In between, his office was swamped with correspondence. "Time and time again he had been requested by President [John] Fernley to give much of the detail work to his assistants," one account noted, "but Mr. Cahill, so strong was his heart in the sport, believed that if one wanted a thing done right to do it himself."

His doctor prescribed a long vacation, but the trip Cahill took that summer only steeped him further in the game. Invited at short notice to play a series of matches in Sweden, the USFA hastily formed a squad of "All-Americans" and appointed Cahill to take them across. American soccer had never strayed far from home—and certainly nowhere near Europe—but the Swedes hadn't forgotten Cahill's Olympics visit in 1912. Judging by the account in Spalding's 1916 *Guide*, they treated him with genuine affection:

> Mr. Cahill, as the representative of the Americans, was picked out as the recipient of a rather strenuous honor they pay to people they like in Sweden, which in the vernacular is called "den hiss." Hiss is merely the Swedish word for "hoist," and the ceremony consisted in a half dozen Swedish giants seizing Mr. Cahill by arms and legs and in three times tossing him to the high ceiling, but each time catching him before he could hit the floor.*

If Cahill was still not feeling up to par, he at least had cause for celebration. "I do not know just how it will strike you people, but to me it seems that our United States Football Association has some reason to be proud of its achievements," he told his Swedish hosts. "Here we are, in only the third year of our national existence in the world domain of association football, sending a team for a series of games in this far country." There had even been a cordial salutation from King Gustav V, who watched the first match from the royal box. (The king later attended one of the two baseball games the Americans played on tour—both meticulously detailed in Spalding's *Guide*—and was said to have been "so interested that he had an interpreter explain the detailed play to him.")

Though hastily assembled, the American team proved up to the task: playing before crowds as large as 20,000, it lost only one match of six. Cahill returned to New Jersey weighted down with medals, trophies, and tributes—and utterly convinced of the game's future in America. Yet he wouldn't have had a team to manage, let alone cross the Atlantic with, had the newspaper *Göteborgs Morgonpost* not given the Swedish association $6,500 to finance the tour (the USFA had but $2,500 in its treasury). And while the secretary had pledged to his hosts he would "not rest until we have had the opportunity to welcome a team from the Scandinavian

---

* The Swedish phrase is actually "*att hissa*" (to hoist someone).

states to our shores," he would be dead for over a quarter-century before the United States hosted Sweden in a full international.

Cahill could be forgiven even for assuming his country had only just begun to stretch its international wings. Certainly he was smitten by the progress of the game in St. Louis, where American-born and American-coached teams had become among the strongest in the country. In 1917, he boasted to one St. Louis paper that he could "pick eleven men from this city and, by hard training, put an eleven in the field that could not only win the American title, but face any eleven in the world and win." It was, he thought, purely a matter of conditioning: American players were "seldom in the best shape" and "20% better when trained."

That chance never came, but Cahill was given two more opportunities to accompany teams to Scandinavia and drew further encouragement from the results. In 1919, he managed Bethlehem Steel's formidable collection of largely Scottish imports (plus a few standouts from other teams) to six wins and six ties in fourteen matches. He returned the following year with an American-born team predominantly from St. Louis, one he apparently chose himself and immodestly deemed "50% stronger" than either of the others (see Chapter 5).

The trips won Cahill many Swedish friends, though not at the expense of his fierce competitive streak. On the eve of Bethlehem's departure, he exhorted to the team:

> You are not going over there to steamroll a weak and yielding opposition. You are going to tackle as fine an article of football as you have ever seen. These Scandinavians have the combination game down perfectly. They have had the advantage of English and Scottish coaches and of competitions with English teams, and the only way we defeated them three years ago was by superior speed. . . . Friendship is friendship, but friendship ceases when it gets down to the serious business of winning football games from such worthy opponents. . . . We've got to win, and, with good co-operative teamwork from top to toe of the expedition, we will win.

Speed alone wasn't always enough. But Cahill again shook hands with royalty, and his conviction that he was building a soccer superpower was even shared by some across the Atlantic. "We are sure that in a few years the Americans will be leading the world in soccer football," wrote the *Morgonpost* in the wake of Bethlehem's tour, "as they are leading in any other sport they are interested in."

World war would frustrate his aspirations. Yet Cahill believed that the presence of American forces in Europe ultimately would advance the game back home. "The Civil War gave baseball its true start, students of the game agree," he wrote, "and those who follow the fortunes of soccer are convinced that the Great War will accomplish, eventually, for soccer what the Civil War did for the diamond game."

He added:

> Soccer was in a far more advanced state at the outbreak of this war than baseball was in 1861 and, when the present war is over and the boys come home again, there is no question but that there will be a tremendous growth in soccer popularity, and it behooves those of use who are left behind to keep the game and its organization in such shape that the returning heroes will find their opportunity for indulgence in the game ready for them.

The war did introduce the sport to millions around the world, but largely as a byproduct of socioeconomic and political change. Its impact on the United States would be limited: baseball was already established as the people's game, and an "American" one at that.

Cahill recognized that his country wouldn't embrace any sport that wasn't seen as true-blue. Transatlantic tours may have demonstrated the benefit of conforming to international protocol, yet he was bitterly disappointed by FIFA's intransigence over substitutions ("A game that does not permit of substitution for injuries surely can make no appeal to an American public") and in 1923 even suggested "a 12-yard zone across the center of the field wherein no player could be penalized for offside," presaging the NASL's contentious thirty-five-yard line by over half a century.

For him, though, what was needed to make soccer a national pastime wasn't so much alterations in the rules as a change in the contestants. In particular, he was desperate for the professional game to wean itself from a dependence on imported players. Of the major centers, only St. Louis turned out American-born teams in any number; others found it easier and more effective to take in established talent from the British Isles. This exasperated him. "Imagine the professional game of baseball giving preference to foreign players rather than to those who come to the farms and cities to play the national game of the United States," he wrote, "and you may also imagine a debacle for professional baseball. It would lose its national import in a season and with it its national support. . . . I believe promising United States players have been permitted to lie idle and go to seed while the foreign player has reaped a harvest."

The 1922 Challenge Cup final offered a hopeful portent. Scullin Steel of St. Louis, with not a "foreigner" to their name, defeated the largely British-born Todd's Shipyard of Brooklyn. Impressed with what he'd seen—and with the success of the "St. Louis" team he'd taken to Scandinavia still fresh in his mind—Cahill reiterated his impudent 1917 claim: he could pick a team of Americans capable of defeating any team in Britain. "In goal shooting, speed, aggressiveness, and other factors America is equal to or better than the old country today," he maintained. "This opinion is shared in Sweden, Norway and Denmark, elevens from which countries have met football teams from this country and from the British Isles, too. Swedish authorities long ago told me that America had outstripped England in football strength. I believe it."

The British laughed. Fred Milnes, leader of the Pilgrims team Cahill had helped to bring to North America, thought that to "compare the best soccer in America with league football in England" was "really too funny for words," even if the game had "come along by leaps and bounds in the States":

> Although Mr. Cahill is an enthusiastic secretary, his knowledge of a player is his weakness. He is no judge of a player. . . . The best "American-born" team would rank perhaps on a par with Central or Midland League football. The best team chosen from the States, including Britishers, would compare with Third Division football. . . . The popularity of soccer is exceeding the "perfecting" of the play. I know Mr. Cahill longs to see an international game with England. I know it is one of his great ambitions—he has told me so—but more hard work is necessary ere this is accomplished. Had Mr. Cahill any experience as a player, he would know that although "speed" is a great asset it is by no means everything— perhaps it is the least essential. . . . If the Americans challenge an all-British team, or an English eleven, or a Scottish selection, and come to this country they will be taken seriously—and beaten, even if our standard of skill is not yet what it was before the war.

Cahill was unrepentant. He called attention to the "record of the successes of the American teams that have visited Scandinavia," which "appeared to so much better advantage against the best teams of Scandinavia than the British teams had been doing." But this was a woefully naïve assessment. The British teams in question were amateur, hardly the level of English and Scottish League professionals. It's quite possible Cahill was aware of this and was merely trying to drum up interest in a transatlantic confrontation. In any case, the opportunity never came, and he would have to make do with visits from touring English and Scottish clubs, pitted against "American" teams that were usually anything but.

His judgment in domestic matters was more surefooted, though much of his time seemed to be taken up calling attention to fairly obvious encumbrances. In his secretary's report to the USFA for 1920, Cahill noted that many Challenge Cup matches had been played at distinctly unsatisfactory venues (a fourth-round match in Detroit had even taken place on a public park). "The growth of the game cannot be properly maintained unless there are proper fields for play," he warned. "Poor and uncomfortable accommodations for the spectators will soon kill the interest we have been at such pains to develop and if it once recedes, it cannot very easily be rearoused."

But the USFA was still hopelessly under-resourced and its behavior, frustratingly adolescent. Cahill feuded bitterly with a number of officials—enough for the first president to resign and the second to attempt to do the same—and was said to have provoked a number of adversaries into making seditious challenges to the association's authority. Though little of this reached the press, a correspondent of the *New York Tribune,* who was also a USFA delegate, did note in 1918:

> Meetings of the national body have been little better than knock-down-and-drag-out affairs. The most intricate political maneuvering has been resorted to in some quarters. There has been vote bartering. There has been double-crossing. The history of the government of the game embraces also unadulterated middle-age violence. There have been some creditable actions, some calm and collected periods, to be sure, but for the most part USFA affairs in the past have been odoriferous.

According to the *New York Globe,* though, the challenges were more imagined than real:

> The usual rumblings of the formation of a new organization in opposition to the United States Football Association again fills the air. Annually there are a few disgruntled and dissatisfied office-seekers who put such rumors in circulation, accomplished

by [diverse] threats as to what is going to happen at the annual meeting of the USFA. Invariably the meetings of the parent body [have] passed off in the most harmonious manner, with each individual delegate from as far west as Missouri showing the keenest interest in the success of the organization. According to the statements published in several of the newspapers the principal trouble lies in the manner in which Secretary T. W. Cahill runs the affairs of the USFA. Even the men who have opposed Cahill in everything pertaining to his office have admitted that he has done more to boost socker in this country than any one individual. . . . Since the USFA was organized Secretary Cahill has had numerous fights on his hands, and has emerged from all with flying colors.

Fights there were. When the USFA proved incapable of producing a team for the 1920 Olympics, Cahill, secretary of the Olympic committee, squared off with another committee member, former president Guss Manning. Manning accused Cahill of taking more of an interest in accompanying the St. Louis professionals to Sweden than in getting an Olympic team to Antwerp; Cahill thought Manning was merely harboring a grudge over the USFA's decision not to join the British in pulling out of FIFA in protest over Germany's continued membership after the war ("The Olympic episode was merely seized upon as affording a means for the display of his spleen").

If the English-born, German-educated surgeon and the bluff all-American salesman made for an unlikely couple, it was one that had done much to get the USFA off the ground. But their antagonism continued to fester to a point at which some claimed Manning was furtively plotting for Cahill to be replaced. Until 1921, though, the secretary's position was an elected one—and for all the hackles he raised, the incumbent was widely regarded as the best man for the job.

Yet Cahill was also eager to put the game on a higher plane, something he now thought couldn't be done without his moving on. In November 1920, he told the *St. Louis Post-Dispatch*:

I have been secretary of the USFA for a long time and cannot better myself in that body. I have several things in mind, but if I am tied down to the secretaryship, I cannot accomplish these. . . . The plans I have in mind at present are for the betterment of soccer and will also help strengthen the national body. My idea is to put the game on a paying basis, while I also have in mind a plan to form a national soccer league. However, for this a lot of money is needed, and that will be one of the things for me to work out, after I have left my present place with the USFA.

His departure was confirmed at the annual meeting six months later. Well aware of what it was losing, the USFA offered him an honorarium of $2,000—over one-fifth the amount in its treasury—and membership for life. Cahill, "speaking under great emotion," explained his reasons for leaving: far from abandoning the organization, he "intended to go out and open up new fields and make the national body bigger and more powerful than it was today." The USFA, he insisted, was "at the beginning of its brightest years," having "attained its manhood."

This apparently decisive moment in the association's history proved rather more inconsequential six months later, when James Scholefield's indiscretions sent Cahill careering back into the secretary's chair. But by then, his lofty idea had been realized: the American Soccer League, a professional circuit of eight teams stretching from Massachusetts to Pennsylvania, had begun play a few months earlier. Cahill was its secretary and driving force, and his inspiration had come from baseball. Soccer, he knew, would not flourish in America by dint of knockout cups and occasional international contests; it needed regular first-rate competition. He was proud of what his league had achieved in its first year. "Just as in baseball, the professional game has developed the amateur interest to such an extent that every American boy plays baseball from the time he is able to toddle," he noted. "So it is coming to be with soccer. . . . Already this season, there has been more soccer news printed in New York papers than in the entire preceding three years."

The American Soccer League represented a genuine breakthrough for the game in the United States.* Cahill knew its success depended on paying customers and did his best to accommodate them: almost all the teams played in baseball parks or athletic grounds with covered stands, and in most of them matches were permitted on Sundays. The league produced weekly press releases that included kick-off times and venues. And the standard of play, if Spalding's *Guide* can be believed, was

---

* According to the minutes from the ASL's organizational meeting, the use of the word "soccer" was urged "because it would discriminate between the American game of football and soccer, the rugby game being considered football in an American sense." The officials "considered that for press purposes and convenience the title should be as short as possible, and contended that though this seemed at first thought, of small consequences, it was vital from the view point of advertising."

"undoubtedly higher than any with which the soccer public of the Eastern United States has been regularly provided in the past."

Yet it had not gone entirely to plan. After the first season, several clubs folded, withdrew, or changed owners. Attendance was patchy; indiscipline, rife. "It is sufficient to say that the authority given to the American League to operate practically under the direction of Mr. Cahill has not been altogether successful," observed one Philadelphia paper, which would later claim the hometown team had lost $10,000 in spite of winning the championship. To Cahill, though, these were growing pains. "One not need be possessed of the gift of prophecy," he wrote, "to look into the future and see not only a steady and rapid growth for the American Soccer League, but also the formation of similar leagues in other sections of the country." That he would now turn his attention to developing a similar entity in the Midwest—with the winners of the two leagues meeting for a national championship—seemed to many an inevitable next step.

Though one of the reasons he'd left his USFA post was that his "personal interests had suffered," Cahill seemed more embroiled in the game than ever, and Scholefield's absquatulation had left the association with a mountain of work. Returning to the secretary's desk, Cahill tackled the assignments with his customary vigor. A relieved USFA awarded him another honorarium: $500, "in consideration of his untiring efforts to restore order in the affairs of the office which were in chaos at the time." While Cahill agreed to remain secretary, it was with reluctance: the "member for life" was also an ex-officio participant of each of the USFA's eleven standing committees.

The influence of the man some had come to regard as the "father of American soccer" was nearing its peak, and Cahill continued to seek pragmatic solutions to the game's ailments. The scarcity of decent ballparks moved him to write in 1922 that the USFA should "secure permanent grounds, either by purchase or lease," a proposition the association's finances seemed increasingly capable of supporting (around $16,000 came in from Challenge Cup fees in 1922, a record 132 clubs having entered). At the 1923 annual meeting, he again "laid stress on the difficulty of obtaining suitable fields for the playing of big games and urged immediate action," but the delegates could only respond by appointing a committee to "consider the matter of securing a suitable ground in the metropolitan district of New York." Nothing came of its efforts.*

---

* "One interested capitalist wanted to stake us funds to erect a double-deck soccer stadium of our own at 3 percent interest—[an] easy pay-off," Cahill recalled to a writer in St. Louis in 1946. "In the end, caution prevailed and we never cashed in on our prospects."

Searching for the right places to play was something of a preoccupation for Cahill, and it took him on some wondrous flights of fancy. Touring Sweden in 1916, he'd marveled at the all-covered stands of Stockholm's Olympic Stadium, which had no equivalent in the United States. According to the *Post-Dispatch*:

> Cahill . . . brought back a new suggestion for soccer—one which would cost more money than any known promoter outside the asylum would at present care to follow through. This is: That the soccer fields be entirely enclosed in a glass roof of sufficient height not to interfere with kicks. He thinks that this would popularize a game that now has many inconveniences for the spectators, owing to the inclement season in which it is played in this country.

While Cahill had done much to point the game in the right direction, it continued to display a worrying proclivity for ineptitude. In 1922–1923, for the first time, over 100,000 paying customers attended Challenge Cup matches, and nearly 10,000 of them were on hand in Harrison, New Jersey, to watch the final between Scullin Steel and Paterson FC. But the match ended in a tie—an outcome nobody seemed to have considered and one that would embarrass the sport. With several Scullin players due elsewhere for the start of baseball season, the club insisted it could only play the rematch at home. The USFA, clutching its rule book, refused; the final had to be played to a conclusion in the East.

Here were headlines soccer could have done without. Papers in St. Louis urged the association to see sense and replay the final in their city; others suggested a best-of-three series or postponing the match until the following season. Many agreed with the *New York Herald* that the "real final" had taken place in Cahill's office, where the two clubs and the association tried to forge a compromise. But no one would budge. Paterson claimed the trophy by forfeit, and soccer was left nursing an unsightly bruise. Cahill tried to brush aside the disappointment, claiming the controversy had simply "opened the eyes of the East to the bigness of the game." But he knew the damage that had been done.

What he didn't know, though, was how unfavorably the decision would rebound on him—and culminate in what he would refer to as "the biggest trouble of my football career." Anger in St. Louis about the USFA's cup final obduracy carried over into the association's annual meeting a month later. The city's delegates—including Winton Barker, Cahill's longtime associate—voted for a regime change, helping to bring to an end the largely benign four-year reign of Detroit's George Healey.

The new president had previously occupied the position from 1917 to 1919: Peter Peel of Chicago, long a Cahill adversary.* Though losing by a single vote, Healey amiably moved that the decision be made unanimous, but he was in a less charitable mood a few days later. He wrote in a letter to Cahill that his successor was "a nice chap, but the biggest four-flusher in soccer, one who [has] done nothing for Chicago Soccer for years but to use it as an advertisement for himself."

Cahill agreed, claiming also that Peel "had the active assistance of the little group of English and Scotch here in the east who follow the leadership of [Guss] Manning," a cadre apparently still incensed with him for not following the British associations out of FIFA. According to Cahill, Manning "practically retired from soccer except in a small local way" but continued to "[assert] himself in national football politics as a power behind the opposition when he saw a chance to circumvent me." A year earlier, Cahill had made reference in his annual report to "a campaign of hate which has been waged persistently, if under cover, against the administration by a little clique who seem actuated by the idea that if they cannot rule, it is their special province to ruin." Whom he had in mind is unclear; the Manning faction was only one possibility.

Yet there were still plenty in Cahill's corner, and it came as little surprise to see him appointed to manage the 1924 Olympic team. When Peel was named as his deputy, though, the rift between the two men deepened. Cahill soon complained that the president had become "insulting and domineering" toward him; Peel, in turn, was unhappy with the latitude Cahill took as secretary. The denouement came at a meeting on the eve of the National Challenge Cup final. Cahill described the incident to a friend:

> [Peel] began his abuse at the beginning of our committee meeting, and after the meeting adjourned, loudly declared he could take care of me "mentally or physically at any time." As luck would have it, I had my pocket knife in my hand—which is probably why Peel chose that moment—cutting a plug of tobacco. I could not let such a challenge pass and I advanced in his direction, putting the

---

* How much of an adversary? When Cahill announced he was stepping down as USFA secretary in 1921, Peel wrote to pass on his good wishes, noting how bitterly the two had fought during one particular stage of their work. "It is quite true, we battled desperately," Cahill replied, "but it was open warfare, carried on in thoroughly understood hostility. There was no pretense of friendship to furnish an ambuscade from which to strike."

knife away and taking off my glasses. If he had made good on his challenge, there would have been a lovely row, but the two others present intervened, and I left the room. The best evidence they could bring out in the Commission meeting was that at no time was I within five feet of Peel, but he declared I had assaulted him with a knife. He had that story printed in a friendly newspaper in Chicago, and telegraphed from there around the country. Naturally, it did me tremendous harm.

At Peel's beckoning, the USFA dismissed Cahill as secretary for "insubordination and incompetence" and removed him from the Olympic post. He had, according to one account, "been withholding certain correspondence from higher officials of the [USFA], and when called to task about this and other matters . . . displayed a flare of temper which could not be passed without notice."

Peel raised his sword:

> The recent actions of the ex-secretary at St. Louis, when he showed his true colors, were a culmination of many such acts to which national officers were subjected to by Cahill in the past. The removal of Cahill marks the end of his tyrannical reign and soccer fans and followers will undoubtedly relish his relegation to the scrap heap.

It was a premature obituary—and the requital was hardly surprising. One paper wrote how "various foemen in soccer football politics, whom Cahill in earlier years placed in office only to force out later after breaking with them[,] were 'in at the death.'"*

Cahill took up legal advice in an effort to restore his name but was left spitting feathers. Through a commercial agency, he discovered that Peel had filed a bankruptcy petition three years earlier; anxiously, Cahill wrote to a friend that "a $50,000 failure with no assets doesn't augur very well for the future of the $24,000 now in the USFA treasury." Talk began to surface of Cahill seeking to destroy what he created—by pulling the ASL out of the USFA and augmenting it with a second professional league in the Midwest. But such a mutinous change of heart seemed unlikely. As a life member, Cahill still possessed the means to attack the

---

* One official later claimed that "persons belonging to a certain secret society abetted the movement on the sole plea that Mr. Cahill belonged to a Knight of Columbus council." Was there more to his dismissal than a fit of pique?

association from within, and not everyone had condoned Peel's chicanery. Barker and his St. Louis League colleagues hastily passed a resolution deploring Cahill's dismissal and the allegation of incompetence "when we know that Mr. Cahill has, through his energetic and untiring efforts, sacrificed the greater part of his life without recompense for the welfare and advancement of the game."

One thing seemed certain: fur would fly at the USFA's 1924 annual meeting. Yet in the end, Healey and Manning brokered a compromise: Cahill would apologize for his fit of temper at the hotel, and the USFA, though not reappointing him secretary, would offer a compensatory "salary or honorarium" of $2,000. No blood was spilled; one observer even went so far as to claim that "any feeling that may have existed prior to the meeting was absent when the session ended, every one without exception being in harmony."

Privately, though, Cahill still seethed, railing against Peel and vice-presidents Morris Johnson and William Patrick, the two others who had conspired against him in St. Louis and "took over the most prosperous sporting organization in the country that I built up from nothing." Peel declined the nomination for another term as president in 1924, but it was Johnson who succeeded him. The new administration moved the USFA out of Spalding's premises and into offices on Liberty Street (while Spalding, much to the dismay of future historians, stopped producing its annual *Guide*).

Cahill was in no hurry to be secretary again. He still had his foot in the USFA's door and still plowed his furrow for the ASL. Yet this may not have been enough for his employer, especially in the wake of his indecorous removal from office. In fact, Cahill would leave Spalding to focus full time on the ASL, an enterprise he believed was "beginning to lift its head into prominence." While his assertion that soccer would soon rank second only to baseball as the leading professional game may have been self-serving, few doubted that his league could survive as a profitable entity.

But his focus on cultivating the professional game and the desire of its pre-eminent clubs to improve their financial positions would cripple the USFA. Lacking sufficient financial incentive to play in the Challenge Cup, the ASL refused to enter its teams in 1924; it created its own knockout competition, which it believed would draw bigger crowds—and from which it could pocket more of the gate receipts. When the professional clubs from St. Louis, the game's other profitable attraction, also withdrew, Johnson's USFA was deprived of a main source of its revenue.

Revenge? By himself, Cahill could not have overturned the will of the professionals, but it's unlikely he would have made much effort. As it turned out, the ASL/St. Louis "professional cup" attracted nearly 52,000 fans for its eleven games, while the whole of the Challenge Cup drew fewer than 56,000 for 144. "The season of 1924–25 has not been one of great accomplishment," admitted Andrew Brown, the USFA's secretary, claiming among other things that the association's efforts to interest the American League in the Challenge Cup had been "met by undisguised hostility."*

Cahill denied orchestrating the pullout and doubtless would have abhorred the thought of the association digging into the surplus he had scrupulously built up. In fact, he might still have hoped, as one paper asserted, that the USFA would raise the $50,000 he wanted to "erect a monster stadium as a monument to the sport." But if he was merely sending a message to Johnson's regime, it was a devastating one. "The USFA went into eclipse the moment Cahill left it to its own devices," claimed the *St. Louis Post-Dispatch*. "The shadow of Cahill's newly built American Soccer League fell athwart the USFA and blotted it out. The national body's present control seems to lack a master mind and a real executive." In some ways, the association never recovered from the blow. Thoughts of owning a stadium would vanish amid the turbulence of seasons to come; and it would be a very long time before the Challenge Cup again generated the $112,000 in receipts it did the year before Cahill's dismissal.†

All the same, there was plenty of cause for optimism. The ASL was still on the rise: gate receipts had improved substantially as owners splashed out on better players and spruced up their grounds (a few even owned them). Some insist that the quality of its play was as good as nearly anywhere in the world. The clubs also re-entered the Challenge Cup under new terms, restoring prestige to what was still officially the national championship.

For Cahill, though, the game had still failed to address a number of fundamental issues. Among them were "the necessity of playing in cold weather because baseball monopolizes spring, summer and fall," the "wide popularity of, and heavy investments in, college football," and the "lack of the right propaganda to interest American youth in the game." In

---

* This is the same "somewhat antagonistic" Andrew Brown who had been president of the American Football Association in 1913 (see Chapter 2).

† Some random examples: 1936–1937, $36,920; 1950–1951, $1,662; 1962–1963, $7,784.

an interview with the *Post-Dispatch* in 1925, he spoke in detail about the obstacle perhaps closest to his heart:

> I think the time has come when American-born officials should control the national and all subsidiary organizations in this country; when the teams should be made up of as large a percent of American-born material as possible; and when the propaganda of soccer should be undertaken with a view to more thorough Americanizing some of its phases. The country owes a great deal to the Old Country pioneers who brought the game across and kept it alive during its early days. We need their good players, and their presence in a minor proportion on all clubs is highly desirable. [But] at the present time it is almost impossible outside of St. Louis to assemble an eleven of first-class, home-grown soccer football talent.

He was far from the only official to hold such views. "Americanization" had been a key theme since before the USFA's formation, and even foreign-born officials acknowledged the need for the game to become more homegrown. But this was easier said than done. Bethlehem Steel, which won its fifth Challenge Cup in 1926, remained the most famous team in the country and still recruited most of its players from Scotland. Professional clubs were more concerned with winning matches than developing native talent.

In fact, even amid the burgeoning fan interest, few teams in the American League were making much money, and by the summer of 1926 their frustration began to tell. The New England franchises contemplated forming a league of their own (even inviting entries from Canada), and overtures were made to baseball owners, if primarily for their ballparks. Cahill wasn't implicated in the former but tried to leverage his baseball connections, with little success.

Then the sky began to fall. Fred Smith, the English-born Brooklynite who had served as the ASL's president since 1923, gave way to the more "progressive" figure of Bill Cunningham, a onetime football all-America turned sportswriter for the *Boston Post.* Cunningham was also appointed the league's secretary, though there had been a unanimous vote that Cahill's services be "retained in an advisory capacity, at a salary to be determined at a later date."

What appeared to be an injection of fresh blood was actually a coup d'état. At a meeting in Providence, Rhode Island, a few weeks later, Cunningham appointed his *Post* colleague Dave Scott to the secretary's position. When it also emerged that Cahill's advisory role would carry little weight (one paper claimed it was "generally understood he was to be the league's representative in the metropolitan district, taking care of registration forms, publicity etc."), Cahill balked. He told the *St. Louis Post-Dispatch*:

> I considered the offer of an "advisory" post a demotion and a reduction in salary and it looked as if these fellows thought I had reached the end of my period of usefulness and were trying to "take care of me" as they put it. I am not a subject for the poorhouse by any means and I refuse to be subservient to the new officials whom they saw fit to appoint. I have labored hard for this organization and I feel that I am entitled to at least some consideration. They evidently did not want me in because I have always refused to be [a] "yes" man for anybody. They do not realize what soccer means to me. It is in my blood. When they offered the advisory position I challenged them to show me one reason why I should not be returned to the secretaryship and they could not answer.

Hastily, Cunningham wrote to Cahill:

> I can't tell you how sorry I am to have walked into a jam like the one at Providence, and I wish there were some way out. . . . Somebody cabled me an offer of a job I didn't know existed, and I cabled back "Yes" because I felt I had the time to swing it and because I was interested in the thing it was trying to do. I wouldn't have walked on anybody's neck for the world. And when that somebody turned out to be a fellow like you, I want you to know that it broke me up pretty badly.

Cahill shot back:

> Don't bother to try explaining any sorrow you may have, for walking as you call it, "into a jam" at Providence. Put it out of your mind until you walk into a few more and then you will begin to understand the first speech you ever heard from me. Until then you may imagine there is not much to soccer except to kick the ball. A few years from now, if you care to stick at it that long, you

and I will be firm friends, because I am a straight shooter and I think you are.

This proved about as cordial as relations would get between the two men.

Cahill was dazed. Visiting the offices of the *Fall River Globe* not long after the Providence meeting, he "had the same hearty handshake, but his face was that of a person who had suffered the loss of a dear one." Rumors again surfaced that he would turn his hand to some new soccer enterprise or other, the most ambitious of which was a professional league connecting St. Louis, Chicago, Detroit, and Cleveland. Yet it was hockey that came to his aid early in 1927. It even sent him back to Sweden, whose soccer association had regarded him highly enough to have made him the first foreign recipient of its medal of honor.

The Victoria hockey club of Montreal appointed Cahill to manage what was the first venture into Scandinavia by a North American team. In fact, the club would tour almost the whole of Europe, playing in such unlikely frozen-pond venues as London and Venice. The Canadians eased their way to fifteen straight wins and outscored the opposition 162–15, with Cahill dutifully apprising Spalding Brothers of the game's potential ("There is no doubt but what Sweden's winter game of the future will be[:] Ice Hockey developed on the Canadian style of equipment, uniforms, and rules").

Soccer did not keep him away much longer. James Armstrong had become the USFA's secretary, but by the summer of 1927 the English-born New Yorker could only report that the season, "while not of great accomplishment, at least held its own with the preceding season." He did not wish to serve another term. In considering a replacement, none other than Peter Peel—to much applause—declared at the association's annual meeting that "applications for this particular position should be considered entirely on their merits and all previous history of this organization should be lost sight of." Whether this was a direct appeal for the return of his knife-bearing foe or whether all the wounds had healed is unclear, but Cahill was appointed to replace Armstrong without a trace of objection.

Had the USFA finally succumbed to the overwhelming need for unity? The association had grown steadily over its first decade but was losing momentum in the second. It had made few inroads into less familiar parts of the country and achieved little at the junior or scholastic level; its Challenge Cup income had also been greatly eroded by the demands of the professional clubs. Attendance for the competition began to level off, and by 1927 the $24,000 that once sat in the treasury had been whittled down to less than half that.

But it was the decision the USFA made at its 1926 meeting to give professional clubs greater autonomy that proved to be the most damaging. Cunningham's ASL initiated sweeping changes, many of them to do with the game itself: shirt numbers, player substitutions, goal judges (briefly), and hockey-style penalty boxes. Such was its hubris that the referees soon went on strike, and the questionable means by which some ASL clubs had acquired overseas players landed the USFA in trouble with FIFA. In his secretary's report for 1928, Cahill warned that a "grave danger" confronted the association: the ASL coveted the USFA's authority, and its apparent disregard for international convention over players' contracts and suspensions had "given rise to heated comment on the honesty of this sport" and were so severe as to demand "immediate relief." He warned the association to "beware of the thrust from within"—something he had first-hand experience of, even if his lunges had been more honorable.

The association itself remained dysfunctional. "For some time past it has been no secret that the [USFA] was running along none too smoothly," the *Fall River Globe* wrote in May 1928. "It is no dark and deep secret that there have been rumblings of discontent and distrust for at least two seasons past, and that it needed a zephyr to fan into uncontrollable flame the undercover fire. It has been recognized in many districts throughout the jurisdiction of the USFA that constitutional authority was a mere matter of imagination, and that laws existed only as printed in the rules book." The paper claimed that Andrew Brown, who'd become president in 1926, "failed to reach a degree of capability or capacity to follow the constructive ideals of most of his predecessors and became content to slough along or permit himself to be carried along by gush and ego."

The assessment may not have been altogether fair, but Brown's ability to identify and harness the talent within the association was certainly open to question. The process of selecting of a manager for the 1928 Olympic team was a case in point. The *Globe* noted that "after considerable heat and passionate exchanges, a decision [appeared] to have been reached whereby President Brown became entrusted with the task of picking of the party who should manage the team." Cahill, whose fund-raising efforts for the trip to Amsterdam had been typically prodigious, might have expected to have been rewarded with the manager's position, yet he was passed over in favor of Elmer Schroeder of Philadelphia, an inexperienced man less than half his age. (The president later defended his decision with the assertion that he "had to consider the sending abroad of sixteen boys who had never been away from their native country, with but one exception.") Brown did ask Cahill to accompany Schroeder as his adjutant, but with the galling proviso that he raise $500 to finance his trip. Cahill declined, citing "urgent official and personal business matters" but privately seething with resentment. Given the performance of the scrupulously amateur U.S. team in the Netherlands—it lost 11–2 to Argentina—he may have been glad to have stayed home.

But abject defeats on foreign soil were the least of the USFA's worries. Reining in the feisty ASL was proving beyond its means, and the league's increasingly uncompromising stance toward the governing body turned up the heat on the game's most important relationship. In October 1928, the pot boiled over. The ASL instructed its clubs not to participate in the Challenge Cup; when three teams entered anyway, it removed them from the league. Incensed by this decision, and perceiving it as a threat to its own authority, the USFA then revoked the ASL's membership, leaving the league to operate without national (or international) approval.

The men running the game seemed hell-bent on destroying it. Pressed into action, and sensing a chance to slay the beast he had fathered, Cahill hastily formed a rival Eastern Professional Soccer League, picking up the three ASL outcasts and enlisting several clubs from metropolitan New York. As the two circuits traded insults and picked each other's pockets, fans and newspapers lost interest. But the war endured for twelve desperate months. Cahill—for once—may not have been at the center of the battle, yet like everyone else he was swept up in its rhetoric, hurling insults at the enemy and allowing differences of opinion to billow into antipathy. Addressing a meeting in early 1929, he insisted that the war was purely an effort by the professionals to gain control of the game:

> I hope you people will not permit yourselves to be misled by the mis-statements of these men who are in the game for the "dollar" and not for any good they can do the sport. They have absolutely failed in their effort to wreck the USFA. They have also failed to realize that soccer does not belong to the American League, the Eastern League or any league. It belongs to the people, who pay the bills and who are the first to be considered. The USFA is interested in satisfying the people first of all.

But divisive language did soccer no favors. The sports editor of the *New York Telegram* wrote to a USFA official to explain why his paper had all but given up on the sport:

At present, there are three or four contesting leagues and associations. They put on games which draw less than 100 spectators on numerous occasions. They bicker, yap, fight and tear each other's reputations to shreds. Court action is being taken by the rival organizations and players are on the verge of being deported as non-artists.

This was the precarious position from which American soccer entered the Great Depression. Eventually, the USFA brought the ASL back into line, but not before both had bled close to death. The decision of Bethlehem Steel to fold its team in the spring of 1930, partly as a result of all of the in-fighting, was, for Cahill, a kick in the teeth: the club had been "one of the national organization's staunchest pillars," and its passing represented "a stunning blow to soccer football and one the full extent of which the game's followers generally may be slow to appreciate."

Few could imagine how much further the game would fall. Sixty-six when Bethlehem disbanded, Cahill had every excuse to put up his feet or throw up his hands. But he remained steadfastly active. "He is still in the best of health," one paper noted, "a strong, virile man, who has never allowed himself to become physically stagnant." All the same, his star was fading. Again he was denied the chance to lead the national team onto the world stage, this time at the inaugural World Cup. The USFA appointed as manager its thirty-eight-year-old treasurer, Bill Cummings, one of Cahill's adversaries in the St. Louis hotel incident. Cahill also sensed that there no longer was much to the secretary's position; Armstrong Patterson, who began a four-year tenure as president in 1928, was now doing most of the heavy lifting.*

It was time to move on. Cahill wrote to Patterson—just weeks after Bethlehem's demise—expressing a "preference for more activity" and a "personal desire to assist to the best of my ability in furthering the organization." His days as secretary, he affirmed, were over; he and his friends thought he could "be more useful elsewhere."

Patterson agreed. Though quarreling frequently with Cahill in private, the Northern Irish-born Michiganian had not underestimated his value to the game. After arranging a vacation for Cahill at the association's expense ("You have worked unceasingly for a long period"), he

---

* One of Cahill's tasks included finding new premises for the association. Patterson settled on the Cornish Arms Hotel on West 23rd Street, where the USFA would remain until the 1940s.

found an outlet for his perpetual energy and drive. For some time, the USFA had debated the merits of hiring a "field delegate" to survey the game's wider terrain and kindle interest in the more forlorn parts of country, particularly among the young. They now had their man. Cahill spent the better part of six months drumming up support in the South and Southwest, helping to form new regional associations in northern Texas and greater Cincinnati; he also met with various representatives of the National Recreation Association, a group the USFA hoped would help to establish the game on playgrounds. But in cities like Jacksonville and New Orleans, hardly anyone knew enough about the sport to teach it, and not everyone was keen to learn. The superintendent of recreation in Savannah, Georgia, told Cahill that although he was interested in soccer, he had "only been able to get the girls to play the game."

The roots Cahill and his associates had laid down a generation earlier seemed to be rotting. Increasingly, soccer was looked upon as an alien game, even in St. Louis, where the *Post-Dispatch* observed it was "still, except in intercollegiate circles, largely played by the foreign-born athletes." Persistent clashes between the professionals and amateurs left the USFA without a clear sense of direction. Patterson and Cahill may have regarded the development of the professional game as paramount, but not everyone in their ranks agreed.

In 1932, Cahill declared:

> Two soccer bodies are needed in this country. Professional soccer has grown so rapidly that its rights and needs are not protected fully under the present system whereby one organization handles both amateurs and professionals, with the amateurs trying to keep the reins of power. Imagine amateur baseball trying to dictate to professional baseball! All the capital, all the risks, all the stars are in professional football ranks. It of course can't be right for amateurs to jeopardize the investments of professionals by objecting to their plans and policies. Just at this time soccer affairs of all sorts are below par, perhaps. But even so it is the professional teams that create interest and supply most of the funds for the USFA. In my opinion it is only a question of time when the amateur and pro branches will operate under separate associations. And that time is not far distant.

He was wrong about the split—and, for that matter, the "rapid" growth of the professional game. By 1931, the St. Louis League had been brought to its knees, partly by the Depression but also through maladministration, its difficulties made all the more apparent by the thousands who still turned out to watch matches in the city's Municipal League. Visiting in conjunction with his field work that year, Cahill despaired at the state of the pro circuit ("Three hundred persons at a Sunday soccer game? What's happened to the old sport here?"). By the autumn, he'd become its secretary. His efforts at resuscitation included dropping the admission charge to 50 cents, which helped to attract an opening-day crowd of 2,500. Returning east, Cahill felt confident he had made the necessary improvements, but they proved fleeting. Before the end of the decade, the St. Louis League would be gone.

The USFA, too, shivered in the cold. Soon there was no money for field delegates' expeditions or much else besides, and while the Challenge Cup still attracted plenty of entries and the occasional half-decent crowd, it was no longer a cash cow. Often it was its own worst enemy. The *Fall River Herald News* voiced its displeasure in 1931 at the association's decision to change the kickoff time of February cup games, apparently without letting anyone know. For a match between Fall River and Providence, it claimed "over 1,200 fans were forced to wait a half hour in the biting cold." Once the paper had been among Cahill's harshest critics; now it wrote:

> When is the United States Football Association, the governing body of the soccer game, going to snap out of it and do something to build up the sport rather than destroy what interest there is left in it? There was a time, back in the days when Tom Cahill was in power, when the public was kept informed with everything that was going on but now it appears to be the rule to keep everything secret. . . . A little more action and less chair warming in the USFA headquarters would be greatly appreciated by the fans, many of whom are of the opinion that the USFA is only an excuse to provide some favored persons with soft jobs, good salaries and long trips.

For some, the time had come to start from scratch. Edward Duffy wrote in *Soccer Star*:

> Thomas W. Cahill, pioneer of the sport in this country in an organized way, always declared, when he saw the baby he had reared to childhood become recalcitrant, that it needed a dictator and once he attempted to get football to adopt such a man as the salvation

of the sport. He failed and Tom does not hold the position in soccer he once did. The numerical superiority of the inconsequential elements that go to make up the national body overshadow the important elements; and their combined influence have the final say [*sic*] about the multitude of rules and regulations that would baffle even a baseball lawyer. . . . It must be conceded the present system has not brought results. America's success in all its affairs lies in its readiness to discard quickly unsuccessful methods in favor of successful ones. There is no tradition in these United States. What was successful ten years ago is in the ash can now. Let's throw soccer's wrecking influences to the garbage man and retrieve the game before it is entirely lost here, as many a good soccer man fears.

Entering his seventies, Cahill began to spend much of his time in Florida but still pursued opportunities to develop the game. In 1936, he headed a committee to introduce "major" soccer to the southeastern United States "and particularly the Florida resort cities." Nothing major came of the committee's work, though Cahill did help to organize a four-team league in Tampa and introduce the game to students at the university there. At seventy-four, he even refereed the occasional match.

By then, though, the papers were preparing their epitaphs. Sid Keener of the *St. Louis Star-Times,* profiling Cahill and another enthusiast, wrote in 1936:

Old Tom didn't exactly bring the game to this country, but he was the one who stood behind it, plugging and boosting the kicking pastime, and partly succeeding in his efforts to govern the game and promote it on a par with baseball and collegiate football. Cahill visualized a prosperous future for soccer at that time. He talked about crowds of 50,000 and upwards at the national championship he planned. He'd organize soccer on a nation-wide basis, so he said, and he'd have leagues that would compare with major league baseball and stadia that would rival collegiate football fields for seating capacity. Part of Cahill's dream came true. He was instrumental in organizing the [USFA]. . . . Teams, leagues and districts were organized and eventually the west and east met in a grand finale for the national cup. Those were happy days for the old boy. Concrete stadia, with seating capacity of 50,000, however, did not materialize. Cahill's idea failed to click after a fairly successful start. Passing years marked occasional spurts in the grand old kicking game, and the pay-off for promoter and players alike was pretty substantial at times. Then something happened, the game lost its pull with the patrons and here we find a pair of old-time soccer enthusiasts almost at the point of surrender in their thankless efforts to keep the sport alive.

Old Tom refused to surrender. "All we need is some live-wire direction by the national body," he insisted. "We showed them long ago what a little hustling could do." Well into the 1940s, he continued to search for chinks of light that might rescue the game. Robert Burnes of the *St. Louis Globe-Democrat* wrote in 1946:

Less than a year ago Cahill thought he might be on the brink of achieving success. Branch Rickey, an old friend from their days in St. Louis, conferred with Tom on the possibility of setting up a professional soccer league in major league ball parks. He offered Ebbets Field and already had interested Phil Wrigley of the Cubs. ... Current operators of soccer franchises in various cities, learning of the purported deal, instead of lending all the support possible, upped the sale price of their franchises or demanded to be cut in on the operations in the big parks. The minute Rickey heard that, he pulled out—and Tom Cahill's last hope of building soccer to major sport proportions failed. "It's been the same story for fifty years," he said. "I've known, everyone in soccer has known, that until there are adequate stadium facilities, the game will never be a financial success."

The USFA's 1947 meeting, at the Pennsylvania Hotel in New York City, proved to be Cahill's last; prophetically, he was given the chance to speak. "I have devoted 90 percent of my life, when I wasn't working—and that was very seldom—to sport," he declared. "I have given everything from my heart and my very mind to devotion of sport." While the delegates rose dutifully to applaud "this grand old man of soccer," few of them would have appreciated the extent of his accomplishments. In taking American teams overseas and overseas teams across America; in elevating the professional game to a level that would not be matched for another half-century; in identifying and attempting to remove the game's most threatening obstacles; even in simply laying the groundwork for a big Challenge Cup match, Cahill had demonstrated his facility for overachievement.

It's tempting to think that with a little better luck, he would have left a more lasting impression. But too much stood in his way. Soccer had become too marginalized: there were few places where Americans could discover the game, and its most fertile ground remained the sort of immigrant turf on which red-blooded Americans did not tread. Playing through the winter, comfortable stadium or no, was ruinous. And though Cahill's political skills lacked refinement, not even the most able diplomat stood much of a chance in the USFA's fractious and petulant cosmos. Add to this other, more generic impediments—changes to migration patterns, the Great Depression, the burgeoning hostility shown toward soccer by other sports, even the increasing importance of radio broadcasts, which took little interest in soccer—and it's hard to see how one man could have achieved more.

Cahill died on September 29, 1951. He'd been living in a nursing home, having suffered a stroke earlier in the year. The USFA sent flowers, and its secretary attended his funeral, but the grief was far from overwhelming. By then, several men had come to be regarded as "fathers" of American soccer—Manning and Peel among them—and few of Cahill's surviving peers did much to preserve his memory. His groundbreaking trips to Scandinavia had been eclipsed by more recent Olympic and World Cup play; his American Soccer League would scarcely be acknowledged by the "new" ASL that succeeded it in 1933; and in St. Louis, where he learned about the game and helped to put it on solid ground, most of the early successes had faded from memory.

If there is a happy end to Cahill's life, it came the year before he died, with America's victory over England at the World Cup. Twenty-eight years earlier, the flag-waving secretary had been ridiculed for suggesting American speed could overcome British craft. The victory of the United States over England in Belo Horizonte may not have proved him right, but for the next two decades it was the most conspicuous prize soccer in America had to its name. And no one had more reason to celebrate.

Uncle Sam and John Bull muse on their footballing predilections for the *Boston Globe* in the wake of the Pilgrims Football Club's visit in 1905. "Well, John, your game is mighty pretty, and deft, and well done, but there's something about our little old pastime that *does* fetch me."

The Brooklyn Field Club, first winners of the National Challenge Cup, or what today is known as the Lamar Hunt U.S. Open Cup. Bob Millar, "easily the classiest player in the New York district" and the man who would coach America's 1930 World Cup team, is third from the right in the front row; third from his right is James Ford, who scored the winning goal in the final. *(University Archives & Special Collections Department, Lovejoy Library, Southern Illinois University Edwardsville)*

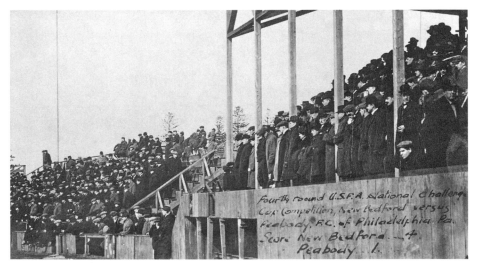

Spectators at the Athletic Ground in New Bedford, Massachusetts, await the start of a fourth-round National Challenge Cup match between the local eleven and the Peabody club of Philadelphia in March 1914. Though designated the home team, Peabody agreed to play in Massachusetts for $225 and 10 percent of the gate. New Bedford's was an all-star team, formed specifically for the competition that year. *(University Archives & Special Collections Department, Lovejoy Library, Southern Illinois University Edwardsville)*

Celtic of Brooklyn face the Rangers of Niagara Falls in the semifinal of the 1914 National Challenge Cup in Paterson, New Jersey. Shaking hands with Celtic's captain Andrew Robertson (3) is Fred Milnes (1), the Englishman who several years earlier had led the Pilgrims Football Club on two seminal tours of the country. Note the precariously supported fence in the background. *(University Archives & Special Collections Department, Lovejoy Library, Southern Illinois University Edwardsville)*

Cigar in hand, Tom Cahill relaxes en route to Scandinavia in 1920, the third such voyage in four years he had undertaken with American soccer teams. As early as 1917, he boasted to one St. Louis newspaper that he could go to that city and "by hard training, put an eleven in the field that could not only win the American title, but face any eleven in the world and win." *(University Archives & Special Collections Department, Lovejoy Library, Southern Illinois University Edwardsville)*

Cahill makes his allegiances plain before an unidentified match in Sweden. "We are sure that in a few years the Americans will be leading the world in soccer football," one Swedish newspaper predicted in 1919, "as they are leading in any other sport they are interested in." *(University Archives & Special Collections Department, Lovejoy Library, Southern Illinois University Edwardsville)*

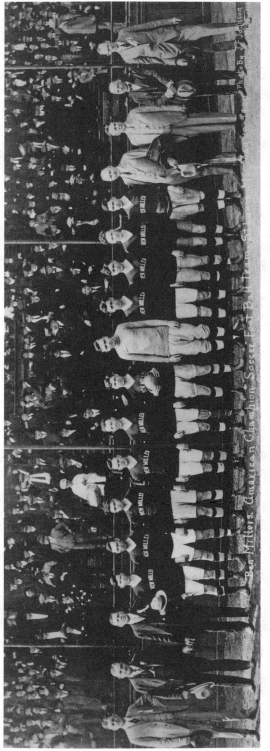

At the 1920 National Challenge Cup final, the Ben Miller club of St. Louis lines up with the great and the good of American soccer. The eponymous Ben Miller is second from left, with Tom Cahill to his immediate left. Peter Peel, who would accuse Cahill of pulling a knife on him in 1924, is fourth from right; to his immediate left is Winton Barker, a key figure in St. Louis soccer of the era. Hats, perhaps straight from Miller's factory, are conspicuously represented. (*University Archives & Special Collections Department, Lovejoy Library, Southern Illinois University Edwardsville*)

93

The mythical "St. Louis Soccer Club" poses before a match in Stockholm in 1920. Seven of the eighteen members of the squad were picked from Eastern teams, including Harry Ratican (front row, fourth from left), who had learned the game in St. Louis. But all of the players were American-born. *(Loan from archive of Gunnar Persson)*

The Scullin Steel team of St. Louis tied 2–2 with the Paterson club of New Jersey in the 1922 National Challenge Cup final, in what was regarded by at least one observer as "without a single doubt the best game seen since the innovation of soccer football in this country." But they forfeited the rematch because four of their players—Emmett Mulvey (back row, far left), Harry Oellerman (back row, center), James Brannigan (front row, fourth from left), and John Rooney (front row, third from right)—were due for baseball spring training. *(University Archives & Special Collections Department, Lovejoy Library, Southern Illinois University Edwardsville)*

The New York Americans take on the Shamrocks of St. Louis in the second game of the 1937 National Challenge Cup final at Starlight Park in the Bronx. It was the sixth straight year the Shamrocks, under various guises, appeared in the USFA's showpiece game. But the club disbanded a year later—and not until 1948 would the city again be represented in the final. *(University Archives & Special Collections Department, Lovejoy Library, Southern Illinois University Edwardsville)*

Bill Jeffrey, whose twenty-six-year tenure as Penn State's coach included tours of
Scotland in 1934 and Iran in 1951—and a nine-year, sixty-five-match unbeaten
streak. "I don't know, but it seems to me when I watch Bill and the boys out practicing they're just like a bunch of kids out playing for the fun they get," noted one
observer. "You'd think that a team . . . would be under great strain and tension
to keep up such a record, but on the contrary, there is no strained atmosphere."
(Penn State University Archives, Pennsylvania State University Libraries)

Fastidiously dressed representatives of Penn State pose aboard the *Cameronia* before their landmark tour of Scotland in 1934. The star of the team, John McEwan (back row, third from the right), had actually graduated from Syracuse University in 1933. Jeffrey is second from left in the front row; to his right is Jack Fletcher, the Penn State captain.

Penn State battles Purdue's club team in the 1951 "Soccer Bowl" on a raw New Year's Day at Sportsman's Park in St. Louis. Post-season play was extremely rare in college soccer before the 1960s; a formal national championship wasn't organized until 1959. (*University Archives & Special Collections Department, Lovejoy Library, Southern Illinois University Edwardsville*)

Tanned by a California summer, Englishman Mel Scott (6) displays his all-star form for the Oakland Clippers in the first match of the 1967 National Professional Soccer League championship series. The Clippers lost but won the return game a week later and "crowned the Eastbay with its first major league championship." *(From the archives of the National Soccer Hall of Fame and Museum)*

Dimitrije Davidovic (18) scores the Clippers' second goal against Manchester City in 1968. Oakland defeated the English league champions 3-1 in front of over 25,000 at the Oakland Coliseum, but three days later attracted only 2,512 for a home league match. *(From the archives of the National Soccer Hall of Fame and Museum)*

Aleksandar Obradovic, the Clippers' manager, displays one of his many talents after a match with St. Louis in April 1967. The Belgrade-born doctor of medicine led his team to a league championship that year. "You wait, in two, three years the Clippers will be good enough to play anywhere in the world." *(Courtesy of Getty Images)*

An ebullient Phil Woosnam, commissioner of the NASL, is flanked by the heraldry of the league's eighteen franchises in 1977. "I sell this game because once I believe in something and it makes sense to me, I will make it happen. This sport will take off. There is absolutely no way that it will not bypass everything else." *(AP/Wide World Photos)*

Kevin Hector (11) of the Vancouver Whitecaps tangles with the New York Cosmos' Vladislav Bogicevic (8) in the second game of the NASL's National Conference final in 1979. In what many regard as the greatest contest in the league's history, the Whitecaps eliminated the Cosmos after nearly three hours of play. *(AP/Wide World Photos)*

4

Mild Bill

Bill Jeffrey, Penn State, and College Soccer between the Wars

Said one freshman: How is the game up here, Bill, pretty rough? . . .
Jeffrey, that genial Scot, smiled and replied: No, we're technicians up
here. We don't use that Gas-house Gang stuff. If they play rough, we
kick 'em in the pants. And that's the way it goes. Every man on Bill
Jeffrey's team is a man who can handle the ball with his brains as well
as his feet. There is no reliance upon brute strength.
                                    —*Penn State Daily Collegian,* September 1937

I'S TEMPTING TO THINK that college soccer didn't amount to much
before the 1960s. Across huge swathes of the country, it didn't even
exist. Twelve states—among them Arizona, Texas, Washington, and
Wisconsin—hadn't a single varsity team. The first national championships didn't take place until 1959, by which time the game had developed
an appearance uniquely its own. Penalty boxes had become semicircles;
slide tackling was banned; and throw-ins had been replaced with kick-ins.
Matches consisted of twenty-two-minute quarters, and late in the final
periods time was stopped if the ball went out of play. When a goal was
scored, referees in striped shirts made the signal for a touchdown.

Such audacious efforts to Americanize the game failed to rescue it
from obscurity. On most campuses, soccer remained at best a foreign
quantity, at worst an unknown one. Wilkes College of Pennsylvania
began its first intercollegiate season in 1949 without any of its team having ever seen the game being played. In upstate New York, Rensselaer
Polytechnic had fielded teams since the 1920s, but among the varsity letters it issued in 1952 was one to the Uruguayan who served as the team's
translator. Elsewhere, the foreign presence was so overwhelming in parts
of the country that some schools ignored "official" college rules and
played by international ones.

Expertise was scarce. Most coaches knew almost nothing beyond what they'd picked up in PE class; many leaned on their experience of field hockey or lacrosse. Books were few and largely out of date—perhaps explaining why many schools persisted with tactical formations the rest of the world had abandoned. Learning baseball in Bolivia may have been more challenging, but not by much.

Not surprisingly, fledgling teams tutored by floundering coaches did not provide a great deal of entertainment. The typical college soccer match was crude and disjointed—and, in the heavy rain and snow of the late season, prone to farce. One of the era's most successful coaches, Earle Waters of West Chester College, was nicknamed "Muddy" not from any interest in Chicago blues but because of his teams' penchant for foul weather.

Some colleges did find coaches who understood the game. Unfailingly, they were foreign—and in the early years of the game they were also unfailingly British. One of the most enduring was Tom Dent, a Scotsman who had spent time at Aston Villa hoping to make it as a professional there. Dent took the job at Dartmouth College in 1924 and was still its coach in 1959.* Such a long tenure wasn't rare. Donald Baker, who was born in Pennsylvania, coached at Ursinus College from 1932 to 1971; Hugh McCurdy was in charge at Wesleyan University from 1922 to 1963. By 1961, no fewer than thirty men had been college soccer coaches for at least twenty years. The eldest of the elder statesmen, Allison Marsh, had started in 1916 and finished in 1957.

Did such long incumbencies develop because so few of the faculty knew anything about the game, or because so few institutions gave it much thought? Under Dent, Dartmouth was hardly a soccer powerhouse; losing years were nearly as common as winning ones. Baker, a professor of classics, was even less tainted by success ("My premise is that soccer in college is for fun and health")—he recorded just four winning seasons. Lehigh's coach from 1921 to 1940, Harry Carpenter, won only six of his last sixty-six matches. Even Sam Fletcher, a standout player and key figure in the American Soccer League of the 1920s, managed only one victory in each of his first five seasons at Brown.

Some, though, took winning rather more seriously, and in the early days of college soccer the most conspicuous of them was Douglas Stewart, a Scot who for thirty-two years presided over the program at the University of Pennsylvania with all the sinew of a drill sergeant. As a young man,

---

* In 1927, Dent was appointed Dartmouth's lacrosse coach and spent the next thirty-five seasons in charge of that team, as well. He is still ranked as the school's most successful coach in the sport, though he'd never played it.

Stewart had played for teams in Glasgow and London; he then enrolled at Canada's Royal Military College, where he was said to have starred in several sports, playing lacrosse as well as soccer and "pulling a fine oar on the crew." Settling in Philadelphia, he soon helped to form Pennsylvania's state soccer association. In 1910, whip in hand, he began his coaching duties at Penn.

One coach wrote of him:

> With his army background he regarded himself as the officer and his players as the enlisted men. He called everyone on the team by his last name and was known to frequently whack an erring player across the legs with his walking stick. In his extensive soccer program Stewart was aided by an assistant coach and a corps of student managers. Even the managers viewed Stewart as somewhat of a tyrant as he required them to bring to his home prior to 8 P.M. a daily typed report of each practice session.

Tyrannical or not, Stewart knew the game, and his program became one of the most successful and visible of the era. During the 1920s, Penn fielded as many as six separate soccer teams and played before healthy crowds. One writer even claimed that soccer "became a cult at Penn, and he was its high priest." Certainly Stewart cut an authoritative figure: elected vice-president of the USFA in 1915, he also held key positions in refereeing and collegiate circles. For years, his All-America selections appeared in Spalding's *Official College Soccer Football Guide,* as did essays replete with his trenchant observations and schoolmasterly advice. His book *How to Play Soccer,* first published in 1934, can still be found on a few library shelves.

But Bill Jeffrey's name has worn much better than Stewart's. Anyone the slightest bit familiar with the patchy World Cup history of the United States can place him on the touchline in Brazil the day America beat England in 1950. By then, the mild-mannered Scot had completed his twenty-fourth season at Penn State and become, at least in the narrow confines of the college game, a coaching wonder. He retired in 1952 with his teams having lost just twenty-four of 206 matches. From November 1932 to November 1941, they didn't lose at all, a sixty-five-match unbeaten streak that, were it recognized by the National Collegiate Athletic Association (NCAA), would represent the longest in the game.*

---

* Between 1948 and 1959, the University of San Francisco lost only one of ninety-seven games.

Suffice it to say that college soccer has changed considerably since then. The official unbeaten record of forty-six matches, held by Indiana University, was set in just two seasons, 1983 and 1984. Jeffrey's teams never played more than ten times a year, less than half the schedule confronting the modern coach, and they rarely traveled far from State College. Their opponents often had only a tenuous grasp on the game—something that cannot be said of teams today, when even the most successful school encounters defeat each season. Yet Jeffrey's achievements remain exceptional. With no athletic scholarships and few of his players possessing more than elementary soccer skills, he may have been limited to assembling serviceable teams from the natural athletic talent at his disposal. But he succeeded in a way his contemporaries did not.

While the competition during Jeffrey's tenure was much more limited—the number of varsity teams never exceeded a hundred, rather fewer than the 750 or so men's programs there are now—the game's reach was surprisingly long. Even in the early 1900s, students at many institutions could take up soccer as part of their PE requirement. For many, this was a more enticing alternative to the dreary regimen of the gymnasium. Interclass tournaments were a recurring, if unassuming, feature on many campuses; the first at State College took place in 1910. Soccer may not have been well understood, but its value as a form of exercise found favor with PE instructors and gung-ho coaches who recognized its fitness value. Typical among them was Bill Hayward, track coach and "physical director" at the University of Oregon, who was said to have pushed hard for soccer's introduction at Eugene "because he wants to make a few 'high brow' students turn out for something besides 'class work, debates and YMCA meetings.'"

On Hayward's and other campuses, the game did sputter along for a number of years, propelled by the visits of the Pilgrims and Corinthians and the intractable difficulties associated with football. By 1911, the NCAA's ears had been pricked. At its annual meeting, it formed a Committee on Association Foot Ball (one that included basketball's James Naismith) and, having "officially taken up soccer," set about trying to do something with it. But the assured view of its secretary, James Babbitt of Haverford College, that the game was "destined to become a favorite outdoor sport" was not shared by all in attendance. One account claims that a skeptic at the meeting, "the question being asked as to injuries, remarked that the only man ever hurt in soccer was a spectator who laughed himself to death."

The committee was undaunted—and hopeful. "No game in America is making more rapid strides in this country than Soccer," one of its members wrote in Spalding's 1913 college soccer *Guide.* "Club Soccer is coming fast, but collegiate and scholastic Soccer is coming to the fore with even greater rapidity." It charted an erratic course, one that in the 1910s passed through some unlikely places. Auburn's football coach, Mike Donahue, brought a soccer team to Atlanta in March 1912 for what the *Atlanta Constitution* deemed "the first soccer football game played by a southern college." The following year, a Baylor eleven, coached by "Scotchmen familiar with the game," played a series of matches with the University of Texas, its own team founded by a student from Wales. A number of other schools—among them Kansas, Minnesota, Ohio State, Southern Methodist, and the future Oregon State—tried to fly the flag, but it fluttered only briefly. One by one, their programs disappeared.

Seeds at State College found more fertile soil. The school's first varsity eleven—of a sort—took to the field just days before the NCAA's 1911 meeting. The players were mainly from prep schools in and around Philadelphia, and they supplied their own uniforms; some "tacked on cleats" to an old pair of shoes. While there was no official coach, the team was looked after by Walter Savery, an undergraduate who had learned the game at Westtown Academy in Philadelphia (and whose teams would include a number of Westtown graduates). A talented athlete, Savery ran track and cross-country at State College and played basketball and lacrosse, as well. Offered a scholarship to look after the interclass and varsity soccer teams, he turned it down, insisting he didn't need one.

The 1911 varsity season consisted of a trip to Philadelphia during the Christmas holiday. On consecutive days, the Nittany Lions played Westtown and reserve teams from Penn and Haverford, returning with two ties and a defeat. "As this was the first time that the Blue and White was ever represented by a soccer team in the east where the sport is so popular," the *Collegian* student newspaper observed, "the outcome of the series was somewhat doubtful. However, the result was most creditable."

Over the next three seasons, progress followed similar lines. Underwritten by "Mr. J. G. White, of the class of '82, who is intensely interested in the development of soccer as one of our sports," State arranged a modest schedule against a few colleges and prep schools that were prepared to cover their expenses. "Whether or not soccer football will be a successful venture here is yet to be discovered," the *Collegian* mused in January 1912. "At the present, the game is a little too young at this institution to take hurried steps. It is an assured fact, however, that with the keen, growing interest and the support of the student body, soccer football has come to stay."

With the game largely dependent on the charity of an alumnus, steps were anything but hurried. All the same, by October 1913 the student paper claimed that soccer's growth had been "so rapid and consistent that it bids fair in time to become one of the leading sports of our institution." Given that the varsity continued to play all of its matches away from home, the assertion was rather curious. But these were propitious years for the sport. "It is spreading faster than any other game in this country," claimed Spalding's 1914 college *Guide*, "and it would be no exaggeration to state that in the last ten years this game has gone ahead five hundred percent, more than any other game in America." At State College, though, candidates for the varsity may have been enticed less by the sport than by the prospect of being excused from Wednesday afternoon "drill." Thirty-five men reported for the first practice of the 1913 season, and few of them would ever have kicked a ball before.

In April 1914, the Lions at last made an appearance on their own campus, trouncing Lafayette 6–0 before a small but appreciative crowd. "The band was out but was not needed to start enthusiasm," observed the *Collegian*. "Cheerleader Hill found the stands very responsive to his call for cheers." Indeed, such was the level of interest that the athletic association at last consented to underwrite the team. Its obligation was modest. Though rivals like Penn took part in as many as twenty matches a year, as late as 1921 State played no more than three. Many were against prep schools; Westtown remained on the schedule until 1916.

But the support at least meant there was a proper coach—Jimmie Crowell, an instructor in Spanish at the college—and the prospect of a minor-sport letter. Players still provided their own uniforms and footwear, but their technique began to improve. In a 1941 master's thesis, Harry Brown claimed that State had heretofore relied on "the long passing type of game," but Crowell, a Haverford alumnus, "set about immediately to develop an effective system of team play while the men developed more individual skill."

Play may have remained fairly rudimentary, but the results were impressive. Under Crowell, the Lions never lost a match. By 1920, they'd even beaten his alma mater. Brown also noted that the sport had outgrown its confines:

> The response for candidates was so great in 1920 that the squad was crowded for practice ground. . . . This crowded condition was partly created by the fact that fifty sophomore and seventy fresh-

men reported for soccer practices in preference to physical education classes. Two soccer fields were constructed on the drill grounds at the rear of the Armory. Even with this increased facility, candidates had to come out at different hours.

After the 1920 season, Crowell left to pursue a doctorate at Cornell—and in the five seasons that followed, four coaches came and went. The last of these was Ralph Leonard, "secured with considerable difficulty" in 1924 to coach soccer, wrestling, and lacrosse. A year earlier, Leonard had led the Williams College eleven to a 2-4-1 record, but his two seasons at State produced only one defeat in eleven matches.

Amid such accomplishment, fan interest only flickered. The *Collegian* claimed that the first game of the 1922 season, a 1-1 tie with Lehigh staged on the football practice field, had attracted "the largest crowd in the history of the sport, at this institution." It did not provide a figure, though, and whatever it was would not have rivaled the thousands of State fans who traveled to Philadelphia a few weeks later for the gridiron clash with Penn, swelling attendance to more than 50,000. Not even Leonard's 6-0-0 team in 1924 won the campus over. "Entering the sixth year of undefeat," the paper had noted, "the Nittany booters continue to battle, year after year, oft-times with but very few spectators on the grandstand."

Wherever the grandstand might be. Soccer, shunted as it was from one patch of ground to another, had no permanent home at State College. It wasn't unusual for matches to take place on the New Beaver Field gridiron, often with a football game to follow. But early arrivals were few and largely unwilling to follow the team beyond the stadium.

Brown, who for his thesis interviewed a number of coaches and participants from this period, noted a number of other difficulties, as well:

> In 1921, Professors William V. Dennis and Thomas C. Pakenham coached the team. Professor Dennis [recalled] that the biggest problem was getting the boys to train. He had to appeal personally to several boys to keep themselves in condition by proper training methods, which called for no drinking. . . . According to [Dennis], the players supplied their own equipment except balls in 1921. There were very few balls though and only one was usable. They formerly oiled balls to preserve them which caused them to resemble basketballs. The first indication on record of the college furnishing any equipment for the soccer team was in 1922.

It was still a primitive game, "knock-'em-down and drag-'em-out foot-ball," as Dennis recalled, and not for the fainthearted. The *Collegian* reported that in the 1924 season finale against Navy, one State player was knocked unconscious and recovered only to tear up his ankle; three other players were seriously hurt, while "minor injuries were sustained in the majority of the other members of the team." State won, 2–0, but the "rushing clipping attack of the Midshipmen" had left them "badly bat-tered. . . . [T]o play further games would be out of the question had there been more on the 1924 schedule."

Though Leonard returned for a second season, he was troubled by his fledgling lacrosse program, which had yet to enjoy a winning season "chiefly because the players never had the game at heart." Apparently beset with a similar lack of affection for soccer, he resigned as coach in 1926 in favor of drilling his stickmen through the winter. (A year later he left for Michigan State, where he concentrated on wrestling.) But his greatest gift to athletics at Penn State may have been the match he arranged against the Altoona railcar shop in 1925. The visiting coach that day, who doubled as the inside-left, was Bill Jeffrey. While the match ended goalless, in the eyes of the *Collegian* the works team "demonstrated a skill at kicking seldom displayed in collegiate contests" (though the col-legians naturally "had the advantage over the Altoona aggregation in fighting spirit").* It may have been this proficiency that persuaded State's athletic director, Hugo Bezdek, to consider Jeffrey for the job. Before appointing Leonard, Bezdek had approached Bill Smith, an earlier Altoona coach, who turned down his offer. Jeffrey, granted a three-month leave of absence from work, did not.

It was an improbable fate. Born near Edinburgh in Newhaven, Scot-land, in 1892, Jeffrey had captained his team to a scholastic champion-ship in 1906 and shown considerable promise as a young amateur. But a long period of convalescence from a knee injury turned his mother against the idea of a professional career. In 1912, he was sent to America to live with an uncle in Pennsylvania—to "get away from the game," as he would contend—and as an apprentice engineer he readily found employ-ment in Altoona. But he also found its soccer team, rife with old-country

---

* It wasn't unusual for a college to include works teams—even if they weren't amateurs—on its schedule. In 1917, State had faced the Juniata Shops team of Altoona (they had also intended to play them the year before but were beaten by the weather). One of the more prominent encounters of the era was Bethlehem Steel's 3–1 defeat of Penn in October 1919. Bethlehem, national champions that year, fielded a weakened team, as many of their players had yet to return from the club's tour of Scandinavia.

migrants who were just as keen on the sport as he was. Within months, he'd become their starting center-forward.

The rest of his playing career is less clear. Some sources claim that Jeffrey played for Bethlehem Steel in 1921, the first season of the American Soccer League. That team, though, had effectively been transferred to Philadelphia that year, and records do not indicate that he ever played in the league (though he did appear in at least one exhibition match). It is possible that he played for the Bethlehem Football Club that was formed in the wake of the Steel's exodus, but records of that team are sketchy. Jeffrey is also credited with having played for teams in Homestead and Braddock, though his time there is no better documented.

In any event, his arrival at State College drew little attention. He was the sixth soccer coach in seven years, and though the Lions had lost only once during that time, it had not mattered to many. The *Collegian* had a hard time spelling his name. Yet his timing was fortunate, given the inroads the college game was making in the East. In January 1926, the decades-old Intercollegiate Association Football League, which had never extended its membership beyond a half-dozen Ivy League schools, disbanded in favor of a broader-based confederation, the Intercollegiate Soccer Football Association (ISFA; "of America" would be tacked on later). The new body added six schools—including State, which had long been excluded from the old league. (Dennis thought the team's uncultured playing style was partly to blame.) Membership was perceived as a reward for State's success on the field; according to the *Collegian,* it "would bring to the Nittany valley the gratification of a desire which has long possessed the Athletic Association, the soccer coaches, the players and the student body."

Among other things, the ISFA believed greater freedom in scheduling would help to raise the overall level of competition. By and large, though, the established soccer schools continued to face the same old opponents—and standards would remain primitively low for decades to come. No one could teach the game to the coaches, let alone the players; good teams tended to rely on foreign students and natural athletes. As late as 1939, Douglas Stewart used the college *Guide* to bemoan the "great number of teams who are appallingly ignorant of anything approaching ball control and who rely entirely on their speed and strength to make up for their deficiency in skill."

Jeffrey's first match in charge, a 3–1 loss to the Altoona team he'd left behind, underlined this primitive approach. "Because of the different style of play used by the Penn State booters and the Altoona combination, the coach declined to make any definite comparison between the two teams," the *Collegian* reported. "According to him professional soccer teams used a close style of play, emphasizing dribbling and short passes, while collegiate booters depend upon long passes and aggressiveness to score goals."

The affable Scot would spend much of his life trying to point the college game in another direction. But to young American men, hefty kicks, determined running, and fierce physical contact were practically second nature. Speed and muscle were the defining traits of college soccer, as was the "playing with pain" that defined gridiron heroism. According to the *Collegian,* the University of Toronto's visit to State College that season produced from the Canadian goalkeeper a "brand of grit the like of which has seldom been seen in a soccer game here":

> Entering the game with one hand swathed in bandages as a result of a painful fracture, he was afforded only the use of one arm. When the going became fast around his post he would be forced to undergo pain while both hands were used. Near the end of the initial half [he] received further injury in a scrimmage and time was called. After a rest he resumed play but black and blue marks on his arm were mute testimony of the fact that he was able to use but one arm thereafter.

Two five-minute periods of overtime against the "intercollegiate champions of Canada for three years" failed to produce a goal (even in the early days the desire to avoid a tie flouted international convention). But the results against Altoona and Toronto were the only blemishes on a 5–1–1 season. Jeffrey's team had held Swarthmore and Springfield scoreless and put five goals past both Syracuse and Navy, handing the latter its only defeat of the season. They had also claimed a gritty 1–0 win over Penn "in the dust of River Field, Philadelphia."

Not for the first time, the Lions could lay claim to one of the best playing records in the country. Yet the desire of the ISFA to improve the game through wider competition left the criteria for determining a champion in the hands of a committee, one that clearly did not attach the same level of significance to the matter that would be expected of it today. Weeks after the season ended, the *Collegian* bemoaned how "no reports have been forthcoming from the league officials as to the actual standing of the teams or as to the conditions on which the championship will be awarded." Not until January—nearly two months after State had ended its season—did a verdict arrive: the Lions were to share the putative title with Haverford (8–0–2) and Princeton (5–1–1). "To rise in one season to a level with Princeton and Haverford, where soccer is an old, well-established sport, speaks well for Penn State's booters," the paper wrote.

While it was anything but a one-season rise, Jeffrey had certainly made his mark. Bezdek found him a position in the industrial engineering department, and over the next twenty-seven years the quiet shopman ("I wouldn't want to be any more than an instructor because it might keep me away from soccer") would take the college game about as far as it could go.

One might expect to see a long list of championships appearing under Jeffrey's name, yet only twice did he lead his team to sole possession of an ISFA title. The reasons for this have less to do with the performance of his teams than the way champions were decided—or, for many years, not decided. Post-season play was still a curiosity in college sport, and playoffs were not the overwhelming compulsion they would eventually become. In rowing, tennis, and golf, "championships" had been held as early as in the 1890s, but these were modest in scope. Equivalents for basketball, gymnastics, swimming and diving, and cross-country weren't established until the 1930s; the first College World Series didn't take place until 1947.

There was, then, nothing peculiar about settling a soccer championship by a ballot, however impossible it might have been for anyone to make an informed comparison among the candidates and however susceptible the arbiters were to politics or prejudice. The mechanics of the process were not made public (and no documentation seems to have survived), but the distinct over-representation of Ivy League schools in the roll call of honors suggests it was driven by the Eastern elite.

The same is certainly true of the selection of All-America players. At the time, there was no official All-America team in soccer or any other sport, though the elevens chosen by Douglas Stewart and printed in Spalding's college *Guide* are often read as such. Not surprisingly, they are laden with representatives from Penn and its opponents. But with the formation of the ISFA—and a nine-man selection committee that included Jeffrey—the composition of the teams began to change. Fullback George Lippencott and outside-right Ed Pecori, chosen in 1926, are generally regarded as State's first All-Americas. But equally talented players from earlier years undoubtedly missed out on recognition merely because Stewart never saw them play—and because other lists failed to survive.

The notion of a committee, though, doesn't seem to have lasted long, and, of course, there was nothing to prevent a coach from naming his own All-America teams. The *Collegian* noted in 1929 that Stewart, Al Nies of Princeton, and Jim McPete of Haverford had all done so (Jeffrey selected five Penn State players for his eleven). By 1934, the State coach was making his choices "with the assistance of three Philadelphia soccer enthusiasts," likely to have included Stewart and McPete. All the same, if the greatest player in the country were enrolled in a college west of the Appalachians or south of the Potomac, hardly anyone would have noticed him.

Moreover, as many of the best players were only passing through the country, All-America talent wasn't all American. A case in point at State was Egyptian-born Mousa Serry, who had captained the rugby team at an American university in Cairo before becoming a "familiar figure at the practice sessions of many sports" at State College. Serry's desire to make the football team aroused the curiosity of newspapers across the country—his photo made the sports pages—but it was his prowess as a soccer forward that earned him recognition on All-America teams in 1927 and 1928.

Serry would also be named to his coach's all-time State team in 1943, but it wasn't until after he left that the Lions claimed their first undisputed ISFA title, in 1929. Being the only unbeaten team (6–0–1), their selection was relatively straightforward—but, as the *Collegian* noted, the association realized it had been fortunate on this occasion:

> Difficulty in determining the leader . . . in the event that no team remained undefeated, prompted the conference to seek a new method of organization and champion selection. Henry W. Clark, graduate representative of Harvard and vice-president elect of the Association, suggested the formation of divisions among the league teams, the leaders of which would meet in a post-season play-off to decide the champions. The plan proved feasible following announcement that three colleges, Amherst, Williams, and Wesleyan, had applied for admission to the Association. If the applications are accepted, there would be sixteen teams in the circuit, enough for at least two divisions.

It seemed sensible enough, yet the plan was never adopted. Talk of championship games would persist for decades, yet not until 1950 did any sort of match-up take place. The ISFA habitually blamed "difficulties of scheduling," geography, or even Christmas vacation. No one seemed particularly bothered by this—or, at least, not enough to make any changes to the leadership of the association. From 1922 to 1939, the presidency of the ISFA and its forerunner was held by just two men, Princeton's Edward Keyes and Haverford's Arthur Cookman; from 1922 to 1933, the only secretary-treasurer was Penn's Morris Johnson. (A stockbroker, Johnson was also president of the USSFA from 1924 to 1926; he never graduated from the university.) While by 1939 the number of colleges playing intercollegiate soccer had grown to around eighty, the game remained in the same few hands.

Some schools had formed soccer conferences—as early as 1915 there was one in eastern Pennsylvania—but State continued to operate as an independent, constrained not just by geography but by the indifference to the sport shown by many of its traditional rivals. The University of Pittsburgh didn't field a varsity team until 1954, a curiously belated inception given the success of amateur teams in that area. (As early as 1927, Heidelberg had won the U.S. amateur championship.) One might attribute Pitt's lack of interest to its status as a gridiron powerhouse during the 1920s and '30s. Yet Jock Sutherland, the school's celebrated football coach, had played the game as a youngster in his native Scotland. That aside, Pitt was hardly the only school to have developed an acute case of football fever. Indeed, for all its "remarkable" progress, soccer was still left to gather whatever crumbs it could find. Jeffrey drew a curious level of encouragement in 1932 from the decision of State's student body to grant varsity soccer players the "larger" letter awards issued for basketball, baseball, and track (football honors being on an altogether higher plane)—it would, he believed, "help the rise of the game all over the country."

But events later that year showed how far it had to go. After a wearying two-day bus trip to Massachusetts, the Lions lost close games to Springfield and Harvard. But to Jeffrey, the school's first back-to-back defeats since 1914 weren't nearly as embarrassing as the "failure of the athletic authorities to supply the soccer team with proper facilities and conditions for travel." Candidly, he ascribed the results to "the poor condition of the players, because of the long hours they were forced to ride in a bus in such cramped positions." The team, he noted, had left State College on Thursday night and spent all but a few hours on the bus, arriving late on Friday, "just in time to go to sleep, all tired and cramped." They lost 3–1 to Harvard the following afternoon. ("We went after the ball but our legs could not get us there the way they always do," one player noted.) There was less of an excuse for the 2–1 defeat at Springfield two days later, but matters had only been decided by a last-minute goal, and the winning coach was impressed enough with the contest to declare it "the finest exhibition of college soccer that I've ever witnessed."

At State College three weeks later, defeat by Syracuse left the Lions needing a win in their final match to avoid their first losing season since the war. In the teeth of a driving rainstorm, they beat Army 2–1 to finish with three wins and three losses. Nine years would pass before they lost again.

Oddly enough, Army would end the sequence in 1941. But invincibility often mattered little to the ISFA. As an independent, State had no conference to reign over, and the association's appetite for post-season play remained faint. When State and Penn both finished their 1933 seasons without a loss or tie, a showdown match seemed perfectly feasible; the *Collegian* even claimed that the mood on campus seemed "highly in favor of challenging the Red and Blue squad." But within weeks, the paper was left relaying the news that there would be no playoff "because the expenses to be incurred were cited as being too high."

Admittedly, the Great Depression was casting a long shadow over college athletics. That season, State had played host to the University of Illinois, whose team had survived a decision to drop the sport in 1931 only by agreeing to fund itself. With the Big Ten still impervious to soccer, the Illini traveled thousands of miles in search of competition. At the end of their 750-mile trek to State College, they were beaten, 4–0. They would give up on the sport a few years later.*

State persevered, though interest in its team remained fragile. While Jeffrey had little difficulty in finding players (many of them from the same prep-school wellsprings Walter Savery had relied on a generation earlier), attracting fans was another story. The *Collegian* did its best to rally the student body, but proud declarations that State was the equal of any team in the country counted for little. Jeffrey, for all his success, often appeared as "Coach Jeffries" in the paper, and match reports could include unfathomable references to "backfields" and "line play." In its account of the Illinois game, the paper wrote that the visitors "could not offset the offensive drives of the aggressive Blue and White team" and that one State player "came out of a brisk scrimmage on the twenty-five yard line, and marched straight down the field" to score.

Football, it seemed, was on everyone's mind, no less so at State College than anywhere else. But the collective delirium associated with a successful team was leaving many to question the sport's bloated role on

---

* Intersectional games had taken place as early as 1927, when Ohio State traveled to Princeton and lost, 7–0. The Buckeyes dropped intercollegiate soccer after the 1931 season and did not take it up again until 1950.

campus. In 1929, the Carnegie Foundation published a report exposing a number of disreputable recruiting and subsidization practices. Yet most colleges found it difficult (or disadvantageous) to rein in the enthusiasm of the alumni and community. Many all but ignored the findings.

That wasn't true at Penn State, where action had been taken action in advance of the report. Under President Ralph Dorn Hetzel, control of the football team had passed from the "board of athletic control" (effectively, the alumni) to the college, which instituted a program of "de-emphasis." Among other things, this did away with athletic scholarships in favor of identifying and developing "the latent athletic ability in the general student body." Quite predictably, it also resulted in a string of mediocre football seasons and outrage from pennant-waving alumni. Policies were soon relaxed. By the mid-1930s, football players were receiving subsidies through fund-raising campaigns and other indirect sources; a decade later, as part of its "sanity code," athletic scholarships were effectively permitted by the NCAA.

But in 1933, de-emphasis left State's gridiron team playing just seven games—and the last eleven on the football field that autumn was Jeffrey's. A 2–0 win over Springfield, with "Major Tommy Thompson and his Blue Band strutting their wares," drew a crowd of nearly 2,000. This was an encouraging turnout, but it still left around 28,000 seats empty. "With all due credit to the soccer team," one disgruntled fan wrote to the *Collegian,* "how much more could a grid encounter with a major foe have been enjoyed by the student body Saturday?"

All the same, these were heady days for soccer at Penn State, and the announcement that the team would play a series of matches in Scotland in the summer of 1934 broke new ground not only for the school but for the game as a whole. Already the Lions had attracted international interest: in 1933, they'd been asked to represent their country at the International Confederation of Students' Games in Italy, and the president of the Bermudan Football Association invited Jeffrey to bring across an all-collegiate team to face a group of local all-stars. Nothing came of either proposal, but in a way this was apposite. College soccer had still to venture beyond North America and the overseas country most deserving of the game's maiden voyage was surely the one in which Jeffrey had been raised. Scotland had furnished the United States with many of its best coaches, players, and referees; Scots were disproportionately active in administrative circles; and the visits of Scottish clubs such as Rangers and Celtic had produced some of the largest, most enthusiastic soccer crowds America had seen.

The college itself put very little weight behind the trip. Each player was told to raise $100 toward his expenses; according to Jeffrey, "The only thing the school supplied was new equipment." Perhaps as a result of this, seven of the fifteen letter winners from the previous season stayed at home. It left the thirteen players who boarded the liner *Cameronia* that August resembling neither the 1933 nor the 1934 varsity. They included inside-right Eddie Finzel, who had already completed his senior year, and three sophomores whose playing experience had been limited to the freshman team. One of them, Bill McEwan, would prove talented enough to earn All-America recognition at the end of the season. It was, though, the inclusion of McEwan's older brother in the party that proved the most propitious—and sensitive: John McEwan wasn't even enrolled at State College and had in fact graduated from Syracuse the year before.

In a country as thoroughly steeped in the game as Scotland, Jeffrey knew even his best eleven would struggle ("If we make the contests close, I'll be more than satisfied"), but the team's first test came rather earlier than expected. Six days out to sea, the *Cameronia* encountered a violent storm; according to *The Scotsman,* one man was lost overboard, twenty passengers were injured, "crockery to the value of between £200 and £300 was destroyed, 195 chairs were smashed, tables were broken and cabin equipment damaged."

The paper added:

> An American amateur football team from the Pennsylvania State College travelled on the Cameronia. . . . A member of the team, William M'Ewan, the son of Scottish parents, said he was in the writing room when the waves struck the ship. "I was looking out the port hole watching the storm," he said, "when the vessel went over on her side. I went right across the room and back again."

No one in State's party was hurt, but there was little time for reflection; within the week, the Lions were facing their first opponent. They would take on seven more during their three-week tour, visiting nearly every part of the country and, in the words of the team's captain, Jack Fletcher, being "shown every possible courtesy everywhere we went."* Banquets, sightseeing trips, meetings with local dignitaries, and other manifestations of Caledonian bonhomie kept them assiduously occupied; the *Collegian* even made reference to three dances "for which several of the bon-

---

* In Fletcher's case, the courtesies included the acceptance of his offer of marriage in 1936 to a woman he'd met on the tour.

niest lasses of the countryside were imported." The visitors accepted such hospitality with grace; to one Highland reporter, they were "a jolly lot" who "certainly brightened up the town."

On the field, though, the shortcomings of even the best American college team were laid bare, and the local papers made little attempt to conceal their disappointment. State's arrival in Edinburgh had been anything but low-key: handbills promoted them as "America's amateur champions," which, of course, they weren't, and their first game, against an amateur team from nearby Leith, was staged at the home of first-division Heart of Midlothian. The Lions were soundly beaten, 6–4. "The football played by the majority of the Americans was a trifle crude," the *Edinburgh Evening News* noted. The notable exception was John McEwan, who had scored all four of State's goals—enough, apparently, for the *News* to play up his chances of appearing for Hearts themselves. "He was speedy and he could take the ball in his stride and carry it with him," it claimed, "while he put in as good shooting as has been seen at the Heart of Midlothian ground for a considerable time."

Two days later, in the southern town of Galashiels, the Syracuse alumnus was joined in the lineup by another interloper: Jeffrey himself, a sprightly forty-two. But against Gala Fairydean, stalwarts of the East of Scotland League, State needed more than a half-decent center-forward and a wise old head; they lost 7–2. "There was no comparison between the two sides," wrote the local *Border Telegraph*. "The College men have much to learn in the game. Though keen enough they are very hesitant to go in to tackle, and their half back play is weak. The visitors' forwards are better than their defence, and J. M'Ewan was the star of the side, and had the best idea of the game."

Nearly every match of the tour would be reported along similar lines. Feted as a championship team on arrival, the Lions would then be excoriated for their limitations. In advance of the third match, against Inverness Caledonian of the Highland League, the *Highland News and Football Times* referred to the five State players named to an All-America team in 1933 as "internationalists" and insisted that the team would give "a splendid performance against their more experienced opponents." But the ease with which Caley claimed a 10–6 win left the paper describing "an amusing display of football":

> The Americans were outclassed in every department, and there was every reason to suppose that if the Blues cared they could have added to their score, and prevented the tourists securing at least

three of their goals. The general impression amongst the large crowd was that the visitors have a lot to learn about the game. They have not yet acquired the proper method of tackling, their shooting was weak, and their combination [play] left much to be desired.

McEwan added two more goals to his burgeoning total and a hat-trick the next day against Thurso Pentland. But with Ben Palmer, the only goalkeeper in the party, out with an infected foot, the Highlanders had little difficulty in running up a 12–4 victory. The six-foot-four-inch Palmer missed the rest of the tour, leaving Bob Dallas—a sophomore half-back without a varsity match to his name—to guard the net against Elgin City. The emergency custodian was doubtless comforted to see his coach spearheading the defense, but the charity of the opposition did him no less a favor. "Elgin did not seek to demonstrate their superiority in goals," the local *Courant and Courier* insisted of its team's 5–4 win. "Rather was it their aim to show the tourists the most profitable method of getting within the danger zone of their opponents' goal. The City might have counted several times in the opening fifteen minutes."

The *Northern Scot* noted:

What the visitors lacked in craft was made up for by enthusiasm, and it is obvious that with practice their deficiencies in regard to positional play can be remedied. Flashes of clever play, which the crowd did not fail to appreciate, were evident at times when the attack got going, but the centre-forward was the only man who knew where the goal lay.

Ironically, the Penn State player who attracted the most attention wasn't even from Penn State. One wonders how much more lopsided the scores would have been without the Syracuse graduate in the lineup: he'd been responsible for thirteen of State's twenty goals. To the *Northern Scot*, McEwan was "one of the most dangerous centre-forwards seen at the Elgin enclosure for many a day."

He was without question one of the most talented players the college game had seen. As a sophomore in 1931, McEwan had helped Syracuse to its best-ever season; as a junior, he featured on almost every All-America team and even scored the winning goal in the Orangemen's first-ever victory over State. Owing to "a technical deficiency in his school work," he then sat out his senior year, but the *Syracuse Herald* was in little doubt as to where his future lay. "It is very likely that he will now accept the offer of the Glasgow Celtics, world champions," it wrote, "and join them when they tour the country in the spring."

Not that there were "world champions" of club soccer, Scottish or otherwise, and Celtic's next visit to the United States didn't actually materialize until 1951. McEwan never played for the club, though he did end up in Glasgow shortly after State's tour. While Board of Trade regulations prevented American citizens from playing professionally in Scotland, McEwan—born in Glasgow—did make a few appearances for the reserve team of first-division Queen's Park, an amateur club. A few months later, though, he returned to America and ended up playing professionally in New York.

If there was a weakness to McEwan's game, it was his temper. At Queen's Park, he would be thrown out of a match for striking a referee, and on tour with State, he came undone against Falkirk Amateurs. "He was warned by the referee for raising his hands to one of the players," reported the *Falkirk Mail,* "but apparently resented the 'lecture' and had to be sent to the pavilion." Crushed 10-1, with outside-right Don Masters now assuming the role of harried goalkeeper, the Lions singularly failed to impress the *Mail's* correspondent:

> There was little element of contest about the game. . . . With few exceptions the Americans' idea of the game was crude. Their unorthodox style seldom got them anywhere. Their tackling lacked "body." One saw little of their reputed speed apart from occasional spurts on the left wing. As a matter of fact generally speaking they gave the impression of not being well enough trained.

How little the Scots knew. Despite his expulsion, McEwan returned to the team's lineup for the next match and again did all its scoring. But the 5-2 defeat in Greenock had not, as some American newspapers claimed, come at the hands of a high school team; the opponents were actually alumni of the school, "former pupils" who drew a crowd of more than 2,000 to Cowdenknowes. Among them was a correspondent from the *Greenock Herald* who professed to being "rather tickled" by the visitors' machismo:

> Their antics savoured more of the American type of football than of "soccer." One of their backs received an awful smack on the stomach from the ball, and, though he flinched, he did not give in. "That's how to take 'em," shouted one of his colleagues.

Heavy rain nearly canceled the final match of the tour, a 9–5 loss to Kilmarnock Academical. If the collegians' technique had improved, the Scottish press wasn't noticing. "The Accies played real football," sniffed the *Kilmarnock Herald*. "The efforts of the Yanks, on the other hand, were often very crude. Their centre-forward was the only member to show an elementary knowledge of the game."

There had been nowhere to hide. In eight matches in Scotland, Jeffrey's team had lost as often as they had in the eight seasons he'd been at State College. The *Collegian* partly excused the size of the defeats with a reference to "the turn on the Scottish fields, a thick springy cushion that prevented them from timing their kicks accurately." But, as Fletcher acknowledged:

> Losing to a superior team is not a disgrace, and we found that Scotch soccer is superior to ours in every department of the game. And since the real aim of the trip was to bring back to America some idea of how the game should be played, and to spread this knowledge through the country in order that soccer may gain a stronger foothold here, we feel that our tour has been in every way a success.

Back home, embarrassing defeats gave way to resounding triumphs. Bolstered by seven players who had paid their Scottish dues, the Lions tore apart Gettysburg (9–1), Lafayette (7–0), and Navy (7–1) on their way to an undefeated season. It ended with a 10–1 win over Dickinson, described by the *Collegian* as "a rather listless game, in which the players moved swiftly to keep warm rather than for any other reason." Six of the ten goals came from Bill McEwan, whose twenty for the season broke the school record— by ten.

Only two ISFA teams finished the year without a loss: State (6–0–1) and Cornell (5–0–2). Jeffrey was not alone in asserting that his was "the better team," but the association found it impossible to ignore the particulars of State's overseas venture—namely, that he, John McEwan, and others ineligible for the varsity had taken part in matches. Retroactively, the ISFA suspended State for the 1934 season and named Cornell the sole champion. It was a merciless decision. Rather than being applauded for their ambition and mettle, the Lions were reprimanded for relative technicalities (transatlantic tours, after all, were hardly routine constituents of collegiate soccer). Fingers pointed, the *Collegian* leaped to the school's defense:

It appears that some of the Association officials have made asses out of themselves by hewing so closely to the line in making their decision, but Penn State is not entirely blameless of deliberately violating the sacred Association covenants. Coach Jeffrey became Player Jeffrey when one of the other lads who made the trip became ill. . . . [He] was doing the only thing he knew of to prevent the scheduled games from being cancelled—a development that would have reacted decidedly unfavorably to American soccer. . . . The trouble surrounding the whole situation was brewed in Philadelphia. Ex-Secretary [Morris] Johnson is the colored gentleman who hangs out in the woodpile. The [association] has too long been dominated by persons who have not gotten over their undergraduate patriotism for the University of Pennsylvania.

It may have been a prejudiced view, but it wasn't without foundation. Johnson's successor as secretary in 1934, E. Paul Patton, was a graduate of Penn; so was the assistant secretary appointed that year, Wilson Hobson, and his predecessor, William Lingelbach Jr. Neither Patton nor Hobson would vacate his position until after World War II., while Douglas Stewart—still the doyen of college soccer coaches—would maintain an imposing presence up to his retirement in 1942.

Whether these were really the men behind State's punishment isn't clear, but there was little the school could do but look toward the new season. Years later, Jeffrey would rate the 1935 team as the best he'd ever coached; it's not hard to see why. Starting with a 4–0 win over Gettysburg and ending with a 2–0 defeat of Navy, the Lions won all six of their matches without conceding a single goal, all but confirming the *Collegian*'s pre-season assertion that they were unlikely to face an opponent as strong as their second team. In a 4–0 victory over Temple, "play during the first half was so completely under control of the State lads that it bordered on the ludicrous"; a win over Syracuse by an identical score "developed into a regular Penn State cross-country meet, with Orangemen pursuing the Lions all over the field"; and Army lost 6–0, its only defeat of the season, with the ball "almost continuously in State's possession."

Come January, though, the ISFA stood ready with another penalty: Jeffrey's team had played only three of the fifteen "active" members of the association when four were required for championship consideration. The oversight had only arisen because Syracuse, ordinarily an active member, had been demoted to associate membership for a similar lapse the season before. Soon the ISFA would abandon the distinction between full and associate members, but in 1935 it named unbeaten Yale as its sole champion. Calls for a playoff between the Lions and Bulldogs came to nothing; so, too, did a more fanciful idea of a trip to California, where the University of San Francisco, "undisputed soccer champions of the west coast for the past four years," were interested in a showdown of their own. The sports editor of the *Collegian* could hardly conceal his frustration:

> We aren't permitted to play for a championship; we are compelled to wait until January and then we go to New York and fight for it. For the last two skirmishes the score stands: [ISFA], 2; Penn State, 0. Is there a white hope existing that will do something toward restoring the soccer supremacy where it belongs? . . . This department doesn't like to stand by year after year and see a fine coach, a fine team, and a fine game get kicked around by a bunch of muddle-heads.

It's hard not to conclude that the men presiding over the college game were more interested in using their authority to score points and settle grudges than to advance the sport. In this respect, they may have been little different from the USFA. But few Americans had ever heard of the USFA, an organization that existed on the periphery of American sports. College athletics, altogether more conspicuous, may have represented a better opportunity for developing the game; it turned out the sort of true-blue American sporting heroes soccer desperately needed to establish itself as an indigenous pastime. Yet the ISFA was the domain of administrators for whom soccer was just one of many responsibilities—and who seemed more loyal to their alma mater than the sport to which they'd been entrusted.

Whether aggravated by protests or seized by a growing sense of futility, the ISFA gave up on naming champions altogether in 1936, preferring merely to recognize "outstanding teams." It continued to do this until 1944, which, though minimizing the risk of slighting worthy candidates, also diluted the significance of the award. For State, 6-0-2 in 1936, this meant sharing honors with unbeaten West Chester (7-0-0) and Syracuse (6-0-2), as well as Princeton, which had lost to Haverford but was, of course, Ivy League. The Lions could take some comfort in producing three members of the "all-eastern" team chosen by Jeffrey and seven other coaches. It included Bill McEwan, who the *Collegian* claimed was "generally considered the outstanding player in college soccer" that year and one of two collegians to reach "the final Olympic tryouts" that summer.

In his varsity career—which consisted of just twenty-one matches—McEwan scored forty-six times, including nineteen in his final season; he'd been every bit as prolific as his older brother.*

Several of his goals had played a vital role in preserving State's unbeaten run, which by 1936 had stretched across five seasons. A last-second effort salvaged a 4–4 tie with Syracuse ("The most spirited game I have seen in my eleven years at Penn State," noted Jeffrey); another, the following week, averted defeat against Western Maryland. Such efforts contrasted sharply with those of the football team, which hadn't produced a winning season since 1929. "When all else in the Penn State athletic picture is obscured and foggy," pondered the *Collegian,* "this one aggregation stands out like a beacon of hope, shining and glamorous."

Glamorous? Two-and-a-half-thousand people may have wandered into New Beaver Field to watch Jeffrey's team open its 1935 season against Gettysburg, but most had come early for the gridiron clash with Western Maryland that followed. Most of the Lions' soccer victories were earned in obscurity; usually, the team had the stadium to itself on Saturdays, playing when the football team was away. Jeffrey did what he could to drum up support, though not all his efforts found favor. His practice of recruiting co-ed mascots to perform ceremonial kickoffs aroused largely the wrong kind of interest and was abandoned.

The *Collegian* attempted to rationalize the apathy:

No. 1, the world in general and the metropolitan press in particular have failed to appreciate this fine bunch, and the Penn-dominated association State is in has always belittled her every effort to gain recognition. No. 2, the student body is bovinely indifferent to the sport. True they may brag a bit at home when all other conversational stand-bys have been exhausted, but their support otherwise is [sadly] missing.

Not much changed in 1937, when the Lions conceded only a single goal on their way to a 7–0–1 record, or in 1938, when they won all eight games

---

* The McEwans' soccer pedigree is worthy of note. The other collegian to have played in the final phase of the 1936 Olympic tryouts was Dave, a younger brother. Neither Bill nor Dave made the team (not until 1948 would an Olympic player be selected directly from college), but by then they were also playing alongside John for the New York Americans and helped them win the ASL championship in 1936. The brothers later played for St. Mary's Celtic of Brooklyn, which reached the final of the National Challenge Cup in 1938 and 1939.

and were the only school recognized by the ISFA as "outstanding." Some even suggested their success had become monotonous.

By 1939, though, the likes of Duke, Clemson, and Virginia had brought intercollegiate soccer to the south; UCLA and San Jose State were active on the West Coast; and Oberlin and Wheaton had established programs in the Midwest. To be sure, college soccer remained largely confined to the Northeast, yet even there the complexion was changing. Penn's teams of the 1930s lost nearly as often as they won (the 1933 Quaker team remains the last to win the national title), and by 1941, Haverford, Princeton, and Yale were being eclipsed for ISFA honors by the likes of Rider and Amherst.

The team of the 1930s, though, was Jeffrey's. Unbeaten throughout the decade, it had held opponents scoreless in forty-five of seventy-two matches. Indeed, its toughest opposition—the ISFA aside—seemed to be indifference. "Little do Penn State sport fans realize," the *Collegian* grumbled, "that one of the most brilliant intercollegiate competitive teams is playing under their collective noses."

Or maybe they just couldn't warm to the game. Jeffrey, too, seemed less consumed by success than by the pressure the unbeaten streak had started to put his players under. After the 1940 season, a wire-service report claimed that he feared his team "might lose the 'joy' of soccer by playing under the pressure of upholding the record" and was "wondering whether a loss next season 'might not be a good thing.'" Mastering fundamental skills, playing as a team, using the head for more than making contact with the ball—these were the things that mattered to him, and they were still largely absent from college soccer.

Several years earlier, Jeffrey had produced an instructional book, *The Boys with the Educated Feet,* that was still being reprinted in the 1950s. This passage appears under the heading "Playing the Game":

> The essential thing while playing the game is perfect technique; i.e., proper and complete control of the ball in all circumstances. Today in every phase of life, save that of the recluse, the artist, and the scholar, speed is the curse of the age. The world itself does not revolve more quickly, but the dwellers on earth are simply crazy for speed; the fastest trains, automobiles, and what-have-you all bear witness to man's application of science to his inventive genius. Such phrases as: "the quickness of thought" and "time is money" have permeated the mind and have driven us all mad. The craze has even spread to sports and pastimes. Soccer in the opin-

ion of many, has followed the fashion. So we assume that to run with the ball at racing pace is the ambition of every forward. On this theory, the finest forward[s] should be the fleetest players. Are they? A truthful answer would scorn such an idea, because it is contrary to experience. The first duty of the footballer is to be master of the ball; to manoeuver the ball so that it is under control at once and to bring in every artifice so as to hoodwink an opponent by footwork.

Kicking was a particular fixation. To Jeffrey, too many Americans treated the ball as if it were oblong and to be knocked through a distant set of uprights (doubtless influenced by the frequency with which the press referred to them as "booters"). They "kicked from the hip, with a full swing of the leg" when it "should only be from the knee." This had "little place on the soccer field. . . . No power kick can ever put the ball in a specific spot."

Frustration led him to the volleyball court, where propelling the ball into the right space demanded more precision and control. By today's standards, Jeffrey's "soccer-volleyball" invention may seem no more than a novelty, but he regarded it as key to the success of his program. All the same, it was practice matches that consumed most of the training time—and gave him an excuse to keep playing. Well into his sixties, Jeffrey would assign himself to one of the teams, turning out in tennis shoes to remind everyone that kicking wasn't done with the toes. With an affable disposition and more than a trace of boyish enthusiasm, he was about as far removed from the archetypal stentorian coach as he could be. Yet he seemed to earn as much respect from his players as the harshest taskmaster. "While most other coaches either yell out their orders or else command the players as to what they should be doing," noted the *Collegian*, "Jeffrey simply suggests in the softest manner a better way. This method seems to produce results, since 'Mild Bill's' teams have been outstanding for the past decade."

The team's student manager observed in 1940:

I don't know, but it seems to me when I watch Bill and the boys out practicing they're just like a bunch of kids out playing for the fun they get, or maybe the exercise. You'd think that a team, undefeated in 60 contests, would be under great strain and tension to keep up such a record, but on the contrary, there is no strained atmosphere. Everything is run on the most informal terms. . . . Bill always seems to have a helping remark or a funny one to keep his boys laughing, and incidentally, Bill's attitude is as though they really were "his" boys. They always end up by playing a game and if their coach is on the losing team he takes a lot of good-natured kidding.

State made the ISFA honor list every year from 1936 to 1940, but in 1941, on a gray November Saturday at West Point, their unbeaten streak came to an end. Out-muscled by the perpetually well-drilled Army team, they lost, 1-0. "It was the old, old case of Penn State finesse pitted against an opponent's ruggedness and power," wrote the *Collegian*. "This time, power won out." "Army deserved to win," Jeffrey conceded. "They were the better team. Although rough, they played clean soccer and outscored us."*

Bizarrely, defeat achieved what decades of success had failed to do. On the players' return from West Point, close to 3,000 were waiting on the outskirts of State College. They hooked a rope to the team bus and towed it sympathetically into town, then staged a pep rally to console the disheartened occupants. Jeffrey was reduced to tears; the gesture had been "the greatest tribute ever paid to Penn State soccer" and "the nicest thing that has ever happened to me in my life."

Within a few months, though, World War II would leave its mark on State College and the whole of intercollegiate athletics. By 1943, the number of college soccer teams had been reduced by more than half. State's survived, though not hardily: from 1942 to 1945, they lost eight times, more than they had in the previous fourteen seasons put together. Jeffrey spent two months in Italy, teaching at the Army's sports training school and making a brief return to his birthplace. Not until after the war did his teams regain their familiar roar—and only once during the rest of his tenure did they lose more than one game a season.

By then, the National Soccer Coaches Association of America, formed in 1941, had assumed responsibility for selecting the national champion. While the process still involved little more than identifying the schools with the best playing record, there were a lot more teams to choose from.

---

* The star of Army's team—and included in Jeffrey's All America eleven that year—was Bill Guckeyson, an all-conference football player at the University of Maryland who in fact graduated from there in 1937. (His prowess as a soccer player had helped land him an athletic scholarship.) Drafted by the Philadelphia Eagles, he turned down pro football and entered the military academy where, under the rules of the day, he was eligible to play soccer for the varsity. Guckeyson was a fighter pilot during World War II; his plane was shot down on a mission over Germany, and no trace of his body was found.

Military units, headed by the Navy, had introduced the game as part of their conditioning regimen, and many undergraduates serving overseas had developed an affection for it. The ISFA grew from thirty-six schools in 1939 to sixty-two in 1949, making particularly strong headway in the Mid-Atlantic states.

But the team at State College was still the one everyone wanted to beat—since the ISFA's formation, no school had won more games, lost fewer, or scored as many goals—and Jeffrey was at the top of the coaching tree. In 1946, he and Tom Dent were selected to choose and coach teams for an all-star match, the first college soccer had ever staged. Fifteen hundred people saw the "dream game" in the Bronx. The following year, Jeffrey took charge of a college squad that played a series of trial matches in preparation for the 1948 Olympics. He took another group of collegians on a short cross-country tour; and he and his 1948 State eleven were invited to an abortive pan-American tournament in Guatemala.* In 1949, the coaches' association named him the recipient of its "honor award," asserting that he had "probably organized and participated in more amateur, high school and college soccer clinics ... than any other individual" and was even "a man whose influence has been woven into the stuff of other men's lives." All the same, he was still occasionally "Jeffreys" in the *Collegian,* and press releases from State's own athletic department admitted that "the undergraduates never think of giving up a football game to see their booters play." Jeffrey could never fathom the appeal of the gridiron; to him, it was "played with an out-of-shape ball," while soccer had "more thrills in five minutes than you can find in a whole game of football."

Football, though, was leaving an unmistakable impression on college soccer, not only in the rules by which it was being played but in the appetite for the sort of unremitting and radical change that had shorn the gridiron game of its rugby roots. Elsewhere, American soccer continued to be led by immigrants who saw little need to break with international convention, but the colleges were confronted with a raft of inexperienced players and officials and, lacking the time and resources to train them, found it easier to devise their own rules. By the 1950s, a sizeable rift had developed between the college game and the one the rest of the world played, as assiduous rules committees were turned loose in an effort to Americanize the game.

---

* In 1947, his college all-stars lost 5–2 in Pittsburgh and 3–2 in Chicago but won 2–0 in St. Louis. The opposition consisted of teams drawn from local clubs.

Precedent had been established as early as 1925, when college matches were split into twenty-two-minute quarters (the NCAA didn't return to two halves until 1972). Overtime periods dated from the 1910s; for a few seasons, time was kept by representatives from each school instead of the referee. After World War II, the changes became even more pronounced as a growing fraternity of coaches, few of them grounded in soccer, chased a desire to expand the game's appeal. The use of two referees was adopted as the "preferred system" in 1949, having been hailed in the *Official NCAA Soccer Guide* of 1948 as having "proven itself to be close to 100 percent perfect." In 1950, with similar headstrong abandon, throw-ins were replaced by kick-ins. "I have received a great many letters during the past season commenting on the improvement in the game with the change from throw-in to kick-in," wrote the editor of 1951's *Guide*. "As one writer commented, 'Now we are really getting away from basketball and down to football.'"

But they were also getting away from soccer. Two men with firsthand experience of the era, Mickey Cochrane and Len Oliver, describe a particularly radical deviation of the late 1940s:

> In the first five minutes of the game between Yale and Dartmouth in New Haven in the fall of 1948, a spectator well versed in soccer would have been bewildered when the Dartmouth wing-half took the first throw-in. He approached the touch line, reared back like an outfielder in baseball, and threw the ball 40 yards one-handed. No whistle! The New England Intercollegiate League had sanctioned the one-handed throw-in for a brief time in the postwar era.

An equally startling modification occurred in 1952, when the Midwestern Conference voted to abolish the offside law, something coaches had identified as "a drawback in the promotion of soccer." The mind boggles as to the level of goalmouth chaos the decision would have produced; yet only by one vote was the experiment dropped for the following season.

The most obvious of college soccer's idiosyncrasies, though, was its liberal approach to substitution. Almost from the start, it had permitted replacements, first one and then, in 1913, two, "one to be regarded as a legitimate reserve and the other to be allowed in a game in case of injury sustained by a member of the regular eleven, subject to the approval of the referee." By 1934, the number had increased to five, with three re-substitutions; the limit on re-substitutions was removed in 1954; and by

1964, sixteen players could be shunted in and out at the discretion of their coach.

In truth, college soccer had become its own worst enemy. Whether the majority of coaches possessed much of an affinity for the sport is moot; certainly, few had any background in it and little desire to learn from those who had. Rather than face up to their own inexperience and short-comings, they preferred to blame the game, changing its rules with giddy regularity.

Jeffrey's views seemed unequivocal enough—"We should leave the rules alone and play it like the rest of the world"—though at least one source cites him as "favoring the indirect free kick from touch and sub-stitutions." Certainly, he was not averse to replacing an injured player or clearing his bench when the outcome of a match was no longer in doubt. But platoon soccer was anathema to him. Often, he stuck to the same eleven players—Jack Fletcher didn't miss a minute of the 1935 wonder season—and won matches without the aid of a single substitute ("If a boy is good, he can go the whole way").

While the doggedness with which the colleges pursued their own rules was hardly unique to soccer, few of their other sports were so mani-festly international. The NCAA's window on the wider world, though, was provided by the USSFA (as the USFA had become), a pinprick on the American sporting landscape that possessed neither the resources nor the appetite to bring the colleges more closely in line with convention. "For years I've been trying to interest the USSFA in college soccer," Jeffrey lamented. "It has always been my contention that the college boys play a fine brand of soccer, but our leaders have been slow to concede this point. They still look to the sandlots and ballparks for their talent. Seldom do they look in the direction of the college campus." This might have been because so few collegians were used to playing an entire ninety-minute match or more than handful of games a year.

Even on Jeffrey's later teams, a novice with innate athletic ability could quickly establish himself on the varsity. In 1948, a spot of "faulty goal-handling" that contributed to a 4-0 loss to Navy early prompted him to look for a new goalkeeper. The *Collegian* described how he found him:

Big Ed Taggart, an eighth-semester journalism major, was cover-ing soccer innocently enough for the *Centre Daily Times*. But when he approached Coach Bill Jeffrey one day for an interview, the Jolly Scot—always on the lookout for potential soccermen—drafted Ed for his team. The next thing we saw was Taggart guarding the

net for dear ol' State in last Saturday's game with Maryland. He
had never played soccer before being recruited last week by Jeffrey,
and, for a journ student, we think he makes a crackerjack goalie.

State won the match, 1–0, on the way to a 7–1–1 season, and Taggart kept
his place in the team. The following season, duties were split between
George Lawther, a tennis letterman, and Ron Coder, who ran track; neither had played the sport before. Even with these novitiates, the Lions
won all eight of their matches. They included a come-from-behind 2–1
defeat of previously unbeaten Temple, a match in which Jeffrey declined
to make any substitutions.

By then, the ISFA had reclaimed responsibility for naming the national
champion and decided that State should share the title with the University of San Francisco, the first school from the West Coast to earn such
recognition. While the association's indifference toward post-season play
(to say nothing of the NCAA's aloofness toward soccer) showed little sign
of changing—by 1949, even boxing was holding an intercollegiate championship—other parties had become impatient. Pestered by the likes of
Jeffrey, the USSFA seized the initiative: its affiliate in Missouri invited the
co-champions to square off in St. Louis.

The "soccer bowl" played on New Year's Day of 1950 was effectively
the first championship game the colleges had staged in nearly thirty
years.* While press interest in the match disappeared beneath the day's
football, few college teams had ever played in front of a crowd as large
as the 4,660 who filed into Sportsman's Park that afternoon, and the
Lions and Dons responded with a laudable advertisement for the college game.

Dent McSkimming wrote in the *St. Louis Post-Dispatch*:

What looked at first glance like a hazardous undertaking turned
out to be a most refreshing and satisfying experience. It took a lot
of nerve to bring a team from San Francisco and one from Penn
State College to St. Louis for a national title match in midwinter.
College soccer has been something of an orphan and there was
danger that St. Louis sports followers would ignore the show. Bad
weather, long overdue, could have ruined everything. But the class

---

* Princeton defeated Penn 3–1 in a playoff in 1922 after the teams finished tied for first in
the Intercollegiate Association Football League. The match, at Franklin Field in Philadelphia, was said to have attracted a crowd of "about 8,000 intensely interested spectators."

of football shown by the collegians and the white-hot fervor of their play through the latter quarters of the game left a crowd of 4600 happy. At first surprised and then fascinated, the spectators gave the players a hearty round of applause when the thrilling game ended in a 2–2 draw.

It had ended with a dramatic flourish. San Francisco, its team consisting almost entirely of foreign students (a Nicaraguan at fullback, two Filipinos on the right flank, a Nigerian prince at halfback), clung to a 2–1 lead with seconds remaining, only to give away a penalty. Harry Little, State's inside-right, scored from the spot with almost the last kick of the match. Satisfied with an honorable draw, the two coaches decided against any overtime. But for many in attendance, the four quarters of action hadn't quite been enough. One fan told the *St. Louis Globe-Democrat*:

> I saw the Notre Dame–Southern Methodist football game at Dallas last month and this soccer game and that football affair had one thing in common. When the game was over, in each case, there was no mad dash for the exits. Each time the fans stood up, cheered the players as they left the field and seemed reluctant to depart themselves. The impression was that the fans were digesting the enjoyable spectacle that they had just seen—and just sorta hoped or wished that there was a little bit more.

Had the college game arrived? Another soccer bowl took place the following season, but it was contested by teams with no title pretensions. State's hopes of an unbeaten season had been ended by West Chester, the eventual ISFA champions, but they ended up in St. Louis just the same. Their opponents were not San Francisco—still the pick of the West and unbeaten in 1950—but Purdue, a club team that hadn't even finished first in its conference. The second soccer bowl was thus little more than an exhibition, played in bitterly cold weather before a mere 1,673; State won easily, 3–1. Bad weather forced the 1952 event out of Missouri, and the promoters lost interest after that. Not until 1976 was another "bowl" played—and then in upper case, by the professionals of the NASL.*

---

* Temple and the University of San Francisco rearranged their 1952 "soccer bowl" for Kezar Stadium in San Francisco a month later. The Dons were beaten, 2–0, their first defeat in forty-one games. Though the attendance of 10,000 was said to be the largest a college match had ever produced and "large enough to be profitable," the event was never repeated.

Jeffrey, meanwhile, had—at short notice—accompanied the national team to Brazil for the 1950 World Cup. Though elated by his side's astonishing 1-0 victory over England ("I've never gotten as big a kick out of anything as I did, sitting there in a cold sweat, after the game had ended"), his influence on the outcome had been minimal. Because he'd been appointed to the position with only weeks to spare, he, in the words of one player, "didn't have much time to do much coaching, and he was smart enough not to try." Defeats against Spain and Chile on either side of the England victory left the United States eliminated at the earliest hurdle, but most of the country had taken no notice of it. At State College, the *Collegian* relayed the happy news:

> Writing to friends in State College from Belo Horizonte, Brazil, [Jeffrey] said "my boys really rose to the occasion by defeating England, 1-0, in the World Cup championships. It still makes me feel that it was a splendid dream—but it must be true, the papers are full of it."

Just eight months later, he was on another plane, this time with Penn State. The U.S. State Department had received an invitation for a soccer team to play a series of matches in Iran, then at the center of an East-West power struggle. While the decision to assign a group of undergraduates to a high-profile ambassadorial role raised eyebrows (Jeffrey claimed to have no idea why his team had been chosen), clean-cut, genial collegians doubtless represented less of a diplomatic risk than hyphenated Americans from the semiprofessional netherworld. Thus, for two weeks in the spring of 1951 the activities of a college soccer team became front-page news. Part of this was attributable to Iran's political vulnerability, heightened by the largely British ownership of its oil reserves at a time of rising nationalism. In the weeks leading up to State's departure, the Iranian prime minister was assassinated, and Parliament had voted to nationalize the oil industry. The unrest threw State's visit into doubt.

In the end, alarmist stories gave way to reports of a diplomatic triumph; one account even claimed there had "never been a group of Americans who have caused so much enthusiasm on the part of the Iranians, from officials to the man in the street." Locals followed State's players with the zeal of groupies. After one match, they hoisted goalkeeper Ron Coder onto their shoulders; after another, they needed to be restrained by police from carting off the whole team. The *Collegian* was told that small boys would often "sidle up to the Penn Staters just to try and touch them."

Coder received his escort on the back of his performance in a 3–0 win in front of 5,000 in Shiraz. State lost their other two matches, one of them 5–0 to a prototype national team, but by then dysentery had affected the squad to such an extent that Neil See, the team's manager, was threatened with suiting up. Only by pushing the kickoff back a day did a quorum of players emerge from the lavatory.

Once again, the Lions had been humbled in the face of foreign competition. ("It's the same old story," Jeffrey reflected, "a kid must crawl and yawl before he walks and talks.") But with the Truman administration ever more fearful that Iran would fall into the hands of the Soviet Union or succumb to extremists, scores had mattered little. In the eyes of the American ambassador, the tour had been a "stunning diplomatic success"; the assistant secretary of state praised the way the team had "discharged" its "responsibilities"; See wrote of "tremendous ovations wherever we went"; and Jeffrey quipped that "oil was well."

It wasn't quite the last hurrah, but Mild Bill, approaching sixty, was nearing the end of his time at State. His team finished 5–1–2 in 1951 and 7–1–1 in 1952, struggling in particular against the muscle of the service academies. Navy proved the most obdurate foe: through 1942, Jeffrey's teams had won thirteen of fourteen encounters with them but took just two of ten thereafter. Army was almost as successful, though its tactics left Jeffrey cold. "The Cadets have always played a rough type game," he noted after a 1–1 skirmish in 1952, "but some of their tactics were dirty and uncalled for."

At season's end, he accepted a six-month teaching assignment in Puerto Rico, though it ended up lasting much longer. Jeffrey's final game in charge at State had been the stuff of cliché: down 2–0 away to Penn after just ten minutes, the Lions labored through the mud to win, 3–2. All three goals came from sophomore Jack Pinezich, a Brooklyn-born center-forward whose twenty-three goals broke Bill McEwan's single-season record. Close to retirement age, and fond of the "little paradise" he'd found in the Caribbean, Jeffrey ended up spending seven years at the University of Puerto Rico, running machine-shop courses and gasping through the soccer season ("We have to play all our collegiate games in the afternoon, and frankly, it is too hot"). But, according to Jack Infield, who produced a master's thesis on Jeffrey in 1973, soccer in Mayagüez was a different proposition to the one at State College:

Jeffrey was never happy with soccer as the Puerto Ricans played it. Even though his players were far superior in skill than the American boys he had coached, they lacked the varsity enthusiasm displayed by those he had directed at Penn State. Jeffrey found himself in the role of a club manager rather than a coach. The players came to practice when they felt like it (if they came at all), did not respond well to coaching directives, and often displayed individualistic characteristics which would hamper team play.

There were other, more tragic complications. In 1957, Virginia, his second wife, disappeared. A former PE instructor at State College, she was a keen swimmer, and Jeffrey assumed she'd been swept out to sea; her body was never found. Twenty-four years earlier, his first wife, Doris, had died in an automobile accident; Jeffrey had been watching a match in Philadelphia and did not learn of her fate until he returned the next day.

Not one to openly mourn his losses, Jeffrey returned to Pennsylvania in 1959 and married for a third time. "Life is too short—and you are gone a long, long time—to be spent thinking of all the tragedies in your days," he reflected not long before his own sudden death. "We must all live with a wee drop of spirit in our souls." For a man prone to reciting Burns or a more prosaic verse of his own, who as an "inveterate correspondent" kept in touch with his players long after they'd left State College, and who'd even agreed to dress as a leopard to publicize a college gymnastics event, the joys of living were not hard to find.

His own life came to an end at a coaching conference early in 1966. Addressing a delegation one morning, he collapsed from a heart attack and, in the words of one attendee, "died, as he lived, in the hearts and arms of his friends." It darkened an otherwise luminous year for soccer in the United States, one that included the announcements of the country's first coast-to-coast professional leagues, Pelé's first matches on American soil, and national television coverage of a World Cup final. CBS even took its cameras to Berkeley to film the year's collegiate championship match between San Francisco and Long Island University.

Missed opportunity or lost cause? It's difficult to imagine an alternative course of history in which the colleges propelled soccer to national prominence. The collegiate coaching fraternity was abecedarian and self-absorbed; the players had largely the wrong idea of the game; athletic departments were indifferent or even antagonistic; and the likes of the ISFA lacked foresight and ambition. Would things have been any different with a few dozen Bill Jeffreys? Even at Penn State, with a team that played comparatively skillful soccer and hardly ever lost, interest was meager. Half a century after the Pilgrims had tried to introduce the game to the colleges, there had been little change in campus attitudes. Soccer was not football, and football was what mattered.

Many of the fingerprints Jeffrey left on college soccer have faded. The sport is now an altogether more competitive proposition, one that cuts a wide swath across the nation's campuses. Since 1972, though, State's soccer teams have played their home matches at Jeffrey Field, and the coaches' association has honored long-term service to the game with an award in his name. While the World Cup defeat of England—ironically, the achievement that probably required the least of him—has come to mean the most to American fans, Jeffrey's greater contribution was in demonstrating, to any college that was interested, how appealing the game could be if played with skill. For a mild-mannered Scotsman who came to America to get away from the game, it's an unlikely legacy.

5

Dash, Desperation, and Deviltry

St. Louis and the "American Style"

No doubt St. Louis boys hear a lot about the superior British style and have been charged with being over-energetic, rough, even foul. Fudge! We can never equal the British in sheer skill. We have not patience enough or time enough to acquire the perfection of the virtuosos. . . . My advice . . . is to play the St. Louis game. Forget the fouls. Never mind the falls of defeated players, lie fit. Play hard. Win! A Britisher refuses to punish himself that he may win, whereas the American will kill himself to win. Therein lies the great advantage which the American has over the European. He will work harder to succeed. And to our mind American soccer players should always remember that their assets against European players are (1) superior physical condition, (2) superior wallop, (3) the will to win[;] and seek at all costs to nourish and cultivate them.

—*St. Louis Globe-Democrat,* December 5, 1921

THOSE OF A CERTAIN GENERATION may recall the keen sense of anticipation that accompanied soccer's encroachment on the American sporting landscape in the 1970s. The performance of native-born players had started to count for something; native-born coaches were being hired by professional clubs; and a critical mass of native-born fans had developed a hearty appetite for the game. As "Americanization" became a critical part of the lexicon, those familiar with the varied tactical approaches to soccer in different parts of the world began to contemplate the evolution of an American style of play. Would it resemble the high-tempo, physical game favored in northern Europe and among many teams in the Anglo-centric NASL? Or might it take its cue from Latin America, with a greater emphasis on possession and individual skill? One thing seemed certain: the country was starting from scratch, since there was no legacy of homegrown teams on which to draw.

So it was thought. Yet several generations earlier, one city's approach to playing the game had become distinctive and pervasive enough to be labeled the "American style": native soccer as played by the native-born. This was St. Louis, Missouri, then the fourth-largest municipality in the country and a home for the game like few others. Here, soccer was played in major-league ballparks and wrote headlines in the newspapers; for a time, it was the winter's principal spectator sport, as familiar in the frosty months as a scarf or a pair of iceskates.

By the 1970s, this had been all but forgotten. Yet the game had endured strongly enough for the "style" to have survived. Paul Gardner offered this description of it for a 1975 edition of the *Sporting News*:

> It is primarily an off-the-ball style—that is, it involves a good deal of movement and running by players who are not in possession of the ball. The progress of the ball is accomplished mainly by first-time passing. It is rare to see a St. Louis player dwelling on the ball, or engaging in a protracted dribble. . . . Individually, the players tend to be well-built and gluttons for work. They shield the ball well and strike it accurately. The shooting of a St. Louis team is invariably impressive. Overall teamwork is excellent, and the game is played at a rip-roaring pace, with the emphasis on attack.

Descriptions from the earlier part of the century were rather more vague and facile; usually, they were steeped in jingoism. One of the more lucid accounts, almost as breathless as the style it describes, appeared in a 1917 edition of *Sporting Life*:

> The American game is very fast, is wide open, short passes being unusual, and sufficient science is used to take the utmost advantage of the speed of the players in advancing the ball. The effect of the combination of speed and skill demonstrated in a game where an American team[,] having a strenuous time defending and having pulled out of the opposing halves and backs, suddenly clears the ball to one of the wings or the center or an inside well down the field, who, with his mates, makes a breakaway and a lightning attack on the opposing goal that sweeps the fullbacks off their feet and leaves but the goalkeeper to stop it.

This high-tempo approach went down well with St. Louisans—and in the hands of athletically inclined young men it proved remarkably effective.

It also left St. Louis sportswriters—including this one from the *St. Louis Globe-Democrat* in 1921—flushed with expectation:

> I believe that at no very distant day America will turn out soccer teams that will more than hold their own with the best British amateurs if not with the Great British professionals. My reasons for so believing are that the American plays more earnestly to win, puts more punch into every game that he plays than the European does. That we shall ever exceed the British in soccer is doubtful. That we will excel him in vigor of action, intensity of purpose and in physical condition, hence defeat him at soccer, is very probable.

The opportunity for such a showdown never really materialized. Once the Pilgrims and Corinthians had gone home, St. Louis would have to wait until after World War II for another crack at a British team.* By then, soccer's star had fallen, and few Americans in Missouri or anywhere else were bothered about where their teams stood in any international pecking order. The game may have survived in St. Louis better than it did in other places, but its aura had faded.

FOR A CITY far removed from other major conurbations, soccer established itself in St. Louis remarkably early. The historian Melvin I. Smith has identified a contest between "blond lawyers" and "brunette lawyers" on May 28, 1875, as the earliest played under association rules, but better documented in the city's newspapers is a match played on Thanksgiving Day in 1881. The charity occasion was meant to include a five-inning exhibition of baseball, but cold weather limited play to an association football contest between the Athletic and Mound City clubs. It produced only one goal but wasn't short of incident; according to one paper, "The affair was a lively one in a vigorous way, young Shepley was injured, while Larry Daly was badly bruised."

Matters would proceed along such pugnacious lines for decades to come. Soccer in the Mound City was not the game played by the more genteel denizens of New York or Philadelphia: it drew a fair proportion of its participants from less salubrious quarters. Most conspicuously, this

---

* In St. Louis on May 28, 1939, an eleven representing the Scottish Football Association— by no means the full national team—defeated by ten goals to two a team of "Western all-stars," around half of whom were recruited from Pittsburgh or Chicago. The first British professional club to face a true St. Louis eleven was Liverpool, who defeated an all-city eleven 5-1 in May 1946.

included the near-north side's "Kerry patch" of rough-hewn Irish migrants. One writer's assertion that the Irish "looked upon the football game as a good excuse for a fight" may have been couched in prejudice, but referees were rarely given an easy afternoon. "I'd say we used our fists as often as we used our feet," one player later recalled, "but that was what made soccer an interesting game."

Plenty of fans seemed to agree. Yet others were attracted for more virtuous reasons—like the honor of the city. As early as 1884, an eleven from Toronto played two matches with local aggregations over the Christmas holidays, winning 9-0 and 5-0. It didn't take long for teams from St. Louis and Chicago to begin squaring off for the putative "western championship," though their encounters were not always undertaken with the best of grace. A five-game series in 1891 was abandoned at one victory each after the Chicagoans complained about the officiating and were "also much put out over what they term the discourtesy of the St. Louis athletes, who they claim did little to entertain them." (They returned to Missouri a month later and won the deciding game, 11–1.) Another clash in 1896 saw the beleaguered referee "forced to abdicate his position" after erroneously awarding a goal. St. Louis, well ahead in the match, apparently "did not make any remonstrance."

Such intercity contests, not all of them so fractious, quickly became a regular feature of the holiday calendar; often, they were the highlight of the season. But out-of-town visitors were not especially responsible for the game's remarkable rise. Rather, it was the attachment of the city's Catholic institutions to soccer that would weave it into the local sporting fabric. One of the earliest manifestations of this took place in 1893 with the formation of the Sodality Foot Ball League. Drawing its teams from Catholic sodalities with a combined membership of close to 4,000, the league was said to have attracted the largest crowds for football of any code in the city.

Another early wellspring was Christian Brothers College, a Catholic teachers' school whose enrollment included a substantial number of migrants with an enthusiasm for soccer (one account claims that "the Brothers even went so far as to have members of their order transferred from England to St. Louis in order that the boys might obtain expert advice about the game"). Its own team, among the strongest in the city, regularly competed against professional clubs; it even finished second at the three-team Olympic tournament of 1904. But it was the college's wider involvement in the city's recreational affairs that proved more telling. James Robinson detailed this contribution in a 1966 doctoral thesis:

First, the Christian Brothers had junior teams—intramural teams in today's parlance—that played a series of games and among which great rivalry existed. These junior teams were willing to play all comers under 16 years age. Secondly, not long after this order of teachers was established in Saint Louis (1850), the Brothers staffed many of the parochial schools in the city. . . . Thus youngsters were able to learn the rudiments of the game. Finally, graduates of these parochial schools continued to play soccer long after graduation (or dropping out) in numerous clubs and sodalities that sponsored association football clubs.

In a city teeming with Irish Americans, the exceptional interest of the Catholic church helped soccer attain a degree of popularity unique among America's major cities. Other parts of the country may have been no less Irish, but they lacked the same ecclesiastical patronage; they may have pursued the game with similar enthusiasm, but not in such scrupulously organized competition—and certainly not with hordes of native-born youngsters. Most of the principal soccer clubs in St. Louis also fielded youth teams; one league staged its matches on the Christian Brothers campus. At its inception, the Sodality League secured "the three best and only grounds suitable for foot ball in the city"; it was, one paper insisted, "undoubtedly the best managed organization of its kind in St. Louis."

Yet it did not last long. While soccer quickly found a home in St. Louis, its entities led a fleeting existence not uncommon for the era. In December 1885, five teams calling themselves the "Western Foot Ball Association of America" agreed to a regular Sunday schedule, playing on Sunday mornings at the Browns baseball park and on Sunday afternoons at the Union diamond on the corner of Cass and Jefferson avenues. If this was truly a football "league," it predated the first in England by more than two years. A certain J. W. Peckington offered a fancy silk pennant to "the club winning the greatest number of games during the season" but soon found the locals' rough-and-tumble methods difficult to stomach. Matters came to a head after a match between the Hibernian and Thistle clubs; he declared that the former had "acted in a very ungentlemanly matter in all their contests" and had been "so rude that, should they succeed in winning the most games, I do not think I will give them the pennant." Days later, the Thistles withdrew from the league after two contests they'd assumed had been tied were declared defeats. The exasperated Mr. Peckington soon withdrew his prize, never to soil his hands with the game again.

Plenty were willing to take his place, though, and in the years that followed, leagues in the city formed and disbanded with alacrity. A six-team St. Louis Foot Ball League came to life in 1889, playing sixty-minute games at several venues across the city; its participants included the likes of Hibernian and the Shamrocks, two names that had featured in the Western Association. Other circuits included the Lindell League, which staged its matches on the infield of the trotting grounds at Forest Park.

While the game of this era remained largely the pastime of migrants from the British Isles, the seeds of native-born success did not take long to gain purchase. City honors for 1891 were claimed by Kensington, a team composed largely of locally born youngsters. "Very few of the players had attained their majority, some of them were even students at local institutions," noted Spalding's *Association Foot Ball Guide* of 1905, "but they won from the veterans who had been instructed in the game's intricacies in their cribs in the old country."

In 1895, the St. Louis and Sodality leagues combined to form a six-team circuit, which was often referred to merely as the "association league." Two of its strongest entrants were St. Teresa, conquerors of the Lindell League champions two years running, and the Cycling Club, an ambitious collective that had spent freely in pursuit of local supremacy. The latter's lineup included Dick Jarrett, who had played internationally for Wales before migrating to Chicago via Canada; he'd been enticed to Missouri with the promise of a job by a sympathetic businessman.

First place was at stake when the two teams faced off in January 1897, and almost inevitably tempers frayed. "There were phenomenal plays at critical points; there were good hard fights between the players; and at one time about 2,000 people swarmed out onto the field to mix in if necessary," the *St. Louis Post-Dispatch* noted. The pedalists won, 5–1, but St. Teresa protested the outcome, claiming the referee had conspired against them. At a meeting, the matter was put to the clubs; when they voted to let the result stand, St. Teresa withdrew from the league. Finishing the season as an independent, the team hosted, among other things, a two-match series with the Shamrock club of Cincinnati. This they won easily—with members of the Cycling Club on hand apparently to cheer on the visitors—though St. Teresa thought highly enough of one of the Shamrocks to sign him up.

While the Cycling Club finished the season in first place, its triumph rang hollow: St. Teresa was still seen as the team to beat. Keen to prove their supremacy, the new champions arranged for a showdown with their rivals and drew a crowd of over 6,000 paying customers—perhaps 10,000 in total—to South Side Park on Easter Sunday.* Not for the last time in the city, the match revealed a notable contrast in playing approaches. Jarrett and his cyclists had adopted the familiar close-passing style of contemporary British teams, but St. Teresa was a band of mostly locally born youngsters said to have put "life, vim and a bit of roughness in the game" and sometimes criticized for their belligerence. ("The Welsh, Scotch and English on the Cycling Club would fight too, but had been trained to play first the ball, then the man," one commentator recalled. "The St. Teresas always played the man first and paid less attention to the ball.")

On the day, technique may have counted for little. With gate receipts riding on the outcome and fans screaming lustily from the touchlines, the game boiled over with fights and disputes. St. Teresa won, 3–1, although, as the *Globe-Democrat* reported, not without the benefit of some questionable refereeing:

> During the progress of the game some excitement was caused and play delayed for a short time by a collision between Patrick of the [Cycling Club] and J. Daley of the Saints. Patrick fouled Daley, some claim deliberately, and Daley responded by socking him with a left hook. Umpire Rogers saw the blow given Patrick by Daley and ordered the latter's removal from the game. The sodality men protested long and earnestly against the decision of the referee and after considerable time elapsed he reconsidered his decision and permitted Daley to remain.

This, the most famous of the city's early showdowns, would prove to be the high-water mark in St. Louis for some years to come. Though soccer had become a conspicuous part of the city's sporting landscape (Christian Brothers College even traveled to Buffalo to play at the 1901 Pan-American Exposition), it also struggled to overcome a rank level of lawlessness. Crowds of a few thousand were rolling up for big matches, which made it possible to pay players—it wasn't just Jarrett who'd been lured down from Canada—but thuggish behavior and ugly disputes kept many others away.

Spalding's *Guide* claimed that the formation in 1903 of an Association Foot Ball League of St. Louis, with Tom Cahill as its secretary, "noted the return of the game's popularity." This, though, was far from the whole

---

* On the same day, an exhibition baseball game between the St. Louis Cardinals and St. Paul of the Western League drew just 4,000 to Robison Field.

truth. The four-team league had secured a lease on the Browns' baseball diamond at Sportsman's Park and indeed attracted some fair-sized crowds for its Sunday afternoon doubleheaders. But it couldn't keep everyone to heel. In February, after police had arrested two players for fighting (an incident not without precedent that season) the Browns told the league to find another home. The schedule was never completed.

The league found new premises in time for the 1904–1905 season at Kulage Park, a baseball diamond near the intersection of North Newstead Avenue and Penrose Street, and was joined by a rival entity operating out of Sportsman's Park. Neither took prisoners. Fistfights and willful collisions were considered almost part of the game—so much so that newspapers frequently attached a curious premium to a team's weight—and such was the lack of respect for officiating that teams irritated by a referee's performance often just walked off the field. These predicaments were hardly unique to the sport; even the major-league baseball players of the day could get out of hand. But soccer in St. Louis had no Ban Johnson to make them think twice.

The arrival of the Pilgrims in 1905 pointed the game in a more hopeful direction. While the home side was trounced in the two matches the team played in Missouri that autumn—and all manner of excuses were offered for the lack of resistance—the technique of the English had been a revelation. "The game in America consisted of kicking the ball as hard as possible and running all over the field without set positions," the *Post-Dispatch* asserted. "Instead of weight figuring in the results, as has been too often the case to the detriment of the game, the professionals have changed their tactics and are playing the game along the lines exhibited by the Pilgrims. . . . As a consequence, spectators are now witnessing games that are noticeable for fast, clean action, science and skill."

No American soccer match for the next twenty-one years would draw as many fans as crashed through the fences for the Pilgrims' second encounter, swelling attendance to perhaps 28,000, and the eager onlookers had been rewarded with an exhibition of the sport played not only to a high standard but in the right spirit. Before the British had even left town, new clubs and a new league had been formed; a team called the Pilgrims was even readied for the following season.

Had the city really embraced the style and sportsmanship of their English conquerors? It's hard to imagine bands of feisty young St. Louisans suddenly developing a mastery of more measured soccer. Among other things, the game's popularity far outstripped the available local expertise; it was one thing for Catholic institutions to encourage their patrons to take up the sport, but quite another to drill all the eager participants in its finer points. Perhaps it wasn't even necessary if, as one contributor to Spalding's 1905 *Guide* noted, "the local public feel confident that St. Louis has the greatest Socker players in the United States."

Certainly it had produced its share of successful teams, and one in particular—St. Leo—would enjoy a remarkable ascendancy. Formed in 1903 as an amateur side, the club by 1905 had been honored as city champions; they then joined the professional ranks and for the next eight seasons proved impossible to dethrone. Six thousand people were said to have watched them defeat St. Matthew, winners of the amateur league, for city honors in 1907, with mounted police doing their best to keep the field clear. Yet the club's success does not appear to have been predicated on whatever the Pilgrims may have shown them. "Possessed of a fast forward line every one of which can shoot, and a great trio of halves, they play a rushing game," Spalding's *Guide* observed in 1909. "Speed is the watchword with them. They do not play a fancy game but they get there. They keep going at top speed all the time." Such perpetual motion wasn't enough to stop them from being clobbered 12–1 by the Pilgrims in 1909. But by then they'd been feted by the St. Louis press as the greatest team in the Midwest.

They were not without their rough edges, though, and for all its successes, the game in St. Louis continued to make trouble for itself. Players kicked and punched each other; referees were chased from the pitch; and clubs made threats when they didn't get their way. The *Globe-Democrat* observed in January 1911 that it was "nothing unusual to hear the spectators in the stands making remarks that they are tired of seeing so much roughness and so much browbeating of the referee"; it urged the players to "be careful of the spectators and not try to kill the goose that lays the golden egg." That year, Spalding's *Guide* noted that one league had found it necessary to split its season in two and drop two clubs "owing to dissention and poor playing." A match between St. Leo and Innisfail in December 1911 abandoned in the wake of a free-for-all (with St. Leo losing, 6–1) would not have been the only one to end in ignominy that year.

All the same, the professional game had learned how to finish its seasons and seemed to have taken root. The four-team St. Louis Soccer League, which included the likes of St. Leo and Innisfail, typically drew around 3,000 fans for its Sunday afternoon doubleheaders at Athletic Park. This might not have been a dazzling figure, but it was roughly the same as the baseball Cardinals and Browns averaged across the season. Moreover, and unlike baseball, the players were paid a percentage of the gate receipts rather than a salary. Among other things, this put a premium on favorable weather and an attractive opponent. Marrying the two wasn't always easy. Top teams from places like Chicago and Detroit usually demanded hefty financial guarantees before considering an expedition to Missouri, and there weren't many fans prepared to brave subzero temperatures or curtains of snow.

Yet rarely did Christmas pass without a visit from at least one out-of-town attraction, and by 1911 there was enough money in the jar to tempt one from the East. Tacony, arguably the strongest eleven in Philadelphia and characteristically British in composition, played two games in the city, both of them on a pudding of a pitch at Athletic Park. The opposition for the first was none other than St. Leo—and so strong were the two teams that at least one paper regarded their confrontation as being "for the soccer championship of the United States." But on the glue-pot surface, and with a ball said to be "encircled with mud at least two inches," neither side could demonstrate clear superiority; the match ended 4-4, with a crowd of 3,772 earning each member of the home team a welcome $51. (Innisfail beat Tacony, 3-1, a day later.) Not even the sea of mud could obscure the disparity in the two styles. "There is as much difference between the play of the Easterners and that of the Western men as there is in day and night," the *Post-Dispatch* noted. "Like most of the foreign teams, the Quakers play clean football. On the other hand the rough work, not always intentional, of the St. Leos could be easily spotted." The *Philadelphia Record* was less charitable. "Everything goes on the soccer field in St. Louis," it claimed. "Out there they play a combination of Rugby and soccer, and this style of game completely bewildered the Eastern players. . . . The only fouls that are called are for hitting the ball with the hand or offside play. There was no net inclosing the goal [*sic*], four linesmen being used, two on the sidelines and two at the goal." Against Tacony, the paper noted, the referee, "instead of tossing the ball in a scrimmage, set it down as they do in Rugby and St. Leos rushed it into the goal."

The local game was certainly rife with idiosyncrasies, many of which ultimately worked against it. Most leagues played thirty- or thirty-five-minute halves; some allowed substitutes (even, it seems, for players thrown out of the game). Tempers were permitted to fray; misbehavior was readily forgiven. All of this may not have forced teams to go full pelt—few knew any other way—but it did little to move things in a more enlightened direction.

A year after meeting Tacony, St. Leo took a trip of their own, the first team from the city to venture east. They played five matches but won only one, blaming lavish hospitality and a procession of sightseeing and social engagements for their lack of success. In truth, the "Most Famous Soccer Team in the United States," as Spalding's *Guide* would label them, wasn't necessarily the most assiduous. Interviewed before the tour, the club's manager, William Klosterman, blithely asserted that apart from warming up before each match, his team never practiced—and seemed to regard as more noteworthy the fact that twelve of his fifteen players were teetotal.*

Within weeks of the club's return, though, the professional game had imploded. On January 19, 1913, a match between St. Leo and Innisfail precipitated a riot. Not even the presence of an "extra large squad of police" could prevent the abandonment of the match, or the veteran referee, Paul McSweeney, from "throwing his whistle over the fence" in disgust. For the likes of the *Post-Dispatch,* the ugly scenes carried an unfortunate ring of familiarity:

> Soccer football in St. Louis is once more going through the usual process of killing off the interest after the sport has reached a point where it is beginning to really flourish. This is pretty near an annual occurrence and can be safely predicted every fall. Then the seasons start off with a big flourish and matters go along with some degree of smoothness until the race gets close and there is a good bunch of money to be divided. Whenever this occurs either one of two things happen: If there are two leagues here of first-class caliber they get into a fight, steal each other's players and kick up a general row. If there is but one big league, the managers get into a row, lose control of the players and what happened last Sunday happens. Then the season drags along to a close and the cycle begins all over again the following season.

The voluble Klosterman announced that he would disband his team but soon changed his mind and merely pulled it out of the league. It was quickly replaced, but before the schedule had been completed, Innisfail had abandoned its obligations in favor of an eastern trip of its own. (Playing teams from Philadelphia, West Hudson, and Fall River, it failed to

---

* St. Leo's trip wasn't a financial success, either—a 7–1 defeat at the hands of Howard and Bullough (a manufacturer of textile machinery) was played before fewer than 1,000 people in Pawtucket and netted gate receipts of just $56. Klosterman said he was left with just $6 to feed his team for the thirty-six-hour train journey home and had to do so with "apples, figs and dates."

win any of its five matches.) The following season, a rival professional league materialized and recruited St. Leo for itself. The city had, of course, been saddled with competing professional interests before, but never at such an auspicious period for the game in America. It didn't help, either, that each circuit referred to itself as the St. Louis Soccer League, the entity with St. Leo taking up residence at Athletic Park and the other, at Robison Field (the Cardinals' baseball park until 1920).

The professional rift may have been the most obvious of them, but organizational shortcomings ran right through the city. There was no central authority to oversee matters like players' contracts or inter-league play. The absence of suitable venues—a predicament hardly unique to St. Louis—left promoters largely at the mercy of baseball. Perhaps most unfortunate of all, though, no one was able to capture the interest of the city's secular educational institutions. Tom Cahill's endeavors to "introduce the winter sport among the public schools" came to little; Christian Brothers College tried to foster intercollegiate play in the Midwest—it staged an exhibition against the University of Illinois in 1910—but was no more successful. St. Louis University would not introduce a varsity soccer program until 1959.

Ironically, the split in the city's professional ranks occurred in the same year Cahill and his kindred spirits were establishing the United States Football Association, an entity that might have been expected to harness the city's enthusiasm for the wider good. Yet local interest in the new governing body proved lukewarm. Though there were perhaps forty soccer leagues in Missouri and southern Illinois, only the one at Athletic Park became a member initially. The in-fighting endured, and the rival professional circuits continued along separate paths, with hardly anyone prepared to watch either of them.

More immediately significant to the city was the creation of an amateur Municipal League by an ambitious and well-connected cross-section of interested parties (key officials included a Catholic parish priest, the director of athletics for the city's playgrounds, and the city's park commissioner—and future donor of tennis's most famous cup—Dwight Davis). In November 1912, play began in what became known affectionately as the Muny League, with eighteen teams split into four divisions; 20,000 were said to have watched the 1914 championship game.

For many in St. Louis, this league would become soccer's chief attraction, if not always for the right reasons. As with the professionals, there was generally a double helping of matches each Sunday, but admission was free. Anyone of a predatory disposition was thus able to antagonize players, bully the referee, or pick fights with other fans. Hostilities often followed ethnic lines (it wasn't just Irish Americans who had warmed to the sport), and on the unenclosed playing fields typical of the league, unruly crowds were difficult to control. There was also the not insignificant matter of professional teams poaching the league's best players, sometimes as they left the field. While a gentlemen's agreement eventually prohibited this, in the absence of a central authority disputes were often left to blow in the wind.

Lack of coordination and weak leadership was a problem for soccer in many parts of the country, but it was particularly regrettable in a city where the game had become so popular. Perhaps things would have been different had Tom Cahill not departed for the East in 1910; as it was, rapacious players and promoters were rarely kept in check. Winton Barker, a wholesale jeweler who had worked with Cahill to bring the Pilgrims back to the United States in 1909 (and would become a USFA vice-president in 1920), may have been regarded by Spalding's 1912 *Guide* as "the biggest man in soccer in America," but whatever efforts he may have made toward unifying the game in the city or strengthening its foundations had little lasting impact.

Not until the spring of 1915 did the two professional leagues merge; to no one's surprise, the new entity was called the St. Louis Soccer League. Strengthened by the truncation of eight professional teams into four, the competition proved too much for St. Leo, who, already past their finest hour, finished last. The new champions were Ben Miller, a team that two years earlier had introduced a new era of nomenclature to the game in the city. Within a few years, all four professional entries would adopt the guise of whatever business cared to back them, changing names with exasperating frequency. Not everyone was enamored with such barefaced commercialism—and it is doubtful we shall ever again see professional teams named Minit-Rub or Pants Store—but the shift away from ethnic designations like Shamrocks and Thistles may have strengthened the city's perception of soccer as an American pursuit.

Ben Miller's name would endure longer than any in the St. Louis League (even St. Leo would turn itself over to the St. Louis Screw Company in 1918, though it would remain active in the Municipal League). While the firm, which made hats, sponsored teams in many sports, soccer was the one that got its name in the national press. In one of the earliest instances, on Christmas Day of 1913, the club handed a 5–1 defeat to the touring True Blues of Paterson, New Jersey.* Not until 1919 would Ben Miller lose the league championship; by then, many St. Louisans regarded them as the strongest team in the country.

It was a hard claim to substantiate. The city had never entered any of its teams in the National Challenge Cup; its only means of asserting supremacy were in exhibition matches against whoever could be enticed to Missouri. Two of the biggest of these took place in 1916; they involved Bethlehem Steel, Challenge Cup holders for two years running and widely regarded as the best side in the East. On Christmas Eve, more than 5,000 turned out at Robison Field to watch a picked eleven from the St. Louis League try to end Bethlehem's fifty-one-game unbeaten streak. Though conceding a goal in the first minute of play, the locals won, 3–1, a result all the more creditable for having been achieved over ninety minutes rather than the sixty they favored. (Substitutes were also permitted for injured players, though Bethlehem balked at goal judges.) "Speed and stamina were the deciding factors in the fast, rough and exciting battle," Dent McSkimming noted in the *Globe-Democrat*. "Coming back in the second half, after having looked like a herd of novices, the St. Louis lads played a remarkably improved game, and, in flashes, exhibited some combination work which rivaled that of Bethlehem in its palmiest moments."

But there was still more than a trace of belligerence in the local game. Ed Wray wrote in the *Post-Dispatch*:

> The bloodthirstiness of St. Louis soccer methods is a byword throughout the country. But to the naked eye it was not evident yesterday. To many it appeared that the Britons were quite as hectic in their play as the locals, although lacking the abandon. A few spills and a little body-checking was in evidence, but nothing of the sort that was once common on St. Louis fields when the St. Teresa, the Cycling Club and other teams mingled in battle royals. [Bethlehem goalkeeper Bill] Duncan was hurt, but not through intentional roughness. He was quite a bit aggressive himself, and invited trouble by rushing valiantly into it. In the club house, between halves, Tom Cahill . . . asked Duncan what he thought of

---

* So miserable was the holiday weather that when the True Blues took on the Columbia Athletic Club two days later, "Only 50 persons—they were easily counted—were present at Athletic Park . . . when the referee blew his whistle at the start of the game." Paterson won, 5–0.

the St. Louis men. "Men? They're not men—they're savages," he grinned, with a Scotch accent as broad as his back. "I don't know when they come at me whether they're going to play or bite." But he laughed when he said it.

With less than a day's rest, Bethlehem took to the field again, this time to face Ben Miller, none of whose players had appeared for the all-stars the day before. The 2–2 tie led many to conclude that St. Louis teams were just as good as the "British" teams from the East. "Pick 11 athletes, with a few substitutes, from the [St. Louis League clubs] and you have the champs of the soccer universe," gushed the sports editor of the *St. Louis Times,* who even claimed that, in the clash of imported and homegrown styles, "the result proved that St. Louis is the winner." Yet he also noted, almost casually: "The Bethlehem kickers are athletes and play soccer more than anything else. They have plenty of time, and they use these moments to master their weak points on the soccer field, with the result that they are experts in passing the leather on the way down the field. . . . Soccer as played in St. Louis has been picked up with but little preliminary teaching."

It was a fertile time for the game in the city. On an agreeable Sunday in 1916, a St. Louis League player could earn $6—not bad for a few hours' work when the average wage was less than $15 a week. The Municipal League, meanwhile, was pulling crowds few other circuits anywhere else in the country could match. Twelve thousand witnessed a remarkable 1916 final between Christian Brothers College and the Missouri Athletic Association, a 1–1 tie that couldn't be broken after two hours of "the hardest kind of soccer, on a heavy field." The rematch drew close to 10,000, with the Athletic Association eventually claiming victory.*

Even when the league charged admission for playoff matches, five-figure crowds were not uncommon. On more ordinary Sundays, perhaps 10,000 fans could be found scattered across its half-dozen venues. One might expect the USFA to have harnessed this astonishing level of interest, but for much of its existence the Municipal League was unaffiliated; its players could not or would not register with the association, either as amateurs or as professionals. A frustrated Cahill mooted the possibility

---

* "In an effort to help the spectators identify the players," the *Globe Democrat* noted before the first game that "the officials of the Municipal Athletic Association have arranged to put a number on each boy's back. The number and the name of the boy will be found in a program which the M.A.A. has printed, and which will be distributed before the start of the game."

of a national municipal cup competition but never got it off the ground. Yet his hopes for the sport were undimmed. "It's the fastest growing game on our shelf," he told one paper in the wake of St. Louis's success against Bethlehem. "And they have to give St. Louis credit for this sport. It is advancing from its independent policy to a national field and eventually you're going to see an undisputed champion of America. St. Louis, I am pleased to say, promises to produce America's champion on the soccer field."

Beyond paying its $15 membership dues, though, the professional circuit had taken little interest in the USFA and even seemed more interested in antagonizing it. The *St. Louis Daily Globe* reported in October 1918 that the league was "facing ostracism from organized football"—something it claimed had become an annual event—for failing to properly register its players. Not that it mattered much; the likes of Winton Barker claimed his city was "too far away" to compete in the cup and that it would be foolish to interrupt the league schedule. "In many of the cities where teams are entered in the [cup] it is only possible for them to get together one strong eleven, instead of four as we are able to put on the field," he claimed. "St. Louis is the only city in the country that has self-supporting soccer."

In truth, neither officials nor players wished to sacrifice a potentially lucrative weekend of league matches for the vagaries of a knockout competition. "Other cities do not patronize football as does St. Louis, so the players who receive a percentage of the receipts in lieu of a fixed salary, insist on the present system," the *Post-Dispatch* noted, before claiming that the percentage pay plan was "the real cause of all local soccer evils." In the era of a maximum wage for soccer players in Britain, those in St. Louis had certainly been given an unusual amount of leverage.

Not until 1919 did the St. Louis League clubs enter the Challenge Cup—they were the only representatives from the area—but their presence was felt immediately. Given byes to the second round, the four clubs played off in a November doubleheader. Around 4,000 saw Ben Miller trounce Innisfail, 6–1—with members of both teams dismissed for fighting—and Scullin Steel defeat St. Louis Screw, 3–1.

Four more victories, all but one of them at home, sent Ben Miller into the final—and the city rallying behind them. Over 3,700 watched the semifinal defeat of Detroit's Packard club, even though the Browns were in town for baseball that day. Other matches may have drawn bigger crowds (one Eastern club attracted 6,500 for a January exhibition) but the Challenge Cup had earned its keep: 3,700 was even a few hundred more

than had attended the final Sunday of the St. Louis League season, with
the championship still in the balance. Barker admitted that the cup games
had "done much to arouse enthusiasm in St. Louis"; he predicted that
five-figure crowds would soon become common for big matches.

It was just such an ample gathering that St. Louis now expected the
final to attract, and promoters made strenuous efforts to bring it to
their city. After some typically energetic lobbying from Cahill, the USFA
accepted their bid, though instead of the more desirable Cardinals stadium it had to settle for modest Handlan's Park. Barker and his men set
about sprucing up the erstwhile Federal League facility, flattening its
uneven pitch, installing several hundred box seats, and circumscribing
the playing field with restraining ropes. It was, he said, "the biggest event
ever promoted in the soccer game here."

The local press built it up as an international showdown. Facing the
entirely American-born—the entirely St. Louis-born—home team was
the Fore River club of Quincy, Massachusetts, all of whose players had
migrated from Britain. "The battle . . . in effect will be a game between an
All–St. Louis and a picked British eleven," the *Post-Dispatch* claimed. "To
all intents and purposes, therefore, the Ben Millers are already the United
States champions with respect to American born rivals."

On a mild Sunday afternoon in May, national honors became official.
Ben Miller claimed a 2-1 win with a goal from center-forward Jimmy
Dunn seventeen minutes into the second half. "In the end," crowed the
Post-Dispatch, "it was the dash and aggressiveness of the truly American
soccer that conquered over the more scientific but slower foreign game."
No one was more overjoyed than Cahill. "I lived to see a St. Louis team
win and also saw all the predictions I have been making come true," he
exclaimed. "In the face of a great many counter attractions, we drew a
record crowd. It is the finest thing that ever happened to the sport."

It certainly did something for the St. Louis League: by the end the
year, one paper claimed, crowds had risen from 800 to around 4,000. Victory also fuelled an already burgeoning heady level of local pride, one that
sometimes mutated into outright arrogance. David Barrett, a frequent
contributor to Spalding's *Guide,* was perhaps the most headstrong propa-
gandist. In the wake of the showing of St. Louis teams against Bethlehem
Steel during the club's 1919 visit, he even laid into the then national
champions:

Here is what I think about Bethlehem. It is [a] flashy, front running combination that lacks the hearts of champions. Unlike the

St. Leos, for instance, it has not the courage to come from behind and snatch victory out of the fire in the last few minutes of play. It is a team that once it gets the jump on an opponent keeps piling up the score, but cannot stand rough going or hard competition.

Others admired the local vigor with more equanimity. In the same edition of the *Guide*, Jimmy Walder, a British-born referee, wrote:

The American soccer footballer plays a fast, aggressive and vigorous game, and the forwards who seem to practice shooting are dangerous at all times and a source of worriment to any set of backs which may oppose them. Truly they have not the fine art of playing the ball back to their halves or that neat little touch to each other that should be used in all games; still when they take up an attack they are not to be feared. . . . What the American player needs most, in my opinion, is to be taught how to get control of the ball properly, to trap, accept and give a pass in the proper manner, and when he has learned these points and mastered them— and the day is near when he will—then other nations beware!

How near was that day? Not everyone had been swept away by the fervor of the times; one *Post-Dispatch* writer conceded that a "match between the champions of Great Britain and the Ben Millers would be about as logical as matching the Municipal baseball leaders with the World's Champion Reds." But less than two months after Ben Miller's triumph came the chance for the "American style" to be tested against bona fide foreign opposition. For the third time in four years, Cahill was invited to send a U.S. team to Scandinavia—and for the first time it would consist entirely of American-born players. But the **ST. LOUIS U.S.A.** sewn into their black jerseys was misleading: seven of the eighteen squad members were actually the property of Eastern clubs.* Many of the best soccer players in St. Louis were primarily connected to baseball, and their summer months

---

* One of the non–St. Louisans, Newark-born John ("Rabbit") Heminsley, had toured Scandinavia with the first "All-America" team in 1916 but was arrested shortly before the 1920 team was due to sail. The *St. Louis Star* reported that Heminsley was held on $25,000 bail "on two serious charges proffered by two Philadelphia girls, 16 and 17 years old. . . . The girls were entertained at the Malta Club a month ago and were arrested recently in a raid on a disorderly house in Newark and implicated Heminsley." Heminsley made the trip but never played a match; Spalding's 1922 *Guide* does not even list him as a member of a member of the touring party.

were given over to minor-league diamonds; bad winter or no, for them
the season ended in April. The Scandinavian party thus included just five
members of the national champions.

While Cahill claimed that this squad was much stronger than the one
from Bethlehem he'd accompanied the year before, their results were
about the same: seven wins, two defeats, and two ties against fairly modest opposition. The strongest team they faced, a representative Swedish
Olympic eleven, whipped them, 5–2, in front of 25,000 in Stockholm,
with another 6,000 said to have been locked out. ("We were beaten but
have no excuses to offer," a member of the party admitted. "The Swedes
are a fine team and deserved to win.") Against provincial opposition the
results were more encouraging, though in a 2–2 draw with the AIK club
of Stockholm they complained that the referee "eleven times during the
first half . . . neglected to blow his whistle for Swedish offside."

Certainly they were enamored of their visit, going to far as to claim
the Swedes had "learned much from the Americans as to individual play,
speed and determination" and had even moved nearer to them in playing
style. But the muscular approach had not necessarily played well to local
audiences. A cartoon in one Swedish paper depicted center-forward Harry
Ratican with the ball at his feet and his elbows willfully connecting with
the faces of two opponents. Sweden's fans were familiar enough with
Ratican, who had been part of Bethlehem's tour the year before. Although
he had since joined Robins Dry Dock of Brooklyn, he'd been born in St.
Louis and learned the game there, with stops at Christian Brothers College, St. Teresa, and Ben Miller, among others.

Ratican would return to St. Louis in 1924, but in 1921 his Dry Dock
team thwarted his hometown's hopes of winning a second straight Challenge Cup. The Western representatives, Scullin Steel, also won the St.
Louis League that year but reached the cup final only with the USFA's
help. After a quarterfinal clash with the Bricklayers of Chicago ended 1–1,
Scullin lost the replay in Illinois but protested that the referee (Alex
McKenzie, respected enough to have worked the previous year's final) had
cost them the match. According to various sources, the man in charge
had called eighteen fouls on St. Louis and just one on Chicago; awarded
an unwarranted last-minute penalty (and then dismissed a Scullin player
for arguing about it); and even extended the halftime interval to twenty
minutes to allow the home team to "bathe and get rubbed down while
the Scullins were left to get chilled outside."

The protest was upheld—petulant St. Louis League officials threatened to withdraw from the USFA if it wasn't—and the replay was even

allowed to take place in Missouri. From there, Scullin's path to the final was less complicated. They beat the Bricklayers 2–0, then drew 7,500 to Cardinal Field for a semifinal confrontation with the Caledonian club of Detroit. A goal in extra time against the "foreign born aggregation" from Michigan gave them a 2–1 victory and their date with Ratican's Dry Dock in the final.

While for even the strongest "imported" team the speed and muscle of an accomplished St. Louis eleven was difficult to subjugate, other factors played into in the city's hands. The most obvious of these was home advantage. Financial inducements offered by St. Louis League promoters almost invariably resulted in cup matches' taking place in their city. Switching home and visiting teams was not something the USFA encouraged—and the St. Louis press stayed remarkably silent about it—but as Challenge Cup receipts were the association's main source of revenue, it could hardly object to the likelihood of a larger gate. Thus, apart from the final, throughout the 1920s teams in the St. Louis League almost never played away from home.

Barker lobbied hard to bring the 1921 final to St. Louis, but the USFA had insisted—for the time being—on alternating between Eastern and Western cities. Odd-year finals were reserved for the East, and this one was given to Fall River, a city still bursting at the seams with immigrant fans. Thousands of them duly turned out to support the event, but they weren't too impressed (one local paper deemed the match "not up to the standard of soccer finals of previous years," having featured "little which bordered on championship soccer"). Robins, largely British-born despite the presence of Ratican at center-forward, scored twice in the second half to break a 2–2 deadlock and win, 4–2. "The St. Louis team gave a real display of how they play soccer in the Middle West," the *Boston Globe* observed. "If that is the best they can do they have a lot to learn yet about how the game should be played, but they sure did have pep, dash and vim." Scullin fans pointed out that illness had forced their regular goalkeeper, Duke Sheehan, out of the lineup. His replacement, halfback Joe Hennessey, had never kept goal before and, thrust between the posts at short notice, "played almost every shot at goal with his feet."

Not everyone in St. Louis was convinced the team had played to its strengths—and there were those who perceived Scullin's compromised tactics as part of a wider trend. One writer claimed that local teams were "abandoning the St. Louis style, the dash, desperation and deviltry" in favor of "the pretty but punchless English style." This, he feared, was "permitting the English spirit of 'What does it matter who wins?' to supersede the panting American spirit of 'It matters everything in the world that we should win.'"

This may have been a naïve view of English football, or perhaps slanted toward the amateur side of the game, but the emphasis on native virtues is not surprising. The America of the 1920s was not particularly enamored of immigrants—all manner of laws were being passed to restrict their ingress—and St. Louisans did not regard soccer as an exclusively ethnic pursuit. U.S. teams with stars born in the old country ran the risk of being labeled "foreign" by the city's press; victory for the home side was often perceived as a triumph for Old Glory. No self-respecting American sportswriter dared to doubt that his country's spirit and endeavor was capable of overcoming anything more sophisticated from overseas, and it was no more true than in St. Louis. Some of its observers dismissed old-country soccer as boring or outmoded; a few even regarded it as inferior. But none was prepared to admit that the local "style" had evolved largely out of necessity. Speed, aggression, and tenacity were useful qualities on the baseball diamond; St. Louis had merely borrowed them in abundance for soccer.

Smarting from the defeat by Robins and keen to re-establish their national supremacy, the four St. Louis League clubs now discussed the possibility of forming one or two all-star teams for the Challenge Cup "and not including any baseball players who might be called to join their ball clubs." But nothing came of it, and Scullin once again reached the final under their own steam. There was something of a familiar look to the opposition, which included Ratican and five other members of Robins's 1921 cup-winning team, but the team was called Todd's Shipyards, an amalgamation of Dry Dock with the inimitable Tebo Yacht Basin FC.

The selection of St. Louis to host the match was a foregone conclusion—no other Western city could possibly have offered the USFA better terms—but bad weather threatened to spoil the day. Rain fell for eighteen hours before kickoff and for some time during the first half; though the field had been covered with three tarpaulins, it was still reduced to mud. Those who thought this would compromise the locals' double-quick approach seemed to be proved right when Todd's scored twice before the rain stopped (owing to the paludal surface, the Scullin goalkeeper "could not move a foot on shots to either side"). But rather than push for another score, the Brooklyn club decided to protect its lead. Scullin pulled a goal back before the break and, with a strong wind at their backs, took control of the match in the second half. Three minutes from time a strike from center-forward Allie Schwarz set the crowd of 9,000 alight;

the locals claimed a 3–2 victory. "It was," the *St. Louis Star* insisted, "a sheer triumph . . . of youth over age, of American methods of going directly to the goal instead of endeavoring to arrive there by indirect and devious methods known as 'combination.'"

Soon it would prompt Tom Cahill into making his infamous claim that the best American team could give the best from Britain a run for their money (see Chapter 3). "The United States owes a great debt to the old country boys who in the past have taught us the fundamentals and who are responsible in part for the present standing of the game in this country," he said. "There are many wonderful old country players on teams in the United States today. But I think the American eaglets are about ready to quit their nests."*

They weren't, of course—as the years to come would prove—but the interest of St. Louisans in their native elevens had done much to boost the game. It had also helped keep the USFA in the black. Nearly half of the $50,000 in receipts generated by the 131 Challenge Cup matches that year were for the fourteen contests played in the Missouri district. The final itself, for which 8,568 tickets had been sold, grossed $8,400, something like $100,000 today.

While no one professed to be disappointed with the turnout for the final, a quarter-century after 7,000 had watched St. Teresa battle the Cycling Club, more might have been expected of St. Louis. Crowds for its professional league had not improved much: gates of a few thousand that dwindled to a few hundred in poor weather and perhaps doubled when everything came together. Forced out of Cardinal Field in 1921, the league had settled for the more austere confines of Laclede Park—or High School Field, as it rather prosaically had become known. For some, including the *Star*, the sport deserved better:

---

* For Todd's, things proved altogether less encouraging. Their manager, John Drysdale, made various assertions about the treatment his club had received at the final. Newspapers reported claims that a Scullin player had "viciously assaulted" a Todd's player; that Scullin's player-manager had "continually abused" the referee; that the visiting goalkeeper had been threatened with a gun; and that the entire Todd's team was "told point blank by a crowd of roughs that if they won they would never walk off the field alive." Drysdale filed a grievance with the USFA, but the association found no evidence to support his charges (though the referee admitted hearing an unidentified Scullin player remark that "if they did not win I would not get off the field alive"). That Drysdale was, as one St. Louis paper reported, "indefinitely expelled" by the USFA, presumably for his apparently spurious allegations, may have contributed to the decision of Todd's to fold its team that summer.

The soccer players should long ago have had a fine football field of their own, especially built for football games, a field that would bring the spectators down on both side lines. Nothing interests spectators so as to be close to the players. No matter how fine the play, if the players are afar off, the spectators never become warmed up to them. . . . The soccer game has made enough money time and time over to build a beautiful field and stands for both soccer and rugby. The soccer players of the past were not unselfish or far-seeing men. They should have put aside a fund for building. Instead, the practice has been to split up the receipts after every game and spend them before midnight on Monday. So soccer football, a very great game, is now facing a serious situation in St. Louis. It has no real park in which to play.

The lack of progress and foresight was all the more frustrating given the enduring appeal of the Municipal League, whose own ambition was somewhat more apparent. One week after Scullin's Challenge Cup triumph, St. Leo defeated Hense in the third and deciding game of the championship final; the very next day, it began a two-game playoff with a team from Memphis, Tennessee, for the "municipal championship of the South" (which it would win 13–0 on aggregate). Three Muny League teams even entered the Challenge Cup in 1921, the first ever to do so.

Progress at the professional level, however, seemed largely confined to rule changes. In 1922, the St. Louis League voted to use two referees for each match—"with two side-linesmen, the goal-linesmen being dispensed with"—and continued to allow substitutes; toward the end of the season, it also dabbled with uniform numbers (and several years later with hockey-style penalty boxes). That its halves were only thirty-five minutes long was apparently not even a topic for debate. Nowhere else in the world was the game played in quite this way, but that was perhaps the point: soccer in St. Louis was the brand advanced by native-born Americans, and even over ninety minutes it had proved itself good enough to beat the "imported" teams.

In the 1920s, though, interest in the sport had grown to where other parts of the country were starting to put together locally born elevens of their own. In particular, a number of coalmining towns in western Pennsylvania formed teams every bit as hard-charging as those from St. Louis. Scullin would play host to one of them, Arden, in the semifinal of the Challenge Cup in 1923. For the *St. Louis Times,* the speed and aggression shown by the visitors—traits it doubtless admired all the more for their country of origin—was a revelation: Arden ranked "with the choicest ever sent out from the East." Led by inside-right Mike Bookie, who in 1930 would be named to the U.S. World Cup squad, they held the lead for more than an hour. But two second-half goals put Scullin into the final once again.

The steelmen would concede the title under the most embarrassing circumstances. A 2–2 tie with Paterson FC—who featured five members of the Todd's Shipyards team beaten in the previous final—was never replayed because four Scullin players were due for baseball spring training (Chapter 3).* The forfeit undermined what had been a cracking match, played to a huge crowd at the International League baseball park in Harrison, New Jersey. "Fans from this vicinity have been used to seeing good hard fought soccer games," the *Newark Ledger* wrote, "but the opinion . . . was that the final was without a single doubt the best game seen since the innovation of soccer football in this country." The hero of the afternoon was the Scullin goalkeeper, Harry Oellerman, whose agility and mettle limited Ratican and his cohorts to two goals. This was no mean feat if, as the *New York Times* had calculated, Paterson forced twenty-one corner kicks during the match.

But in the eyes of some, the level of excitement had been unacceptable. Barker, in from St. Louis for the occasion, claimed that during the second half "the crowd was on the field practically all the time interfering with the Scullins by overt, hostile acts." He said he had pleaded with the referee to stop play and clear the pitch, but the only reply he received was, "What can I do?" No such difficulties had ever occurred in St. Louis, Barker insisted, nor "was such unsportsmanlike conduct ever displayed by St. Louis soccer crowds as a body."

In truth, it was his own city that had been humiliated. The St. Louis papers lobbied hard for the final to be replayed nearer to home—or even at the start of the following season—and many vented their spleen at the USFA for insisting the replay take place in the East. (Some, including Barker, proposed a three-game series, though how that would have made things any easier is unclear.) "St. Louis teams are handicapped in a peculiar way, especially in so far as final cup contests are concerned," a contributor to Spalding's 1923 *Guide* wrote. "The city is a cradle of baseball

---

* According to the *New York American* of April 3, 1923: "Goalkeeper [Harry] Oellerman is with the Hutchinson [Kansas] Southwestern League club; Inside Right [John] Rooney is with St. Paul in the American Association, and Inside Left [James] Brannigan is with Terre Haute in the Three 'I' League. Outside Left [Emmet] Mulvey is with the Mobile Club in the Southern Association."

and most soccer stars are also professional ball players. . . . This condition does not obtain in any other section." That may have been true. Yet there had been no displays of outrage in 1921 when Scullin had been made to travel to Fall River—for a final that took place eighteen days later than the one in 1923. Was the fault with the USFA, or with Scullin?

Dismayed by the Challenge Cup forfeit, the St. Louis League clubs once again debated the merits of holding back star players—particularly those without baseball commitments—and lending them in later rounds to the team that progressed the furthest. Even without such expedients, though, a good St. Louis team was still hard to beat. Vesper-Buick Auto, who'd replaced St. Louis Screw in 1922, won the St. Louis League in their debut season and reached the Challenge Cup final the next. With a lineup that in 1923 included an English-born forward and a fullback fresh from Scotland, they weren't quite the local archetype, but several of their stars did play baseball. Had a benign winter not allowed the Challenge Cup final to take place on March 30 (earlier than ever before), and had it not been the West's turn to host it, the club might have run into the same difficulties that Scullin had.

As it was, they blew into the 1923–1924 final with devastating force, routing the Goodyear club of Cleveland 7–1 and rifling five unanswered goals past Chicago's Bricklayers. But the best from Ohio or Illinois was not on a par with the pick of the East, particularly in the mid-1920s, when the American Soccer League was reaching its peak. The Eastern finalists, Fall River, were well on the way to winning that league in 1923, and their team of imports would prove rather more accomplished than the young St. Louisans were accustomed to.

The final drew a huge crowd to High School Field. Paid attendance of 13,686 set a record for the city; had the left-field bleachers not been condemned, the figure would have been much higher. Anchored by what the *New York Times* regarded as "a smooth running attack and a nigh impenetrable defense," Fall River claimed a 4–2 win. Yet the *Globe-Democrat,* for one, thought the match wasn't nearly as close as the score suggested; the victors had left Vesper-Buick "bewildered so much that at times their actions indicated that they did not know which way to turn."

Little did anyone know, but the professional game in St. Louis—as with the ASL—was nearing its high-water mark. Perhaps soccer had failed to keep up with the pace of other sports; perhaps, as the country's antipathy toward immigrants hardened, attitudes toward "foreign" pursuits had become more entrenched; or perhaps a combination of these and more subtle factors conspired against it. Certainly, selling tickets had always been something of a challenge for the St. Louis League. Some blamed this on the monotony of a four-team circuit; others, on the Municipal League, which continued to put on nearly all of its matches for free. Yet there was still enough interest for players and owners to keep plugging away, even if the two sides didn't always trust each other. When bad weather held down the crowds for the 1924–1925 holiday exhibitions, the players threatened to strike, questioning, among other things, whether they'd been given their fair share of the proceeds.

Ben Miller climbed to the top of the Western tree in 1924–1925, squeezing past Vesper-Buick to claim the St. Louis League crown. They did the same thing the following season and reached the Challenge Cup final even after they'd apparently suffered a second-round defeat. On discovering the victorious Clan MacKenzie club of Akron had used two players from Detroit under assumed names, the USFA overturned the result, which meant Ben Miller got to play Vesper-Buick in the quarterfinals. But the intra-city confrontation did little to rouse St. Louisans. Just 3,109 paid to watch the 2–0 win, nearly a thousand fewer than had seen a New Year's Day exhibition with the All-Scots of Detroit.

When Chicago's Canadian Club, yet another collection of British-born "imports," arrived in St. Louis for the semifinal, paid attendance swelled to 6,538. Ben Miller's "eleven young, dashing greyhounds" placed their faith in celerity. "We cannot hope to beat a well-trained Scotch team by using the short pass or the dribbling style of play," one of them said. "In our fast, swinging, rushing game we have something the Scotchmen have never seen before and are not quite prepared to stop."

In truth, they had seen plenty of it. Four months earlier, they had faced Ben Miller in an exhibition at St. Louis University Field—the latest name for the old Federal League baseball park—and lost, 4–2. Two goals again separated the teams in the cup, both the product of Ben Miller's speedy wings, who tormented the Canadian Club fullbacks all afternoon. "Followers of the Chicago eleven stated, after the game, that they were not impressed by the prowess of the Millers," wrote the *Star*. "They summed it up this way: 'Why, they don't know much about football; all they know is how to shoot goals.' It was quite true: the Millers had much the better shot and in soccer, as in most other games, the team that scores wins." St. Louis's record in the Challenge Cup was unmatched; in each of the six years the city had entered the competition, it had put a team in the final.

Bethlehem Steel would be their Eastern opponents. Though still the most famous name in the game, the club was not the indomitable force they had been a decade earlier. They would only finish a distant third in the American League that season—and against the breakneck champions of the St. Louis League, some expected them to have their hands full. One was the correspondent of the *New York Telegram,* Ernie Viberg, a naturalized Swede who'd accompanied both Bethlehem and St. Louis on their Scandinavian tours. Viberg drew attention to the major change to the offside law initiated that season, one that required just two instead of three defenders between the attacking player and goal. He believed this had adversely affected old-country teams who, unlike Ben Miller, relied too much on the offside trap. In dismantling the All-Scots and Canadian Club, the hat makers, Viberg maintained, had "shown to advantage their perfect wide, swinging game, in which speed of foot is a prime factor"; the final would "be a real game, and any one who thinks it is a walkover for Bethlehem Steel will find out different after seeing the native stars in action."

Certainly, the natives had youth on their side. Inside-left Benny Nash was twenty; outside-left Tal Mulroy and center-forward Johnny Worden both just eighteen. But they had also come to Ebbets Field in Brooklyn without their best striker, Jimmy Dunn, who couldn't take time off from work, and two other players who were injured. Against a veteran Bethlehem team that included the likes of Archie Stark, Malcolm Goldie, and Johnny Jaap, youth betrayed inexperience—and the greyhounds were overrun, 7–2. Rather desperately, Viberg complained that the referee could not keep up with play and had failed to address Bethlehem's "rough tactics." But the victory, which would give Bethlehem its last Challenge Cup title, had exposed fundamental weaknesses in the St. Louisans' approach. The losing manager could scarcely refute that his team had been outplayed; more tellingly, he related that the Bethlehem captain, in offering his commiserations, "told my lads that with proper coaching they would give any team in the country a great battle." Viberg claimed that without Dunn, Ben Miller had forgotten to play their own game and tried to beat Bethlehem at theirs. "The American style will continue," he wrote. "It cannot be changed because the boys have grown up with this style of play since childhood."

That was undeniable. Yet the rise in playing standards in the ASL, brought on by an influx of capable foreign players, had not been matched in insular St. Louis. Not until 1933 would a St. Louis team again lift the Challenge Cup. In the meantime, defeats by teams more distant than Pennsylvania would provide the local fans with plenty of food for thought.

One month after the Bethlehem match, Hakoah Vienna of Austria became the first foreign team in over twenty years to visit St. Louis. The celebrated all-Jewish eleven attracted the biggest crowd of the season to University Field—nearly 9,000—and beat a team of local all-stars, 4–2. "Those St. Louis soccer followers who had no opportunity to witness the defeat of the Ben Millers by Bethlehem ... might have obtained some notion of how the trick was performed had they attended [the Hakoah] match," wrote Dent McSkimming, now at the *Post-Dispatch*. "The visitors outplayed the home-bred lads at almost every angle of the game." Others had been impressed even before kickoff. McSkimming's colleague John Wray noted how meticulous the Austrians were in their warm-ups, in contrast to the local teams, who spent most of their time "taking pot shots at an unguarded goal."

It had not been the happiest of seasons for the professional circuit—bandits had even robbed its officials of over $2,500—and the local press began pushing for changes that only a few years earlier would have been heresy. "Even members of the Jewish eleven said after the game that the local players had everything a soccer team needs: speed, stamina, aggressiveness but no science," claimed the *St. Louis Times*. "Constant practice in the European style of play which in reality is the real way to play soccer will some day put the St. Louis team on a high level in the kicking art. By signing three or four foreign stars to each team the required results will be obtained much quicker."

For Wray, the game in St. Louis was "nearing the end of its primrose path"—and to keep the posies blooming, several steps needed to be taken:

> First—Each local team should hire two competent old countrymen, both as players and coaches. Second—Systematic training should be prescribed and enforced. Third—Two games instead of one should be played each week by each club. Fourth—Contests should be of full legal duration—90 minutes instead of 60 minutes. Fifth—The game should be introduced into public and private schools; and municipal teams should have the benefit of coaching by a professional employed by the Municipal Soccer League.

October would bring another foreign defeat, this one at the hands of Sparta Prague, champions of Czechoslovakia. But not everyone had become convinced of the need for self-flagellation. "We have seen the best soccer team of the European Continent," McSkimming wrote of the 5–3 win over an all-city eleven, "and we are anything but flabbergasted, awed, astounded or otherwise knocked over." Sparta, he conceded, had played well, but the real surprise had been the locals: as late as the seventy-fifth minute, they'd held a 3–2 lead. Over at the *Globe-Democrat*, though, the Czechs' performance represented "a brand of soccer that hardly has been equaled on a local field since the invasion of England's great Pilgrim eleven." The home team had given a strong account of themselves (of course), but they'd been "outwitted and outplayed, bewildered and dumbfounded by a machine that knows no master in European soccer and few, if any, in America."

Six months later a Sparta nearer to home brought the city's Challenge Cup run to an end. This was the Sparta Athletic and Benevolent Association of Chicago, a team consisting of a Scot, a Swede, and nine Czechoslovakians, one of whom had even joined the club from Sparta Prague. Paired in the third round with Ben Miller, the visitors earned a 2–2 tie in "probably the most fiery, thrilling soccer game that has been enacted on a St. Louis soccer field for years." But a week later, a 1–0 loss on Sparta's own jagged cinder pitch—with a lopsided ball that wasn't changed until halftime—ended St. Louis's interest in the competition at the earliest stage it had known.

Expositions of the "American style" were disappearing. "Time was when home-bred players could hold their own with the third-rate foreign-born players who formerly comprised Eastern teams," the *Post-Dispatch* sighed. "Today first-class Old Country men are being used on all the major clubs of the East. A few of them brought to St. Louis might rivet more firmly the soccer championship that seems in danger of slipping today." Barker agreed. "We are convinced from the results of the last three seasons that we cannot hold our own any longer unless we make use of European-trained experts, either as players or coaches," he said, adding that his league would now develop a plan to "inject the best elements of the British short-passing game and better ball control into our speedy St. Louis game."

The expertise wasn't confined to Britain, or even to Europe. The team from Uruguay that arrived in St. Louis in the spring of 1927 may have been the strongest to have toured the United States, including as it did no fewer than eight players who would help their country win the gold medal at the 1928 Olympics. Before a crowd of 6,000 at University Field, the South Americans tamed a St. Louis League selection, 4–1; they were, the *Post-Dispatch* insisted, "quite as perfect as the famous Hakoah and Sparta teams which have appeared here."

The response of the St. Louis League was largely to muddle along. Life at University Field had its drawbacks: smoke from the nearby railroads, stands that were too far from the playing field, and no grass to speak of. A threatened players' strike of 1925 was partly over the abject condition of the clubhouse. Promoters looked for a plot of land to call their own but couldn't find the money. In 1926, they moved into major-league Sportsman's Park, but not once during the season could they attract a crowd of more than 3,000. As complaints grew over the monotony of the four-team professional circuit, Tom Cahill pushed for Chicago, Cleveland, and Detroit to join forces with St. Louis in a Midwestern league. But fan interest in those cities was even more limited. A "Western Soccer Cup Association" involving clubs from St. Louis and Chicago did get off the ground in October 1926, but less than a month later, lack of interest sent it crashing back to earth.*

Greyhounds were falling out of favor. Four St. Louisans, all from the Municipal League, were chosen for the Olympic squad that traveled to the Netherlands in 1928, but none was picked to play in the opening match against Argentina. "Before the game the manager called us into his room and told us that the team he had picked was in his mind the best team to represent our country," one player said, "but you can take it from me that is a lot of baloney. . . . I think all four of us on crutches could have done better than the men who played in our positions." An 11–2 loss hastily eliminated the United States from contention. But a few days later, the four Muny Leaguers were chosen to play (without crutches) in an exhibition match with Holland—"as good a club as Argentina, almost," one of them insisted—and were beaten only by the odd goal in five.

In 1928–1929, the performance of Madison Kennels would encourage some to re-hoist the flag for the "American style." Finishing as runners-up to Tabler Cleaners in the St. Louis League—and led by inside-left "Dinty" Moore—the free-scoring dog harborers popped in forty-seven goals in seventeen games. They were scarcely less prolific in the cup, though their approach provoked some familiar complaints. Detroit's Holley Carburetor, foreign-born to a man, were beaten 5–1 in the quarterfinals, but their Dutch player-manager begged for another crack at them: the lopsided victory had been achieved with "80 percent spirit and 20 percent football skill." In the semifinal, Madison rifled seven goals past Sparta of Chicago, whose own manager proved more charitable; the victors had played "fast football and good football."

---

* Three years later, a six-team "Intercity Midwestern Soccer League," which included teams from Chicago, Cleveland, and Detroit—but not St. Louis—succumbed to similar indifference.

But it wasn't good enough. The Eastern finalist, Brooklyn's Hakoah All-Stars, were essentially the Hakoah Vienna team that had toured the United States (six of them had played against St. Louis in the 1926 encounter), and keeping Madison's speedy forwards in check proved well within their means. In what was now a best-of-three series, Hakoah clinched the title in two games, 2–0 and 3–0, though once again Dent McSkimming saw no cause for alarm. "To have held Hakoah scoreless for 80 minutes of play wherein the pace was killing and the soccer brilliant is tribute to the soundness of the St. Louis game," he wrote after the first match. Hakoah's manager seemed to agree. "All this stuff they have been feeding us in the East about St. Louis boys not being able to play football but only able to run fast is pretty farfetched," he said.*

Soon, though, the Great Depression would sink its claws into the professional game—and the Challenge Cup, for one, would never recover. More than 8,700 had paid to watch the Madison–Sparta semifinal in St. Louis, and for the first leg of the final the figure was 13,937. Never again would the city support the competition in such numbers. At the same time, though, there was no shortage of soccer fans in St. Louis. The match with Holley Carburetor may have drawn only 4,628, but at the same time (and only a few blocks away) close to 5,200 were on hand for the first game of the Municipal League playoff final. That the amateur circuit charged 25 cents admission compared to the mandatory $1 for Challenge Cup ties may account for the surprising parity of the two competitions. It may also explain why the Muny League, though affiliated to the USFA at this stage, rarely bothered with the cup.

None of the St. Louis League teams could advance beyond the quarterfinals in 1929–1930—and such had become the competition's pecuniary significance that the following season, the league agreed to extended its matches from seventy to ninety minutes to help two of its teams prepare for cup games the following week. Whether this was at all responsible for Ben Miller's progress to the semifinals that season is moot; but it certainly wasn't enough to overcome the Bricklayers of Chicago. The eventual finalists tore them apart 7–2 at Sportsman's Park before winning 1–0 on their own pitch to clinch what had become a best-of-three series.

---

* Defeat by such a resolutely imported team did not sit well with St. Louis officials. At the USFA's annual meeting that summer, Barker submitted a proposal requiring all Challenge Cup participants to be at least pursuing American citizenship. This was rejected, but a move the city had long pushed for was approved at the meeting when the USFA finally permitted substitutes in the competition (a maximum of two, but only during the first seventy-five minutes of play).

Whither the "American style"? The USFA sent just two players from St. Louis to the inaugural World Cup in 1930, and only one of them got to play. Baseball may have kept others from consideration, but so, too, might a lack of talent. St. Louis seemed to be facing up to its past: that deficiencies in its instruction and coaching had never been addressed; that many of its best players were beholden to baseball; that early successes had helped to foster an attitude of insularity and complacency—all of this was catching up with the city.

At the start of the 1931–1932 season, the four St. Louis League teams finally agreed to something they'd mooted for over a decade: to leave some of their best players out of the initial rounds of the Challenge Cup and lend them to the last surviving team. Thus, the 1932 finalists—Stix, Baer and Fuller, a chain of department stores in the city—included two players under contract to rival teams. It wasn't enough to help them overcome the Eastern finalist, the New Bedford Whalers, though they managed to force a 3–3 tie in what had reverted to a single-game format. With the Great Depression having all but extinguished interest in the Massachusetts seaport, the teams stayed put for a replay the following week. By then, the Whalers had recovered from the long train journey they claimed had unsettled them in the first game; they won 5–2, with all seven goals coming in the second half. "The St. Louis players appear inclined to get rid of the ball too quickly," noted New Bedford's player-coach, Alex McNab. "They do not steady themselves to see what it is all about. Another thing, they keep the ball in the air entirely too much. . . . But the players have possibilities."

The need for a replay had handed a lifeline to the St. Louis League: so desperate was its financial position that it might have folded had the first match ended decisively. As it was, two crowds, both exceeding 7,000, not only sent the Whalers back to Massachusetts with their reported $3,500 guarantee but pushed the league into the black.

Elsewhere in the city, promoters tried to revive interest with experiments. An indoor doubleheader of football and soccer—the latter pitting "professionals" against "foreign borns"—drew a crowd of 11,000. A four-team "twilight league" extended the season well into the spring, with matches that were fifty or even just forty minutes long. Yet some things were dismally immutable. The deciding game of the Municipal League playoff—"a typical muny championship battle, with fists flying as well as feet"—required police intervention after fans helped along an on-field punch-up. Earlier that year, a veteran referee had resigned after taking refuge in the clubhouse from an angry mob. Over the 1929–1930 season, the league had issued no fewer than fifty-one suspensions. The *Post-Dispatch* complained that its players "come to professional ranks raw and unskilled; and when there, they find that there is no midweek practice and no opportunity to learn combination play and ball control, except against foes who give them no time to learn." John Wray believed the game would "go nowhere very rapidly, until new players and coaches are brought here and the players educated to the fact that only practice makes perfect."

New arrivals would come, though more out of desperation than opportunity; in many parts of the East, the economy had all but seen off the professional game. The ASL disintegrated in the spring of 1932, taking a number of longstanding franchises with it. One of them was the national champion Whalers, whose players had been reaching for their hats even as they were winning the Challenge Cup. "Things up this way are terrible," McNab confessed to the *Post-Dispatch*. "I don't think there is a player on the New Bedford club who would not want to go to St. Louis."

Not that it was much better in Missouri. What money fans had for soccer was reserved largely for the Municipal League playoff series. The 1930–1931 season produced the largest paid attendance in the league's history. This seemed to work against the professional game, which was said to have finished the 1931–1932 season $2,400 in debt.

Yet soccer ran in the blood of many St. Louis League officials, and the opportunity to pick up some of the best Eastern players was too good for them to pass up. Stix, Baer and Fuller's 1931–1932 lineup had been boosted by Scottish-born Willie McLean, who arrived from Chicago (and would play for the United States in the 1934 World Cup). The club finished second in the St. Louis League that season but won it at a canter a year later, largely because it had acquired five of the strongest players in the country: McNab, "Scotty" Nilsen, Bill McPherson, Bill Watson, and the peerless Billy Gonsalves. McNab had also been appointed coach.

Such an imposing team seemed all but assured of success, yet Stix reached the 1933 Challenge Cup final only by the most dubious of means. Anderson Dry Cleaners, a league rival, had seemingly defeated them 2–1 in the quarterfinals, but Stix protested to the USFA that a goal it had scored had been wrongly disallowed for offside. Hardly ever did the association countermand a judgment call by the referee, but in this instance the Challenge Cup committee voted 4–1 to replay the match (a diagram of the incident submitted by the referee himself may have swayed them). Anderson's manager was dumbstruck at what he considered the "rawest ruling I have ever heard of in my 29 years of soccer," and several of his players threatened not to turn up for the replay. But such histrionics merely heightened interest in the rematch—nearly 7,000 turned up, almost twice as many as had seen the first game—and Stix claimed its place in the semifinals with a 4–1 reversal.*

Two victories over Sparta of Chicago put them in the final, which had returned to a best-of-three series. It began at Sportsman's Park in front of a five-figure crowd that on the face of things rolled back the clock. But ticket holders had been treated to an unusual doubleheader, one that began with an American League baseball game between the Browns and the Cleveland Indians. Ticket prices were reduced amid an air of expectation: a seat in the bleachers cost 55 cents. The president of the St. Louis League contemplated a crowd of 20,000, including many who had "never before witnessed a high-class soccer match" and whom he expected to be won over. This was a tall order: not only was 20,000 almost unheard of for the Challenge Cup, it was also rather more than the 1,500 the Browns would average that season. When the final tally was announced as 15,200, no one seemed unhappy, but it begs the question why the experiment was never repeated.

How many remained in their seats the entire afternoon isn't clear—particularly after the Browns slumped to a 7–1 defeat—but Stix provided some late cheer with a 1–0 win. A second-half strike from the diminutive McLean took care of the New York Americans, though the home goalkeeper had been kicked in the head and in the clubhouse afterward "talked incoherently about the 'Hakoah team.'" The second game, played a week later on the Americans' tiny one hundred-by-fifty-yard pitch at Starlight Park, was no less closely fought. Nilsen headed in a corner with seven minutes left to give Stix a 2–1 win, but the man of the match might have been left-half Ollie Bohlman, a seventeen-year-old who'd marked New York's dangerous forward Erno Schwarcz out of the game. Eleven years had passed since a team west of Bethlehem had won the cup, but the 1930s would belong to St. Louis. Over the decade, no city would send more teams to the final.

---

* There was rarely a dull moment for Anderson in the Challenge Cup that season. Prior to the encounter with Stix, they had defeated the Sons of Malta club of Detroit 7–1 in a chaotic match that was nearly abandoned because of fighting. Two members of the losing side were dismissed—though substitutes seem to have been permitted in both cases—and a reserve player claimed to have had his head cut open by a linesman's flag. "If it had been a league instead of a cup match, I would have thrown all the players off the field," said the exasperated referee, who claimed the trouble arose "because several of the Detroit players came on the field under the influence of liquor."

But it was hardly a return to glory for the "American style." In 1932, Gonsalves, McNab, McPherson, and Nilsen had lifted the trophy for New Bedford, and in 1930 and 1931 they had done so for Fall River. In 1934, they would do it for Stix a second time. Not everyone in St. Louis approved of winning honors with such manifestly borrowed talent, but the identity of their game was changing on many fronts. By the 1934–1935 season, Spanish American players had established themselves on each of the St. Louis League teams. The city's Spanish society, La Sociedad Española, sponsored no fewer than four amateur teams and was also said to have "supplied most of the players who composed two more teams playing in East Saint Louis." Most of them had been born in the United States; almost all had learned the game locally.

Widening the ethnic base did little for the professional league. Less than month after sponsoring the Challenge Cup winners of 1934, Stix, Baer and Fuller withdrew its support. Central Breweries took up the franchise while Marre's Tavern replaced the colorful Minit-Rub, whose anointing had lasted all of one season. Unable to pay the rent at Sportsman's Park, the league searched in vain for a place to call its own; nothing came of enquiries Cahill made on a vacant lot on Chouteau Avenue. "We have threatened to disband at the close of each season but there is something to the sport that attracts us and keeps us going," one of the promoters confessed. "I don't think any of us have cleared as much as ten cents through our connection here."

Yet according to the *Globe-Democrat,* things were rather different over in the Municipal League:

> Interest in the game has not diminished, even though the poor attendances at professional matches has made it appear on the decline. The fans simply move along with their friends, the fellow who lives next door or around the corner, and now follow them out to the muny battles where a pal or a friend of a pal dons his regalia and goes forth to do battle for the scrappy St. Agnes outfit, or the Kilkerrys or the neighborhood gang. That is the kick in soccer—where the fans are on speaking terms with most of the players and friendly with the others.

Meager attendance forced the professionals further from the beaten path. Several matches in 1934 took place at Sportsman's Park as preliminaries to professional football contests involving the St. Louis Gunners; some games were staged on weekdays, under lights at Normandy High School.

When this, and a desperate increase in admission charge, failed to turn a profit, the league moved to the low-rent National Softball Park on Enright Avenue. But not many moved with them. One doubleheader in February 1934 produced receipts of $60.50, entitling each member of the two losing teams to 70 cents.

By 1935, the *Post-Dispatch* had turned fatalistic:

Soccer was an infant left on the doorstep of the United States. It has been raised haphazardly and has been kicked around carelessly because no niche for it could be found. For six months of the year, the season when soccer is played in other lands (April to October), soccer in America is shouldered aside by baseball. In the fall when its next best opportunity comes along, the country goes mad over college football. In the winter, the only time left for American soccer, icy fields and biting winds drive supporters of soccer to the indoor sports of hockey, basketball, track and skating. There is, therefore, no place in the United States sport calendar into which this really fine game can fit. Because it came along after all of our American pastimes were fully developed, it is now practically an outcast, almost a pariah.

Perhaps the sporting calendar was rather crowded, and certainly soccer had no business dueling with a Missouri winter. But other factors had also conspired against it. Unluckily for St. Louis, one of the most powerful of them was ethnicity: the city's perception of soccer as an American pastime had been eroded by the sheer number of migrants who'd embraced it. While plenty of mainstream sports fans in St. Louis loved the game, few in other parts of the country wanted anything to do with it. Even if the St. Louis League had managed to build a cozy ballpark of its own; even if its homegrown teams had monopolized the Challenge Cup; even if the "American style" had resoundingly defeated every foreign invader, it's hard to see how one city could have resisted such nationwide indifference. St. Louis had also discovered what would become painfully apparent to the rest of the country several decades later: it was one thing to play soccer or to watch friends or family members play it and quite another to purchase a ticket for a professional match.

The 1935–1936 St. Louis League season began with two false starts and never finished. It had begun hopefully enough with an unprecedented eight teams, including the Spanish Club and the German Sport Club, but within a few weeks had lost half of them. An inclement winter and Challenge Cup obligations left promoters at a loss to complete the season. Perhaps as a result of such disorganization, Ben Miller ended its twenty-three-year affiliation with the professional game—no other commercial enterprise had managed more than seven—and made room for the likes of Town Crier Soda. The national champions, meanwhile, had already lost the patronage of Central Breweries; for a time they were known simply as the "St. Louis club," but they left the league to play independently as "Father Dempsey's Shamrocks" or, more commonly, the St. Louis Shamrocks. McNab, Gonsalves, and Nilsen were still the heart of the team and had been joined by Bert Patenaude, who'd arrived from Philadelphia the season before. The club reached the 1936 and 1937 Challenge Cup finals—six straight appearances in three different guises— but lost them both, latterly to the New York Americans. Not until 1948 would the cup return to St. Louis.

After gasping for most of the 1930s, the demise of the St. Louis League in December 1938 came as little surprise: it had been trying to operate with only two clubs. The Shamrocks had filed suit with the USFA in a dispute over player registrations and folded soon after Gonsalves and Watson refused to re-sign contracts.* Fifteen years after helping Scullin Steel to win the 1922 Challenge Cup, Tate Brady was left shaking his head: "The game has lost its appeal for the young athlete of this generation. . . . I drift around to the old neighborhoods every now and then— Eighteenth and Cass, Jefferson Avenue, Kingshighway and Wabada—and I seldom see youngsters playing soccer. I imagine they're in some dancing school practicing the latest dance steps."

Many had indeed moved indoors. In 1928, the colossal St. Louis Arena—the country's second-largest indoor venue—introduced minor-league hockey to the city. Soon the St. Louis Flyers of the American Hockey Association would attract the sort of crowds soccer had lost. The 1938 Municipal League championship match attracted a paid attendance of 2,506; a week earlier, the Flyers had drawn 8,266 for a playoff game.

While the hockey club would not survive World War II, the Muny League lasted until 1957. As late as 1947, it had featured 119 teams, many of them provided by the Catholic Youth Council. But it never recovered from the council's decision the following year to withdraw its teams and

---

* Gonsalves, McNab, Nilsen, and Watson joined the South Side Radio club of the St. Louis League and helped them to reach the Challenge Cup quarterfinals in 1938. They were eliminated by a club from Castle Shannon, Pennsylvania, in a match the referee had errantly ended after thirty-nine minutes of the second half. South Side's protest to the USFA was thrown out; the club even sued the association over loss of earnings.

start a league of its own. (The council believed it "should exercise more overall control over teams that were based in, and supported by, the various Catholic parish organizations in the area.") The council's own association with soccer, which could be said to have started in 1893 with the Sodality League, has remained strong: thousands continue to play the game under its auspices.

Professional soccer proved more ephemeral. In 1947, St. Louis joined an aspiring five-city Midwestern undertaking known variously as the North American Soccer Football League and the American Professional Soccer League. The club played ten times to sparse crowds before disappearing with the rest of the enterprise. In its place arose a St. Louis Major Soccer League, which operated until 1953 and for its first few years operated from Sportsman's Park. But the most audacious attempt to establish professional soccer in St. Louis—and seventeen other North American cities—would arrive in the summer of 1967. And perversely, it would be undertaken almost entirely with foreign-born players.

6

California Gold

Remembering the Clippers

I know most people so far are gauging success or lack of it by the number
of people who are attending games. This is important, sure, to the men
who are putting up the money to help introduce the game to the American public, but ultimately the real success of soccer will be measured by
how good a game the teams play on the field.

—Aleksandar Obradovic, June 1967

THE FAILINGS of America's flirtation with big-time soccer in the
late 1960s are not difficult to identify. Most can be traced to the
shortsightedness, ignorance, and greed of a band of well-heeled,
self-assured men looking for too much too soon. The whole sorry affair
is usually dismissed with a sneer and quick passage toward the more
glamorous era of a decade later.

To the California Clippers, though, not all the wounds were self-
inflicted. At their final press conference—three days after they had beaten
the champions of the Italian league—blame was liberally apportioned.
The owners admitted that their deep pockets might not have been deep
enough. The public, too, still required "education to the joys of soccer."
But the club's harshest criticism was reserved for the USSFA, "the organization that allegedly governs soccer in this county," and its affiliate in
northern California. Instead of abetting efforts to keep big-time soccer
alive on the West Coast, the authorities were accused of standing in the
way. The Clippers had been forced to scratch matches against foreign
opposition because authorization had not been received in time; they'd
been threatened with the cancellation of others if unaffiliated junior
teams took part in preliminary or halftime games. For an entire month,
the team—though part of the official fraternity—was prevented from playing on Sundays because sanctioned amateur matches had been scheduled

nearby. "It is conceivable that we and others could have nurtured the sport until it achieved more popular and profitable support," one of the owners reflected. "But we definitely could not have succeeded in the face of the aimless difficulties imposed on our efforts by the gentlemen who are the sole arbiters of the conduct of the sport in this country." The club filed an antitrust suit in U.S. District Court, to "try to give the next guys who came along a chance," and won a nominal sum.

Were the millionaires merely piqued that they couldn't control the game as they liked? Or was the USSFA irritated by the forthright approach of individuals with far greater resources than their own? By the summer of 1969, when the Clippers were emitting their death rattle, it didn't seem to matter. Americans had shunned the pro soccer dalliance, and the North American Soccer League had all but disappeared.

It's wrong, though, to overlook the bounding steps the game took during this fleeting era—one that, a decade ahead of the Cosmos band-wagon, introduced more Americans to the sport than any other before it. Relatively few may have passed through the turnstiles, but millions watched on television and tracked it in the newspapers. For the first time, soccer was big-league, coast-to-coast—and out of winter's grip. It was a prodigious leap forward.

If any team from this era is worthy of scrutiny, it's the one that won one professional championship in 1967 and was desperately unlucky not to win another the following year. Not since Bethlehem Steel's indomita-ble collection of Scots from half a century earlier had the United States played host to so talented a unit. Admittedly, in the intervening decades there hadn't been much to choose from. With the demise of the original ASL in the early 1930s, which counted Bethlehem as one of its victims, the game appeared to have shot its bolt. Hardly a sports fan in America could identify a soccer team from anywhere in the world, and certainly not one from the fifty states.

This was as true in northern California as anywhere else. But if up until the 1960s soccer's imprint on the region was modest, it was also enduring. Reports of association football teams and their exploits— among them, references to a "celebrated Oakland team"—appeared in newspapers in the 1890s. As early as 1909, clubs had arrived from British Columbia to contest "the championship of the coast" with all-California selections. Interest in these series was considerable. "The home team scored two goals to the visitors' one," one paper noted of a contest that year, "but the many fast plays by both teams kept the gallery of 5,000 people in excitement to the last minute."

After World War II, opposition began to arrive from more distant shores. Hapoel of Palestine were the first transatlantic visitors, attracting 8,000 to San Francisco's Kezar Stadium for an exhibition in 1947. More famous names from Europe soon followed suit, all but eviscerating the handpicked local opposition. Switzerland's Grasshopper-Club beat one such collection 11–2 in 1955; Manchester City of England won another, 9–1, in 1958; and a selection of players from clubs in Lima, Peru, claimed a 9–0 victory against the far-from-celestial California All-Stars in 1960.

By the time Liverpool rifled fourteen unanswered goals past an unfortunate assemblage in 1964, it was clear that the inclusion of a "home" team was contributing little to the occasion. The following year, promoters arranged for England's Nottingham Forest to take on Hanover 96 of West Germany; they were rewarded with a thrilling match and a gate of 14,000. This may not have been the biggest crowd the Bay Area had produced (15,000 were said to have seen the Manchester City contest in 1958), but it had captured an unprecedented level of attention at a fecund time. Just days later, in fact, the *Oakland Tribune* reported that a nationwide professional league, "structured like our National and American Football Leagues," was up for discussion at the USSFA's annual convention.

Over the next two years, three separate bands of millionaires endeavored to bring big-time soccer to North America. What eventually transpired—the USSFA's authorization of one league, and the other two merging to form an unsanctioned rival—did the sport no favors. Neither did the spurned league's decision to bring forward its first season to 1967, which left it with just a few months to find coaches, players, stadiums— and fans.

While the machinations and subtexts of this period are quite fascinating (and confusing), detailing them all would require a chapter of its own.* Suffice to say that by the end of 1966, North America found itself with twenty-two professional soccer franchises. Twelve belonged to what came to be known as the United Soccer Association (USA), which had been approved by the USSFA. The Clippers and nine others were part of the National Professional Soccer League (NPSL), which had not. (One league, the USSFA insisted, was all it would endorse.) What the NPSL did have, though, was a network television contract with CBS that would bring its games into the nation's homes every Sunday. Sanctioned or otherwise, it was the league the country tuned in to.

---

* One that does this very well can be found in Paul Gardner's book *Nice Guys Finish Last* (1974).

Barely had the ink dried on this contract when the NPSL announced that it had awarded its final franchise to San Francisco because its group in Boston had been unable to find anywhere to play. In the Bay Area, there was no such problem: Kezar Stadium had staged plenty of foreign-tour matches (Germany's Bayern Munich and Scotland's Celtic had squared off that summer before 12,000), while across the water in Oakland, a multipurpose stadium had been built in the hope of attracting a major-league baseball team. The 53,000-seat Coliseum helped to persuade the owners of California Professional Soccer, Inc., to move their operation across the Bay Bridge. But mindful of alienating San Franciscans, they branded their team the California Clippers—a name one sportswriter suggested would "make them a big hit with barbers and North Beach cocktail waitresses"—and even dressed them in colors of "Clipper blue and California gold."

The money behind the team came largely from two oilmen, Joseph O'Neill Jr. and Toby Hilliard. Both were big on sports—O'Neill had lettered in football and baseball at Notre Dame; Hilliard was a "fine golfer and polo player"—and though neither knew the first thing about soccer, both were smitten by the game's potential. "You know, in foreign countries when they build a moat and put barb wire around the field to keep spectators out, there's a little emotion involved there," O'Neill observed. "I don't think it will take too long to win the heart of the community. The sport itself has proved its fundamental appeal."

Eager to offset their ignorance of the game, the owners hired as their general manager Derek Liecty, an American who had been involved with it most of his life. As a sophomore at Stanford, Liecty had appeared in the 1952 Olympic trials but broke his leg; he went on to play in Germany and qualified as a referee in Chile. Thereafter for several years, he also helped Bill Cox bring across big-name foreign clubs to play in summer tournaments the New York promoter billed as the International Soccer League.

But perhaps the greatest help to the Clippers came from a rival team. One of the principal investors in the NPSL's Los Angeles Toros was Dan Tana, an actor and restaurateur who had played for the youth team of Yugoslavia's celebrated Red Star Belgrade. Through Tana, the Clippers' owners met Red Star's manager, Dr. Aleksandar Obradovic. His team had won the Yugoslavian league seven times since the war, most recently in 1964, and on three occasions came across the Atlantic to play in Cox's summer league. Obradovic not only expressed an interest in running the Clippers but indicated he could also bring across Red Star's coach, Ivan Toplak, and a number of good players from that part of the world. The likes of Hilliard and O'Neill may not have known much about soccer, but they could certainly spot an opportunity: on hiring the pair in December 1966, O'Neill remarked that the Clippers had "the strongest coaching set-up in the National Professional Soccer League." It was no idle boast.

True to his word, Obradovic, a doctor of medicine who smoked American cigarettes through a long European holder (and spoke the better English of the pair), recruited several crack players from his homeland. Goalkeeper Mirko Stojanovic and center-half Milan Cop had played for Yugoslavia's national team; halfback Ilija Mitic and fullback Momcilo Gavric had turned out for the under-23s. With the eldest just twenty-eight, all had plenty of soccer left in them. The other clubs in the NPSL launched similar foreign raids, but none produced such a rich concentration of talent. A few genuinely world-class players ended up with rival clubs—Hungarian-born Ladislav Kubala and Mexico's Salvador Reyes, to name two—but only at the tail end of their careers. Other "stars" tended to be products of marketing bluster, rank ignorance, or both.

This, though, was a renegade league, operating without official national or international approval. In some countries, players had been warned of harsh consequences for passing through its gates. In reality, the sanction did not count for all that much—certainly not in Yugoslavia, where Obradovic insisted that the national federation, though part of FIFA, hadn't stood in anyone's way. "There was no problem at all," he said. "Everybody back home is 100% behind us." In Belgrade, he claimed, there had been "1,000 people at the airport in below-zero weather and about four feet of snow to see us off." While no such patronage awaited them in California, there were at least a few familiar landmarks—and, as the *Tribune* noted, all the trappings of Western culture:

> [The Yugoslavs] flew into the Bay Area from Belgrade yesterday, an uprooted, bewildered, amazed, happy group of young men whose sudden dunking into America has to be one of the strangest chapters of sport. They can't believe the cars and the traffic. They knew about but gasped to see the Golden Gate and San Francisco Bay Bridges. They think American girls are something else. One of them is analyzing our salad oil, critically.

Whether they all were so wide-eyed is moot; Stojanovic had kept goal for Red Star in 1964 when the team played in Cox's International League, and the club had even appeared in Los Angeles. Others from equally foreign lands, meanwhile, prepared for Californian immersions of their own.

Scouting in Central America, the Clippers tempted four Costa Ricans into purchasing releases from their club contracts with cash given to them in U.S. dollars. Three of them had played for their country; the pick of the bunch, five-foot-five-inch Edgar Marin, had yet to turn twenty-four.

This peculiar Tico-Slavic nucleus—surely a first in world football—was complemented by other nationalities: a few journeyman English professionals and a smattering from elsewhere. They included fullback Mel Scott, who had spent five seasons with Chelsea before joining Brentford in 1962; Mario Baesso, a blond twenty-one-year-old Brazilian playing in El Salvador; and Ademar Saccone, a veteran utility player from Uruguay. There was also Trond Hoftvedt, a "handsome Norwegian and a girl-watcher at heart" acquired from a second-division team in Sweden. "Brown-haired, with bangs that make him look even younger, he dresses in sharp European cut clothes and pastel shirts," the *Tribune* observed. "Asked how the girls take to him, he smiles impishly and says, 'no problem.'"

It had not taken much to bring any of them to Oakland. Salaries, the Clippers maintained, were "comparable to what the average baseball players make," which in 1967 would have been about $20,000. But the minimum figure was around $8,000, and many were not offered much more than that. "I made $10,000 a year playing soccer in England, but I'll earn less here," insisted Barry Rowan, a wing-half who claimed to have asked eight times for his club, Millwall, to release him. "I came to this country because I reached a point in England where I did not progress financially and football-wise. The game is getting defense-minded over there and I'm offense-minded."

The defense-mindedness of the game was something the NPSL, for all its naïveté, was pointedly aware of. In England, Yugoslavia, and nearly everywhere else, tactics had become predicated more on avoiding defeat than achieving victory. Defenses held the upper hand; goals were drying up. In its search for a remedy, the NPSL decided to replace the game's traditional scoring system. It scrapped the customary two points for a victory and one for a tie in favor of six for a win and three for a tie, with additional points for each goal up to the first three. Not everyone approved, of course—some didn't like the fact that a team that lost 8–3 earned as many points as one that tied 0–0—and in time the Clippers in particular would suffer its consequences.

For most Americans, though, the question wasn't so much whether soccer had lost its attacking flair as what it looked like in the first place. An early Clippers' newspaper advertisement portrayed the game in decidedly gladiatorial terms:

Soccer is a game of fancy footwork and even fancier headwork. The ball control and playmaking are incredible. It's fast. The action comes in big uninterrupted chunks. Soccer is a furious game. Nobody wears pads. Or helmets. Players slam into each other going for that ball, too. (Sure, they erupt, even get out of hand now and then.) Now, should you go see the California Clippers of the National Professional Soccer League? We think so. Especially if you'd like looking in on a major league spectacle that takes skill, guts, stamina. Ninety minutes of it.

As Liecty recalled, it wasn't just the fans who needed to be enlightened:

> We hired as one of our major public relations people Dr. Leo Weinstein, a former youth player with Werder Bremen and a professor of French at Stanford. Leo was one of the most erudite students of the game and a veritable encyclopedia on the international aspects of the sport, tactics and players. . . . Leo's job was to educate the press about soccer. Before each game he would hold forth in the press box explaining game tactics, detailing the qualities of the various players who would be playing that day, teaching the Laws of the Game. The amusing part is that once the game had started, the press box was pretty quiet. With the scoring of a goal, more silence except for Leo explaining over the p.a. system in the press box how the goal was scored. . . . Upon his finishing there would erupt this mad flurry of typewriters clacking as each wrote his story based on Leo's rendition.

The trail of ignorance ran right through the league's front office. The commissioner, Ken Macker, was not a soccer administrator or even a sports executive but a public-relations director and newspaper publisher—albeit one who had been selected from a shortlist of fifty candidates. Clearly aware of what was expected of him, the fifty-year-old pronounced himself in next to no time convinced that the game would soon be "the number one sport in the United States."

The NPSL was also confident of being delivered from its international wilderness, taking encouragement in overtures from the likes of FIFA President Stanley Rous ("Every opportunity must be provided to clubs willing to comply with the regulations to become members"), as well as the irrefutable logic of widening the sport's official fraternity. But approval never came; the rival league had paid the USSFA for exclusivity.

This may not have prevented NPSL clubs from finding players, but it did make a difference to their preparations for the season. Soon after accepting an invitation from the University of San Francisco for a practice game, the Clippers discovered that the humble USSFA possessed a surprisingly long reach. Though the association had only tenuous links with the colleges, it forbade any of them to fraternize with the NPSL. The match was canceled.

Left with only their own kind to play against, the Clippers made do with a pre-season of two matches against the Chicago Spurs, who were training in Arizona, and one each against the Los Angeles Toros and Philadelphia Spartans. In the first of these, which doubled as the last big-league sports event to be played at Oakland's Frank Youell Field, the Clippers beat Chicago 2–1 in front of a crowd of 2,242.* One reporter noted that the crowd remained silent through most of the match, "probably because they didn't understand the rules and tactics of the new game," but "came to their feet five times during the first half when the players looked ready to riot."

Frayed tempers quickly became a league hallmark. A week earlier, the Spurs had walked off the field during their exhibition with the St. Louis Stars ("It was the officiating, we think," a league spokesman ventured); their match with the Clippers included an altercation that led to a member of each team being "asked by the referee to leave the game." For Rowan, the players were too self-conscious. "They've heard so much about all-out smashing in American football and basketball, they think they have to prove themselves in the eyes of the fans," he said. "This will all settle down."

But in attempting to control an international mishmash of playing styles and temperaments—to say nothing of the gamesmanship of wily professionals—the NPSL's humble corps of referees was overwhelmed. Few games were more than a contentious decision or two away from boiling over. With monotonous regularity, the league office handed out fines and suspensions for everything from unseemly pushing and shoving to full-blooded kicks at the man in charge. "If you relish the slicing elbows of basketball, the crunching body checks of hockey, the blind-side tackles of football or the bean balls of baseball, you'll like soccer," sneered one writer, convinced that the sport consisted of "two 45-minute halves of

---

* The $400,000 stadium had been the home of the Oakland Raiders from 1962 to 1965. It was torn down in 1970. Youell, an Irish-born city councilman and undertaker, died only a few months before the match took place.

kicking, fighting, scratching, gouging, punching, biting, twinking, frac-
turing, slapping and saying bad things."

The four exhibition matches did little to rouse the public's interest.
The Clippers beat Philadelphia before 600 at a high-school football field
in Sacramento and lost in Los Angeles in front of fewer than 1,800 in the
enormous Memorial Coliseum. A rematch with the Spurs drew close to
4,000, but it was played in Phoenix, Arizona. The front office duly ramped
up its marketing efforts—soccer was "the go sport" that "really shakes
you up"—and supplemented the CBS television contract with one from a
local station. It was hard not to notice the new team in town: the Clippers
were on billboards and buses, in newspapers and on the radio. They also
moved their front office out of San Francisco and renamed themselves
the Oakland Clippers, "Oakland-based and Oakland-oriented," in Hilliard's words, and "very happy to be so."

The focal point of their pleasure was the freshly minted Coliseum, its
double-deck horseshoe of seats accommodating a soccer pitch more
neatly than most American venues and saluted by Obradovic as "one of
the best soccer stadiums in the world." No one expected it to be full—or,
at least, not for a few years. The average gate of 15,000 cited by O'Neill as
a break-even figure for the first year still left around 38,000 seats empty.
But of course 15,000 was also as many as had ever seen a soccer match in
northern California.

It would be a leap of faith on the field, as well. While Obradovic predicted his club would be as good as the others in the league, the NPSL
was all but a blank sheet of paper on which it was hard to extrapolate
the likely champion. What passed for pre-season forecasts had been left
largely to the few who could identify the world's principal soccer-playing
nations and clubs. "Experts," if that's what they were, gravitated toward
the Clippers in the Western Division and the Pittsburgh Phantoms in the
Eastern—and on the first day of the season, those two teams faced off in
the Coliseum.

No one imagined the Phantoms would go through four managers
and finish the season in last place; so convincingly had they filled their
roster that some thought they should be broken up for the sake of competitive balance. Two of their players, Co Prins and Theo Laseroms, had
turned out for the Dutch national team and were expected to be among
the stars of the league. Oakland's opening-day lineup consisted of the five
Yugoslavians, Scott, Rowan, Hoftvedt, Baesso, Marin, and William Quiros,
a teammate of Marin's in Costa Rica. "We're going to sound like a team

of Joes," O'Neill admitted, "but we've got top first-division players who'll give this area a top brand of soccer."

Would it sell? The front office insisted it expected no more than 5,000 for the big day—which left plenty of room for euphoria when 9,771 filed into the Coliseum. After a demonstration of the rules ("As the public address announcer explains each rule, ball boys will illustrate"), Julie Christie doled out the first ball, and the two teams shared evenly a half-dozen goals, the last a penalty kick from Prins with only seconds remaining. "The final two minutes of play were as frantic as a pro football team trying to go 80 yards for the game-winning touchdown," the *Tribune* explained. Pre-match anticipation gave way to post-match giddiness. Janos Bedl, Pittsburgh's Hungarian-born manager, insisted to reporters that the two teams they'd just seen "were the same quality of Liverpool, Arsenal or any first-division team you'll find in England."

While amid the expectation and fanfare the Clippers had contrived to throw away a 3–0 lead, this seemed less critical than the reaction from the stands. Judging from George Ross's column in the *Tribune*, the day had produced a decisive victory:

> "I'm just too thrilled to express it," O'Neill said at halftime yesterday from the press-level horseshoe overlooking the soccer field. "I'm so pleased with the fans. It's likely that not many of them have seen soccer before and yet they're having a great time." . . . [O'Neill] took a look at the crowd, guessed (optimistically) it was 11,000 and said "This proves to me we're here to stay and damn glad to be here." . . . Commissioner Ken Macker called Hilliard to the phone yesterday at half time, to give him the report from Baltimore: "He said they did just under 9,000 there," Hilliard relayed the word to O'Neill. "And he said, 'Toby, the crowd went wild. We got 'em hooked.'" You don't know yet if Oakland is "hooked" on soccer, but they came out Sunday and they didn't sit on their hands.

Ross himself was more guarded about the league's chances of success. But most of his fraternity, including Sid Hoos, sports editor of the *Hayward Daily Review*, kept an open mind about the sport:

> One didn't need to be able to pronounce [Selimir] Milosevic [or] Ademar Saccone to sense excitement when No. 9 and No. 8 were teamed up with the ball in Pittsburgh territory. Or to applaud a

spectacular rescue by keeper Mirko Stojanovic. . . . It's all there in the open, a panorama of unrelenting movement for all to see from the farthest corner of the stadium, none of it lost to view beneath heaps of elephantine linemen or halted by huddles and whistle-crazed officials. . . . It is easy to be cynical about professional soccer's chances of catching on in diversion-saturated America. The promoters may have to stave off drowning in worse floods of red ink [than] they anticipate at their most pessimistic moments. But they do have an interesting spectacle to sell. Most of the world isn't out of step on that score.

Those who had been thrilled by the new game needed to wait only two days before the Clippers' next home appearance. But for the visit of the New York Generals, the Coliseum was virtually empty. It was, the club pointed out, an evening match played in a chilly downpour; all the same, the 2,600 who turned up to watch a 1–0 win offered a sober warning of what was to come—day or night, rain or shine.

But it would take more than a few empty stadiums to convince the NPSL's officials that the promising figures of opening day were an aberration. Before a month's worth of matches had finished, Macker blithely spoke of expanding operations ("I have on my desk 21 franchise offers from very reputable groups") and moving to a forty-game schedule, even encroaching on the hallowed pro football season. As it turned out, spectators' interest in the NPSL would peak just seven days into the season, when 21,000 in St. Louis saw the hometown Stars face Oakland in CBS's *Game of the Week*. Although the Clippers lost, once again conceding a last-minute penalty, it didn't stop Rudi Gutendorf, the Stars' well-traveled German manager, from declaring them the best team in the league.

Such praise, though, seemed to cut no ice for the Bay Area's soccer fans. That same month, an evening exhibition between Vasas Budapest of Hungary and Fulham of England drew over 14,000 to the Coliseum. The figure was later amended to 8,150, but even this comfortably outdrew anything the Clippers would manage over the next two months. To the *Tribune,* this was excusable. "The display of soccer was more exciting and advanced than that seen so far in the National Professional Soccer League," it conceded. "But part of this is due to the amount of years the Fulham and Vasas players have worked together under the same system. . . . Several of the Clippers could play for either team, however."

Was the ethnic fan really so discriminating? Weinstein, for one, wasn't so sure. "The ethnic groups have been away from European style soccer for so long they are not aware that the game has evolved tremendously," he claimed. "They have a nostalgic regard for an old style of play. When they come to a game here they say 'this is not my game,' but if they went back to the old country they'd find this isn't their game, either."

Newcomers to the sport, according to Dave Newhouse of the *Tribune*, were also searching for something:

> Milan Cop isn't Willie Mays and Co Prins isn't Sandy Koufax in terms of the average American sports fan's interest and this is soccer's main problem. The emergence of box office heroes is the only way the National Professional Soccer League could ease its expected financial skid this year. Because the sport is new and relatively unexplored, instead of Pele, Usebio [*sic*] and Bobby Charlton, Americans find themselves trying to identify with unknown Yugoslavs, Dutchmen, and Jamaicans. The Oakland Clippers . . . would dearly love to see one of their own become the sport's first local celebrity.

The search for a hero became something of a preoccupation for the *Tribune*. An early candidate was Cop, re-christened "the Chopper" in deference to the pronunciation of his surname as much as his tenacious play. ("He comes to the field, puts in his two hours of smooth, almost flawless work, punches out, and is not heard from until the whistle blows for the next game.") But unsung defensive heroics did not lend themselves to celebrity, and not even a glowing midseason appraisal from Obradovic— "There is no question in my mind that he is better than anyone else in the league"—could advance his fame. A goal scorer was the more natural target, but the most obvious candidate, the lithe Selimir Milosevic (a "Yugoslavian Paul Newman"), missed half the season with injury.

In fact, Milosevic's extended absence forced Obradovic and Toplak into a hasty talent search, something that soon became de rigueur for the NPSL and that, for many clubs, lasted most of the season. By comparison, the Clippers fielded a settled team, but in May, just eighteen hours before they were due to play in New York, Obradovic returned from Yugoslavia with two new midfielders. In the media that day, they were referred to as David Dimitri and Ernest Luk; the following morning, they were Dimitrije Davidovic and Ilija Lukic. The pair also featured in reports that the Yugoslavian soccer association had instigated a lifetime ban on anyone joining the NPSL. According to the *Tribune*, Davidovic and Lukic had left the country with two weeks remaining on their existing club contracts, though the Clippers denied any wrongdoing.

While the Yugoslavian federation had grown tired of the exodus of players, its clampdown reflected a broader concern than just an unsanctioned American league. Only a few dozen Yugoslavs had joined the NPSL; far more had signed for clubs in Western Europe, including the whole of the country's celebrated 1962 World Cup team. Pavle Svabic reported for United Press International that money was taking on an uncomfortably significant role in Yugoslavian soccer:

> A new class of dinar millionaires has arisen—and the public is up in arms about it. The new millionaires are the nation's star soccer players, who in the past few weeks have been engaged in some very capitalistic horse-trading. Players have been paid as high as 30 million old dinars ($24,000) to remain with their present clubs for next season, and trades of players have involved sums as high as 45 million old dinars ($36,000). The reaction from the public has been critical. The issue even has been debated in the Federal Assembly (Parliament), where deputies were denounced the deals [*sic*] as contrary to the socialist way of life and have demanded to know how the government-subsidized soccer clubs have come into so much money. . . . *Komunist*, newspaper of the Yugoslav communist party, denounced the "adoration of money" which allows soccer players to earn such relatively large sums and commented: "It is difficult to believe that citizens would let a certain football player earn with his feet more than the brainiest people in this country earn with their heads."

Against the Generals, with the jetlagged Davidovic and Lukic in from the start, Oakland lost, 3–0; curiously, neither player appeared in the lineups the *New York Times* used for its report. The defeat, before barely 3,000 in Yankee Stadium, proved to be the low point of the season. Winless in three matches and still searching for an away victory, the Clippers faced a rematch with the Phantoms in Pittsburgh and took inspiration from a rare Obradovic pep talk (said to have "reached deep into the players' psyche"). Trailing 2–1, they scored two second-half goals, including a long-range effort from Mitic with less than two minutes to play, to win 3–2.

By then, though, the club was embroiled in competition off the pitch as well. The rival United Soccer Association had begun its eight-week "mini-league" with a collection of imported teams, including one based in San Francisco. The Golden Gate Gales were no less bullish than their counterparts across the bay—"Personally, I think soccer can grow to rival baseball," their owner had boasted—and with a ready-made team in ADO of the Netherlands seemed the more cohesive proposition. Over 8,000 had turned up for the club's home debut.

But though the Gales were in playoff contention for most of the season, crowds in San Francisco soon tailed off. The Clippers meanwhile won seven in a row to open up a comfortable lead at the top of their division. The dangerous Milosevic, though rarely completely fit, provided much of their confidence; Obradovic and Toplak had come up empty in their search for a new striker and had been forced into some desperate measures. At home to St. Louis, with their team trailing 1-0, they sent a ball boy into the stands for Milosevic, who changed out of street clothes and entered the match. The Clippers ended up winning 2-1, though the goals had come from Saccone and Gavric. "Sele didn't have to score," Obradovic insisted. "Whenever he plays, the others have confidence. They think, 'okay, now we win'." Then he added: "I have seen all the teams in the league except Baltimore, and we have a chance to beat all."

For the owners, there were more pressing matters. The best attendance during the winning streak was just 4,480—and the trend, if any, was downward. Twice the Clippers had played at home on the same day as the Gales, but neither team had drawn much of a crowd. In fact, as spring gave way to summer, expectations of a steady rise in interest began to ring hollow, and some were even writing off pro soccer entirely.

For Newhouse, such a rush to judgment was too hasty:

Already in the first year of organized pro soccer in the United States, one San Francisco newspaper has already pronounced final rites. "The Bay Area doesn't want professional soccer, and the sooner the two teams realize it and move to other cities—or go out of business—the less money they'll lose down the drain," the S.F. paper had it. . . . But isn't it too soon to entomb the sport or even suggest as much? The same thing was said about the American Football League—an established sport at that!—seven years ago and look where it is today. No, soccer doesn't have the familiarity of football, which means it will have to dig harder. . . . Soccer will be able to challenge, if not buck, the American sports scene, as long as its owners have enough money to lose for the period of time it will take. With foreseeable bigger names and better-organized franchises (the NPSL hasn't celebrated its first birthday), time may be all that soccer needs.

Hilliard smiled through pursed lips. "We're doing about what we had figured," he claimed after the St. Louis victory. "The crowd was 3,753 today when we were bucking a [baseball] doubleheader in Candlestick Park and another soccer game in San Francisco [the Gales]. But I've got to feel that the people who came out to see us today are going to come back. We gave them a nice afternoon."

Little more could have been asked of the team. Halfway through the season, the Clippers had established the best record in the league—and they had done it with an attacking mindset (local sportswriters seemed to take a particular delight in referring to Obradovic's "go-go offense"). On days off, they signed autographs in shopping centers, posed for pictures, held clinics in schools, and tried to establish themselves as good citizens of the community. But the seats in the Coliseum remained just as empty.

It was always going to be hard to sell tickets to an unfamiliar game, but the Clippers had also been handicapped by the league itself. Those who knew soccer could see that the NPSL was not providing the sort of world-class fare it promised. "There is no doubt, so far, the only and real winner in the NPSL this year were a few so-called talent scouts from Europe," Canada's *Tele-Sport* maintained. "With a few exceptions, they sold weary veterans on the down side of the hill, and untested newcomers." Even some coaches seemed to agree. One of them was the fourth (and final) coach of the Pittsburgh Phantoms, Pepi Gruber, who grumbled: "It is impossible to win a championship with a team consisting of only two top players and maybe three or four average players. The rest? Forget about it."

The truth was that most clubs were nowhere near the level of Liverpool, Arsenal or any other team in the English first division—and that the Clippers had stood out from their rivals not merely because of their collective talent but also because of how quickly it had fused together. Toplak, according to Liecty, was instrumental in making this happen. While Obradovic could provide the newspapers with quotes, it was the coach who blended the multitude of playing styles into a cohesive unit and chose the right tactics. Most other clubs spent much of the season fiddling with their lineups, bringing in new players with varying degrees of success. Toplak and Obradovic made just three mid-season acquisitions and didn't get rid of anyone.

By all accounts, including this one from a match program, the polyglot squad had come to feel at ease with their manager:

Since they are average sized men and, since they wore similar
clothes and carried big, black Addidas [*sic*] bags, the Clippers were
mistaken at least 10 times on each trip for a band. When asked if
they were bandsmen, the players would agree. Then they would
point to Dr. Obradovic as their leader, and the good doctor
would always append: "I also play the tuba." . . . Rowan once told
a curious little old lady that they were all sons of Dr. Obradovic.
"How could this be?" she wondered. "Oh, he's been married eight
times!" explained Rowan. "Well, that just beats everything," she
managed.

Come the middle of July, only St. Louis looked remotely capable of over-
taking the Clippers in the Western Division; the greatest threat to their
playoff hopes seemed to be injuries. Milosevic missed most of the run-in
with a groin strain, which forced Mitic to play as a striker; knee trouble
kept Rowan on the bench for seven games; and Scott even managed to
split open a toe on one of his child's toys. Strains and sprains were rarely
given time to heal in the NPSL; clubs found themselves playing twice and
sometimes three times a week, something unheard of anywhere else in
the world.

Even debilitated, the Clippers proved too much for their Western
Division rivals. With a third of the season to go, they lost 3–1 in St. Louis,
which reduced their lead to twenty-two points—but it was as close as anyone would get to them. When the two teams met at the Coliseum a week
later, Oakland cantered to a 9–0 win, the biggest the league would ever
see. "The Stars are very possibly the second best team in the National
Professional Soccer League," wrote the *Tribune*. "But before a screaming
crowd of 4,965 they were made to look like a bunch of ball boys."

The Clippers won the division with three matches to spare. It scarcely
seemed to matter that they would end the regular season with two
straight defeats: they finished with the best record in the league, the most
goals scored and the fewest conceded. In the eyes of *Tele-Sport*, theirs had
been the most attractive and effective team in the NPSL. "[Obradovic]
knew what he wanted," it wrote. "He wanted the nucleus of Oakland to
play the same type of soccer with no possibility of language barriers ham-
pering coordination; he wanted a capable assistant to execute his shrewd
ideas; he wanted a flexible 4–2–4 pattern; but above all, he wanted to win
the league." Other teams, *Tele-Sport* noted, had also moved toward 4–2–4,
but they "didn't have the personnel—and this is the difference."

Indeed, the league's all-star teams featured no fewer than six Clippers: Baesso, Mitic, Scott, and Stojanovic on the first team, and Gavric and Hoftvedt on the second (with no room for Cop, though). But these were still not the sort of stars the fans wanted to see. In fact, the largest crowd to watch a match in northern California that year—and certainly the most rabid—belonged to neither the Clippers nor the Gales but to Eusebio. On August 23, close to 12,000 had peered through the swirling fog of Kezar Stadium for a glimpse of the Portuguese World Cup hero, who was appearing with his club team, Benfica. The opposition, Boca Juniors of Argentina, had an international star of their own in Antonio Rattin, an uncompromising center-half who inevitably man-marked Eusebio to within an inch of his life. It was an evening rife with hysteria. On the teams' entrance, several hundred fans swarmed onto the pitch, delaying kickoff by more than half an hour, and after one player jostled a linesman, there was another frenzied invasion. The match, ill tempered and lacking in goalmouth action, ended 1–1.*

For better and for worse, there had been no marauding fans at Oakland's matches and little in the way of frenzy. The most the club had tempted into the Coliseum had been 9,516 for a weekend game with the Toronto Falcons, but even that had been inflated by hordes of youth groups. This may have been about as good as things got in the NPSL, but with the Clippers through to the championship playoff—a two-match, total-goals series—the meager record seemed certain to be broken.

The Eastern Division was claimed by the Baltimore Bays, who'd fared little better at the box office, though in anticipation of clinching their division they had attracted over 11,000 to their season finale (and then lost). For their home leg of the title series, things looked more promising: advance ticket sales exceeded 8,000—which stadium officials said pointed to a crowd of 20,000, or around twice what the baseball Orioles would average that summer. Not that the media took much notice. Some newspapers noted that the governors of the two states, Spiro Agnew and Ronald Reagan, had wagered a bushel of Maryland seafood against a gallon of Californian wine on the outcome. A few printed a photograph of Bays players angrily kicking balls at placards—printed in several languages—bearing Obradovic's assertion that his team would beat Baltimore nine times out of ten. But with the NPSL having failed to catch lightning in a

---

* Was this a record for soccer in northern California? Wire-service reports initially estimated the attendance at 16,500, which would have made it so. But the *Tribune* claimed that "an official of the California Soccer Football Association, which got a 5 per cent [*sic*] of the gate, revealed the figure as 12,000."

bottle, most papers seemed to have lost what little interest in soccer they'd developed.

But no paper in the country covered its team with more enthusiasm than the *Tribune*. In the run-up to the championship series, its "World of Women" section even devoted an entire page to the wives of the players ("Mara Obradovic volunteered that Slav wives use red peppers freely and find some American dishes less tasty than theirs"). But the team was unable to regain the momentum it had lost at the tail end of the regular season; the Clippers wilted in Baltimore. Urged on by a crowd of over 16,000 with banners and noisemakers at the ready, the Bays scored the only goal of the match. Baltimore's manager accused the Clippers of holding out for a scoreless tie, though Obradovic blamed the seventy-seven-degree heat. "This is not good soccer weather," he mused. "Oakland is much cooler, and we'll play better Saturday, I'm sure."*

He was right. Six days later, the Clippers scored three times in thirteen minutes and coasted to the title. The unlikely hero was another Yugoslavian, Dragan Djukic, whom Obradovic had picked up in mid-season from Los Angeles for all of $2,000. The twenty-eight-year-old headed in the first two goals—from virtually identical positions—and scored a third from the penalty spot, all before the first half ended. "We were undecided between Djukic and Baesso before the game," Obradovic confessed, "but we decided on Djukic because he is the only player other than Milosevic who can head the ball."

The penalty proved to be the turning point of a niggling match. Enraged by the decision, Baltimore's captain, Juan Santisteban, was dismissed after remonstrating with the referee—and taking a kick on Djukic as he lined up his shot. ("He cussed me out in Spanish, which I understand," the referee told reporters, "but you can't print what he said.") The ten remaining Bays produced a goal three minutes later to trim the overall deficit to 3–2, but got no closer. A fifty-eighth-minute effort from the sprightly Marin put the outcome beyond doubt.

For the *Tribune*, the victory was worthy of acclamation: the Clippers had "crowned the Eastbay with its first major league championship" in

---

* The Bays had more than a championship on their minds. Weeks earlier, their front office had made it clear to head coach Doug Millward that he would be relieved of his duties at the end of the season for what was later described as an inability to "maintain proper control of the team." Millward chose the day after the first match of the championship series to go public over his dismissal, claiming that the club hadn't given him any satisfactory reasons for it. He did stay on for the second game, though. "We're professionals, and all we want to do is win," he said, "which I think we will."

"a rough, tough soccer game, making up in excitement and thrills what it lacked in championship skills." But the photos and stories filling its sports pages were probably more than the club had a right to expect. Paid attendance at the Coliseum had been 9,037, fewer than on opening day—and even several hundred worse than had attended the third-place playoff in St. Louis that same evening.

For many, including the paper's Ed Levitt, the entire season had been a peculiar fantasy:

> They came as strangers and leave as champions. And so many of us still cannot remember their names. Perhaps never before in the history of sports has there been a team such as this: organized in Europe, financed in Texas, trained in Redwood City, home-based in Oakland, and winners of a US championship without one American player on the club! Here they were, competing on the same team for six months, yet a language barrier prevented many of them from ever communicating with each other as they traveled and battled. . . . Not once in 17 games at the Oakland Coliseum did they lose a match. Yet their crowds here numbered but 5,000, the club will blow more than $300,000 and still the players say, "We thank the public here for the warm welcome."

In hindsight, the NPSL championship series is probably more remarkable for how it might have been settled than for how it was. Had the aggregate scores finished level, the champion would have been determined by a penalty-kick competition, or what the *Tribune* termed a "special shoot-off." While this might not have been dissimilar to the one in use today, in the 1960s it represented something of a step into the unknown. Not until 1970 would penalties replace the toss of a coin in European club competitions, and it would be several years after that before they were set loose on the World Cup. The paper attributed the plan to Obradovic and Liecty, "who personally don't like the idea but had to do something."*

The Clippers still had one match left to play—against St. Louis, who'd defeated Philadelphia in the third-place playoff—and won it 6–3 to claim the long-forgotten Commissioner's Cup, a decidedly peculiar pairing of

---

* As early as 1952, a Yugoslavian cup match was decided by a variation of this competition. The first penalty series between national teams may have been a friendly match between Taiwan and India in August 1967. Amateur teams representing Venezuela and Bolivia traded spot-kicks for the silver medal at the Bolivarian Games in June 1965, though this is not considered a full international.

first- and third-place teams. "You wait," Obradovic vowed, "in two, three years the Clippers will be good enough to play anywhere in the world."

But attention had strayed well off the ball. Half an hour before the start of second game of the championship, the NPSL had filed an $18 million lawsuit against the USSFA, FIFA, and just about every other soccer organization going, alleging it was being driven out of business. In reality, this was little more than a heavy-handed attempt to force the rival league's hand at a merger—and it would succeed. With FIFA threatening to suspend the USSFA if it didn't bring the two sides together, what one paper referred to as "the most nonsensical struggle this side of Vietnam" finally came to an end in December with the formation of the NASL. It marked the end of perhaps the last major unsanctioned league in world football.

Even this development, though, was all but subsumed by the sea of debt both leagues were drowning in. Estimates of the NPSL's total losses ran close to $5 million—more than six times as much in today's money— with Hilliard acknowledging that the Clippers' shortfall would "be well up in six figures." Some clubs folded; others changed cities. But in Oakland no one, least of all Obradovic, seemed to be giving up. "Next year we will draw 8,000 to 10,000 a game here—that I am sure," he said. "In two years it could go to 20,000. Sure, I am an optimist. Why not? The caliber of soccer in this country will improve. The people will appreciate it more. They will tell their friends. This will sell the sport more than anything."

To the Clippers' relief, the merger did away with the Golden Gate Gales, who relocated to Vancouver. But more formidable competitors for the East Bay sports dollar were already pitching their tents. The American Basketball Association began play in October 1967 with a franchise in Oakland—and Major League Baseball had granted the Kansas City Athletics permission to relocate to the city. Among other things, this meant that much of the green turf of the Coliseum would be peeled away. "Last year we had the best field in America," sighed Hoftvedt. "Now we may have the worst."

As big-time soccer sorted itself out—five franchises folded, leaving seventeen upright—the Clippers spoke giddily of building a dynasty. Liberated by the merger and the removal of sanctions, Hilliard mused that the new league would "make the name of Oakland a household word all over the world" and possibly "the heartland of international soccer through satellite TV." For a club hardly anyone had ever bought a ticket for, it was an audacious notion. The team deserved better, insisted Obradovic; it could beat three-quarters of the first-division clubs in Europe. For Hilliard, 1968 represented the start of a new era. "The soccer world is curious as to how good we really are," he claimed. "The Europeans and the other soccer powers would like to play Oakland to find out. We definitely plan to give them the opportunity."

The first chance came a few weeks before the start of the season, and it produced the largest home crowd the club had ever seen: nearly 14,000 in Kezar Stadium for an exhibition with Guadalajara. The visitors won, 1–0, though they had been tested by their Mexican League opponents. As one paper asserted rather clumsily, "None of the fans were convinced that the neophyte Clippers can't hold their own in international competition."*

It's been argued that pro soccer would take many years to return to the playing standards it set in 1968. Clubs had lost much of their gullibility, and owners had yet to lift their financial drawbridge. Many former NPSL teams made substantial improvements to their rosters; those from the rival USA had been given over a year to populate theirs. Yet in the face of all this, the Clippers stayed more or less the same. Though an unhappy Rowan was traded to the Detroit Cougars ("I was getting $3,000 less than the Slavs"), nearly everyone else returned. They were joined by Stefan Bena, a Serbian fullback obtained from Hanover 96 of the Bundesliga, and Sweden's Kay Wiestål, a forward who would finish the season with St. Louis. In spite of this complacency—or, perhaps, because of it— Oakland was still seen by most as the team to beat. "We will be better this year than last," Obradovic insisted.

The three straight wins with which they began the season—including a 5–0 demolition of the Washington Whips—suggested they were. Obradovic soon boasted that he didn't know of any team in the league that could beat his if they played even to 60 percent of their potential. The Clippers in fact would lose only one of their first ten matches. But the NASL had taken up the NPSL's convoluted scoring system, and two scoreless ties shunted them behind the San Diego (née Los Angeles) Toros in the four-team Pacific Division.

But even at this early stage, it was clear the merger had done nothing to help pro soccer catch fire. The Clippers had attracted just 5,700 to their home opener, and though that was a blessed improvement on the 300 who shivered through the Chicago Mustangs' kickoff at frozen Soldier Field, in a way it was just as chilling. The front office hastily reduced ticket

---

* The rest of the exhibition schedule included two matches against other NASL teams and a 9–0 win over a team of amateur Latin Americans played in front of 500 fans "at the west end of Golden Gate Park."

prices for the next match but still drew fewer than 4,000, and found only 2,600 willing to spend a Friday night watching them battle the Mustangs.

Right across the league, the story was the same—and talk of expanding the schedule and intruding on the NFL season had given way to discomfited silence. By May, reports had surfaced that the NASL was close to collapse. One Clippers official had confided imprudently to reporters that several franchises were close to folding, while the *Atlanta Journal* maintained that the entire operation had been "hamstrung by a weak television contract and hampered by anemic paid attendance. It continues on what could be a collision course with reality—the people simply are not taking to the sport." The doomsaying pushed NASL officials into some awkward corners—"We could lose eight to ten teams and still have a league" was one spokesman's embarrassed response—though not everything was falling apart. CBS, for one, was attracting a 4.3 Nielsen rating for its *Game of the Week,* which, while not NFL-size, was certainly on par with its horseracing, golf, and ice hockey coverage.

But the TV cameras couldn't disguise all the empty seats, and 50,000 of them in the Coliseum were enough to indicate that even a winning team was a losing proposition. The owners reiterated their commitment to the city, but not without a hint of desperation. "If people have any ideas how we can be of more service to the area," Hilliard pleaded, "we're open to advice."

The struggle spread onto the field. Against the Dallas Tornado, easily the league's weakest team, the Clippers could only manage a 1–1 tie, unable to cope with the Texas heat. Only in two of their next eleven matches did they manage a victory, and crowds dipped toward 3,000 even on weekends. Yet smack in the middle of this lamentable run came an unexpected bounty—and perhaps the club's finest hour: victory against Manchester City, reigning champions of the English league, in front of the largest soccer crowd northern California had ever produced.

The English titleholders were nearing the end of a rather embarrassing month-long North American tour. Four times, in four different cities, they had tied Scotland's Dunfermline Athletic (though one match in Los Angeles had been settled on a "penalty goal contest" between two players); in Chicago, they had lost to Borussia Dortmund of West Germany. They'd also been beaten by the NASL's own Atlanta Chiefs, having played, in their coach's words, "like we didn't really want to win." Against the Clippers, their fortunes did not improve: two goals from Baesso and one from Davidovic handed the English their worst defeat of the tour.

Though exemplary, the 3–0 score line was also deceptive. Several of City's best players were back in England, and those who had made the trip were facing their fourth game in eleven days. In the Coliseum, they were reduced to nine men before halftime, thanks to an overly zealous referee (one report claimed that after the second dismissal, the English captain gathered his team together and told them to "take the rest of the afternoon off"). City's manager, Joe Mercer, reacted to the result with an icy silence; there was nothing to evaluate or assess, he sniffed, because "there wasn't enough of a game." The Clippers also kept their perspective. "We would have beaten them eleven against eleven," maintained Stojanovic, "[but] in the English League . . . that's another story, perhaps."

For the *Tribune*, though, the victory was a genuine achievement—and even a breakthrough for the sport:

> The final whistle was like a concerto to most of the 25,237. They stood and screamed for the Oakland Clippers. They booed the British. Soccer, the kind that has hypnotized 80 per cent of the globe, had arrived. The Clippers had drubbed, not defeated, English champion Manchester City, 3–0. It wasn't that close. The only ones who didn't scream were British, obviously. They sided against the rest of the stadium—flag against flags, patriotism burning. There was no doubt; this was soccer.*

But any thoughts that a half-full Coliseum represented the first stirrings of Clipper mania quickly evaporated. Three days later, just 2,527 turned up for a league match with St. Louis. In fact, the crowd for Manchester City would prove to be larger than those for Oakland's next eight home games put together. (Oakland beat St. Louis with penalty kick in the final minute, although the Stars complained that at halftime someone had switched on the speaker in their dressing room and all they could hear was the brass band playing on the field.)

Only once in their next seven games did the Clippers win again. Players remonstrated with each other ("I can't play with Mirko; it's very difficult," grumbled Hoftvedt after a defensive mix-up contributed to a narrow loss to the Cleveland Stokers); Baesso was fined $1,000 for an

---

* Two matches were played in the Coliseum that day. In the second, the injury-riddled St. Louis Stars were forced to play their manager, thirty-nine-year old Rudi Gutendorf, and a few Clippers reserves against Dunfermline. Though they lost, 3–1, Gutendorf insisted that his charges had "made just an effective a performance against a complete team as Oakland did against an incomplete team."

ill-judged expectoration against St. Louis; and the injury list continued to grow. After a 1-0 loss at Kansas City—and with the season barely half over—Obradovic all but conceded the title; the chances of his team repeating as champions were "one per cent." The heart of the problem was an inability to find the net. "At one point or another, it seemed, the complete forward line of Oakland had clear shots at the Toronto goal," the *Tribune* observed after a 2-1 loss to the Falcons. "Either they were blocked suddenly or went high or wide." The loss pushed the Clippers into third place, thirty-three points behind San Diego—the equivalent of four or five victories, as best anyone could judge—with ten games left to play. They would win all but one of them.

The revival started four days later in Detroit. It was led, predictably enough, by Milosevic, who'd been absent during much of the slump. Fit and hungry against the Cougars, he scored all three goals in a 3-2 win, then added three more in a 5-1 drubbing of Dallas and four against the Vancouver Royals. It was a dazzling run of form that, for the *Tribune*, at least, represented the handiwork of a superstar: the Serb with the "soft, charming features" had become "the hottest star in American soccer" and what the league "need[ed] a dozen more of: box office attractions to swell the gate."

Goals suddenly flew in from all directions. The thirty-three-year-old Saccone, whose guns had been silent for most of the season, scored in five straight games, including a hat-trick of his own against the Los Angeles Wolves; eight goals in the final seven matches from Mitic—moved to the forward line, where he would spend the rest of his career—made him the club's top scorer. The one per cent chance mutated into a legitimate play-off bid: San Diego was finishing its season indifferently, and when the Clippers beat New York in a rearranged match at ramshackle Downing Stadium, they overtook the Toros, having played two games more. "I honestly feel the boys have really reached their peak," Obradovic claimed.

The same couldn't be said of the franchise. Amid the string of victories, the Coliseum had remained steadfastly empty; even a Sunday afternoon rematch with Dallas attracted just 3,879. The owners now admitted they were prepared to leave Oakland "if someone would show a serious interest in us." Hilliard was unapologetic. "We've got to make this thing pay for itself, but if we're not going to get any help here, we'd be darn fools not to entertain other offers," he said. "We're taking a terrible bath at the gate, and we're not worth that. Right now, we're the hottest team in the United States, in any sport." Needless to say, serious interest was nowhere to be found; all of the NASL's arrows were pointing downward.

Ironically, that same summer Pelé was touring the United States with his club team, Santos, and demonstrating that America's interest in the game—or, at least, its most famous competitor—was anything but dead. Over 43,000 filled Yankee Stadium to see Santos play Italy's Napoli, close to a postwar record for soccer in North America and more than some NASL franchises would attract over a whole season. Several of the league's own teams had been included on the Brazilians' itinerary; many drew record-setting crowds. The Cleveland Stokers attracted over 16,000, more than had ever seen a soccer match in Ohio; the Whips drew 20,189, easily a record for the District of Columbia. Even the lowly Boston Beacons, who were doused 7–1, pulled in 18,500, more than had watched a match anywhere in New England (even back to the days of Fall River and New Bedford). For this kind of soccer, there was money to be made—enough of it to persuade Santos to come back for more later in the summer.

To the Clippers, left off the original itinerary, this was welcome news: a match was arranged for August 4. But when Pelé picked up an injury, the club faced what looked like a tricky decision. The Brazilians could turn up without their star—for a reduced fee—or they could push the date back to August 30, which was less than a week before Oakland's crucial regular-season finale with San Diego. To a club desperate for gate money, the decision wasn't difficult; even the prospect of key players' picking up injuries in a meaningless contest didn't seem to matter. The Clippers wanted Pelé—and they wanted to face him with their strongest available eleven.

On the night of the match, the man everyone had come to see lived up to his billing. "The whole difference tonight was Pelé," declared Obradovic, his team squarely beaten. "If we had him, we would have won." Hoftvedt did a creditable job of man-marking the main attraction, and Stojanovic performed heroically in goal. But it wasn't the men in Clipper blue and California gold who'd sold the tickets.

Newhouse wrote:

Smack against the center-field wall in the Oakland Coliseum, someone ought to erect a plaque with the following insertion: "Pele, the miracle man of soccer, who performed a miracle in the Coliseum, Aug. 30, 1968." The great one scored two goals and was the primary difference as Santos of Brazil overcame the Oakland Clippers, 3–1, last night. But more than just the score, 29,162 were drawn by this magnetic personality into the Coliseum—a record for any game involving a North American Soccer League team.

No, you're not mistaken. It was Oakland you read about this week where soccer was on its death bed, awaiting final rites. Spectacles do not soccer seasons make, but after the superb effort the Clippers gave last night, a few more than the reliable 2,500 should be back.*

That same night, 4,800 turned up at Soldier Field to see Chicago beat San Diego, 2-1, a result that put the Clippers within touching distance of the playoffs. Victory against the Toros in their final game would earn them the division title; even a tie wouldn't rule them out. "We must score three goals at the minimum," claimed Obradovic. "We must win. We must be sure."

It nearly happened. The score was 3-3 with five minutes to play when Mitic headed a cross from Marin into the net, but it was disallowed for offside. Oakland remonstrated: the linesman had not raised his flag, and Mitic insisted that two defenders had been standing in front of him all the while. "It is impossible for from where Marin passed the ball to be offside," Obradovic fumed. "He was almost on the line." But according to the referee—Eddie Pearson, later the NASL's chief of officials—Davidovic had somehow turned the trick. ("It was a very unfortunate ruling for any official to have had to make.") "We'll file a written protest to the league office," vowed Liecty, "but what chance do we have with no film of the game to question the referee?"

The result left Oakland pinning their hopes on the Los Angeles Wolves, who hosted San Diego three days later in their last match. The Toros won, 4-1—and claimed the division title by one point. Though the Clippers had accumulated the second-highest number of points in the league (twenty-seven more than Kansas City, the Gulf Division winners), though they had won as many games as anyone else, and though they led the league in scoring, their season was over.

Robbed by the referee? In truth, the club had more to regret from their performance three months earlier, when they failed to beat a Dallas team that was still nearly two months away from its first victory and had been outscored in its previous seven matches 38-6. Any kind of victory in Turnpike Stadium would have easily compensated for the offside decision

---

* Once again, the calculation of the "record" crowd is open to question. The *San Mateo Times* wrote that "the Oakland Coliseum turnstile account (according to a Coliseum official) was more like 23,000. . . . Nobody gets into the Coliseum without clicking the turnstile. Even employees, sportswriters, freeloaders and gate crashers are counted. So there's a discrepancy of 6,000, give or take a few."

in San Diego. Even so, fortune had favored the Toros. Under the NASL's peculiar schedule, teams in the same division did not face the same opponents the same number of times—and San Diego had, however unwittingly, been given a much easier ride. They'd played the league's two doormats, Dallas and Detroit, five times to Oakland's three and helped themselves to forty-three of a possible forty-five points. The Clippers, on the other hand faced playoff-bound Cleveland and Kansas City five times to the Toros' three and managed only fourteen points. Moreover, they had the better players. Seven of them were voted league all-stars: Davidovic, Gavric, Mitic, Scott, and Stojanovic on the first team, and Baesso and Cop on the second. No other club managed more than three.*

But the numbers everyone was talking about had dollar signs in front of them. Instead of a rise in attendance, there had been a decline—and losses for some franchises over the two years were said to have run into seven figures. ("Nobody expected to make money," Hilliard reflected despondently, "but nobody figured we'd slide off, either.") Even before Atlanta had beaten San Diego in the championship series, the NASL had started losing teams. Blame was apportioned liberally; among other things, the Clippers complained of there being "more pro sports franchises between Oakland and San Francisco than any place in the world." To many league owners, the problems were insurmountable, and the easiest thing was to bail out. By the start of 1969, most had done so.

The Clippers persevered, but their fate was compromised by geography. The disappearance of San Diego, Vancouver, and Los Angeles left Dallas as their nearest opponent. Moreover, in Hilliard's words, the club had "played 66 league matches over two years and lost money and played five with foreign teams and made money."

Liecty had certainly not regarded the season as a catastrophe:

> The owners wanted to continue with the project, especially in view of their financial investment, the fact that many internal political problems had now been solved, and they were enjoying the experience. Despite losing money, they were the kind of people who loved the limelight and having a good time. After having been through the terrible emotional strain of starting an "outlaw" team, struggling through a merger . . . the 1968 season was a dream.

---

* Not everything about the 1968 season had been a disappointment. "If anything, the players in the NASL appear to be more organized than their predecessors of a year ago," noted the *Sporting News,* which organized the balloting. "When the NPSL players voted in '67, they often wrote down No. 7 or No. 14 instead of the individual's name."

Thus, Dr. Obradovic and I came up with a plan to convince the owners to stay in business. We knew from our experience that playing exhibition games with foreign teams brought in the most money. Our plan was to sit out the 1969 NASL season, keep our outstanding team together, and play a series of exhibition matches until the NASL had a chance to reorganize and regroup. We hoped that within a year or so, the NASL could get its feet back on the ground and that at least two more teams might appear on the West Coast.

Three weeks after the regular season had ended, the Clippers defeated the national team of Israel, 2–1, before a crowd of 4,352—1,200 more than had seen their final home game against Los Angeles. It proved to be their final match under an Oakland banner and their last in the Coliseum. Withdrawing from the NASL, which still wasn't sure what it would do for 1969, they returned to being the California Clippers and pledged to take their game all over the state. "We still have great faith in pro soccer in the United States," O'Neill insisted, "but we feel our international program is the best for the promotion of the game in our area." Obradovic expected "eight or ten teams to follow our example by June," then regional leagues with national playoffs in 1970, and "packed stadiums in three years." He remained as sanguine as ever. "I'm more enthused about soccer here now than ever because of the expanded number of boys playing the game," he said. "I'm so sure we can succeed, I don't see how we can lose money." It would take only a few months for him to find out.

The NASL, meanwhile, came to a decision about its future: for the first half of the 1969 season, British teams were asked to occupy the five surviving cities. The expectation (forlorn, as it turned out) was that a first-division standard of play would galvanize support for the local teams, who would pick up the baton in June. The Clippers were no less concerned about playing standards; their announced intention for 1969 was to bring in "the first or second-best team from ten different countries, nothing less." Yet the major-league budget was gone. The owners had scaled down their support, and Obradovic was left to make some painful financial adjustments:

The players are receiving 50 per cent less than last year. I am getting 65 per cent less. But it must be this way. I couldn't demand a big salary and still face my players. They are sacrificing something to sell soccer in this country. I also must sacrifice. Now that they know I have so much faith in the success of soccer in this country that I will coach for so little, it has to give them the will to continue playing in the United States. They could earn more playing in Europe.

Some already did. Milosevic went to Red Star of the French League, and Lukic joined Heracles, a Dutch second-division club. Scott, meanwhile, had returned to his construction business in England. Those who preferred to stay often topped up their wages by moonlighting in local leagues. Yet the Clippers remained a formidable side, still perhaps the strongest in North America. This was primarily because the NASL's meltdown had left a lot of unclaimed property, including the league's most valuable player, John Kowalik, a Polish international, and Pepe Fernandez, a Uruguayan who'd scored twenty-nine goals for San Diego the season before. The Clippers signed them both; with Mitic staying on, the league's top three scorers had come into their possession.

But the lofty aim of squaring off against the world's elite proved difficult to realize. Deportivo Atlas, the first opponents, were a decent Mexican League side but hardly an international force, and on a January afternoon, just 5,142 paid to watch them at wet and windy Kezar Stadium. All the same, Obradovic took great encouragement from his team's decisive 3–0 win. "After today's performance," he reflected, "we're ready to take on anyone."

It would get better. Obradovic used his contacts behind the iron curtain to pull off a noteworthy coup: a visit from a Soviet club, something American soccer had never produced before. While it hardly amounted to an epic U.S.–USSR duel—there wouldn't be a single American playing—for many in the media it was close enough, and it was written up in distinctly Cold War terms.*

Newhouse wrote in the *Tribune*:

Is it hard calling Russia? "No, it is very easy," declared [Obradovic]. "You call New York and ask the operator for Russia. You give the number, wait one or two hours, and your call is ready." Did Dr. O think the CIA was listening? "Who knows," he said. "We talked

---

* The Clippers did sign a few American collegians but played them sparingly. The NASL had conducted a full-scale college draft the previous June; its intention was for each team to include three North American citizens on their 1969 rosters. One of the Clippers' draft choices was Guatemala-born Luis Sagastume, who would spend twenty-eight years as coach at the Air Force Academy.

soccer anyway, so it is no problem. Later it might be a problem."
... Why haven't the Russians sent a team before? "Baltimore,
Atlanta and ourselves tried last year to get the Russians, but we
went through other people. This time we tried to arrange the
whole thing by ourselves, something I believe had never been done
before, and this must have impressed the Russian federation," Dr.
O said.

With a certain predictability, the Soviets sent across their top team: Dinamo Kyiv, the Ukrainian side that had won the last three league championships. The plan was for a four-match series, something the visitors
claimed to regard as little more than a pre-season warm-up. "It doesn't
matter whether we win or lose," insisted their manager, Viktor Maslov.
Few believed him. "We asked their federation to send some other teams,
now touring South America," said Obradovic. "But no, they wanted to
send the best. They're afraid of losing."

The doctor may have been instrumental in helping to bring the Soviets across, but his efforts had done little to heal the growing rift between
his league-less team and the USSFA. Any match played in the United
States involving a foreign team required the approval of the association's
international games committee, who were doubtless among the "other
people" to whom Obradovic referred. Liecty recalled:

The USSFA, always suspicious of a "private" operation, looked at
the Clippers as now being a hungry exploiter, trying to capitalize
by only playing foreign teams in the ways that some unscrupulous
impresarios had done in the past. Nothing could have been further from the truth. Despite meetings, letters, telephone calls, and
other means, the Clippers management could not convince the
NASL leaders [or] the USSFA that our intentions were legitimate
and, more important, designed to help reconstitute the NASL in
the long run by having an established team already on the West
Coast, ready to re-embrace a reconstituted NASL when it became
economically viable to do so. They were convinced that our operation should be eliminated and they began to put up barriers by
every possible means.

According to Liecty, the barriers included a suspension "pending further
investigation" just a week before the Ukrainians were due to arrive. An
emergency meeting in New York did little to soothe relations, though the

association eventually realized it stood to lose more from a ban than the Clippers did. The matches went ahead.

Three were played. Dinamo won the first, 3–2, on a rain-sodden pitch at Kezar Stadium, though the Clippers thought a shot from Mitic that squirted through the Ukrainian goalkeeper's legs had crossed the goal line and should have been allowed. In a scrappier affair in Los Angeles a week later, their luck appeared to have changed, only for Dinamo to score in the dying seconds and salvage a 1–1 tie. Not until the third match did they finally earn the reward they thought their play had merited. Back in San Francisco, a second-half goal from Kowalik and goalkeeping heroics from Stojanovic gave the Clippers a 1–0 victory. "Maslov congratulated me on our showing," said Obradovic. "He told me after the first game that he was sure we'd win once."

Did it mean anything? According to Maslov—one of the greatest football minds of his time—the Clippers were "a team of good average European caliber." But the Dinamo boss also pointed out the narrow, uneven fields his team had been asked to play on and, in particular, the notoriously sloppy surface at Kezar Stadium. On the whole, though, the series had been the quintessence of diplomacy. "We have been very satisfied with the reception here and would like to express our gratitude to your people," he said. His players, meanwhile, "loaded their suitcases with rock 'n roll records and autographed pictures of Lana Turner," whose performance in *The Postman Always Rings Twice* twenty-three years earlier was apparently still animating Soviet men.

Attendance for the series had been disappointing—fewer than 34,000 in total—and from such modest heights interest in the Clippers would quickly plummet. Generating enthusiasm for an independent team was difficult enough; with officious governing bodies standing in the way, it was practically impossible. "My time should have been spent 100% with the media, getting teams to California, and promotional activities," Liecty later wrote. "Instead it was a daily fight with administrative and bureaucratic problems of a Herculean nature put up by the USSFA." The friction had led to a last-minute cancellation of a series with Ireland's Waterford, something which left the club with only two games to play between late March and early May. In Liecty's view, this was a fatal blow. Yet some degree of cooperation must have existed between the parties: one of the two matches in question was a warm-up with the U.S. national team, which faced a critical World Cup qualifying match with Haiti the following week. The Clippers won, 4–0, but drew barely 2,000 to what is now

Boxer Stadium. Victories over all-star teams from San Francisco (5–1) and southern California (8–1) drew similarly meager gatherings; a two-game series with Club América of Mexico attracted fewer than 9,000.

Would that Pelé had remained in California. But there was no sign of Santos—or Manchester City, for that matter—and the owners' patience was all but up. Hopes of survival came to rest on a four-team international tournament for a "California Cup." The invitees were reasonably strong—Dukla Prague (fifth in the Czech League), VFC Setubal (fourth in Portugal), and West Bromwich Albion (tenth in England)—but lacking in superstars. Most of the tickets went unsold. A Sunday doubleheader that drew 11,500 to Stanford Stadium fell short of expectations, but even it was an improvement on a week earlier, when the Clippers had played Setubal at a high school football field in Fresno in front of just 3,200. Obradovic threw up his hands. "I don't understand it," he confessed. "This is an excellent tournament. If it was played in a European town, the crowd would be 60,000 minimum."

The end was in sight. It came less than a week later, against the newly crowned champions of the Italian league. While the Clippers creditably split their two-match series with a virtually full-strength Fiorentina team, losing 2–1 then winning 4–2, they were on their last legs. (Liecty recalled that in one of the matches they were shorthanded and recruited one player out of the stands.) Disappointing gates of 4,212 in Los Angeles and 7,356 in San Francisco seemed only to vindicate a decision the owners had already made: the club would not play again. "I still remember the last game," Hilliard told the *Tribune* a year later. "Ilija Mitic said, 'When the Clippers die, they die like men.' It brought tears to my eyes."

Even Obradovic had lost his forbearance. In March, he had been "100% certain that in five years soccer will be the second biggest sport in the United States"; three months later, he was on a plane back to Belgrade. "One of the problems here are the American soccer associations," he sighed. "These people are crazy. I don't want to go back, but what can I do?"

Newhouse offered an epitaph:

It was the kind of scene no one likes to see: a man forced to flee from unfulfilled dreams. . . . [T]he doctor lived since early 1967 in relative obscurity in the United States, after years of headlines and mingling with the "best people" in his country. Yet he could adjust, because he had something to prove: that the American fan could and would divorce the slower baseball for the faster game of soccer, "for sure." As attendance proved him wrong, he kept resetting the dates when this change could happen. But he never lost his drive, his enthusiasm until the very end, last month.

Some had left before him. Quiros and Marin jumped their contracts to join the Kansas City Spurs, joined by reserve goalkeeper Leonel Conde. But many preferred to stay in California, even if it meant pursuing other lines of work. Gavric, whose long-range shooting had been a prominent feature of his fullback play, ended 1969 as the placekicker for the San Francisco 49ers ("Fifty yards not so far"). His time in shoulder pads lasted less than a year; he was cut the following summer and rejoined the NASL in 1971.

By then, several other Clippers had also signed for league teams, and some made a lasting impression. Stojanovic was named a first-team all-star while with Dallas in 1971; Mitic spent seven seasons in the league and became one of a handful of players to score more than one hundred goals there. When the NASL finally returned to the West Coast in 1974, Cop, Gavric, and Stojanovic—all nearing the end of their careers—joined the expansion San Jose Earthquakes; Toplak joined in midseason as their coach. Obradovic, though, never set foot in the league again, nor did he manage another team in Yugoslavia or anywhere else. He died in Belgrade on June 22, 2000.

Two factors more than any other contributed to the collapse of professional soccer in the late 1960s. The most significant of these was the absurdity of two professional leagues, not so much for the undesirable competition they created, but because they had forced each other into too hasty a startup. Had the USSFA been able to convince the rival ownership factions to band together as one unified, FIFA-sanctioned league, a number of things would have happened. Play could have started in 1968 or even 1969, giving the franchises time to recruit stronger players and mold them into half-decent teams. The clubs would also have been entitled to arrange the sort of international exhibitions that proved so important to the likes of the Clippers in 1968.

More significant, though, was the breathtakingly naïve assumption that soccer was merely a commodity whose success in North America required little more than marketing. Too many executives and officials were hired on the basis of their understanding of North American sports rather than for any appreciation of the game, and in many cases, the "marketing" that took place was not particularly sophisticated. ("The idea was to shout 'Major-league soccer,' as loud and as long as possible," one writer claimed, "as if the wish would father the reality.") No one can deny that the owners had lost a lot of money by the end of 1968, but the lack of an emotional attachment to the game made their decision to bail out all the more predictable.

In 1978, the NASL made a transitory return to Oakland as the Stompers. With a nod to the past, Stojanovic was appointed head coach, but the team was weak, and he was replaced after only a handful of games. The team moved to Edmonton the following year. By then, though, the strides being taken by pro soccer had grown much wider, and the NASL had produced at least one team every bit as good as the Clippers. And by then, the fans were waiting.

7

Shot Out in Jersey

NASL 1979—The Beginning of the End

> It is very tempting to focus time, attention and resources upon the longer term goal of attracting . . . supplemental income sources. The proponents of this view reason that in order to be "big league" the NASL must possess a marketing company, a national television contract, and must seek immediate rapid expansion. Of course, harvesting revenues from ancillary incomes is a goal and strategy greatly to be desired. This cannot be accomplished, however, unless the NASL is able to deliver to the respective purchasers (television networks, advertisers, manufacturers or potential franchise holders) the single most important indicator of a sports industry's success—attendance.
>
> —NASL Strategic Plan, October 1977

S OCCER IN NORTH AMERICA had never known a year like 1976. It was an Olympic summer, and the gold-medal match between East Germany and Poland had attracted 71,617 to Montreal's Stade Olympique, a record for the continent. In the United States, the national teams of Brazil, England, and Italy had been invited to compete against an NASL all-star team for a "Bicentennial Cup"; crowds as high as 40,000 turned out to watch. And the NASL was scaling dizzying heights of popularity, in no small part because it had signed Pelé to one of the most lucrative contracts in sports; even before the regular season started, 58,000 turned up in Seattle's Kingdome to watch him play. Other World Cup heroes, like Bobby Moore, Eusebio, and Geoff Hurst, had signed for NASL teams; George Best turned out for Los Angeles. More than 25,000 filed into the Kingdome for the league's championship game—easily a record for the occasion, even though it kicked off at eleven in the morning—and five-and-a-half million watched it live on network television.

In seven years, the NASL had been dragged from the brink of collapse to the threshold of respectability—and its British-born commissioner had presided over the transformation with the zeal of a prophet. Interviewing him in 1978, one writer thought Phil Woosnam "spoke as if he were on a divine mission, baring his teeth and clenching his jaws"; another noted how, "when moved to talk about the soccer paradise that awaits the USA if it follows the righteous path, his accent takes on the singsong Welsh rhythm that otherwise seems to have eroded away after more than a decade in this country." Once a high school physics teacher, Woosnam had played first-division football in England and appeared seventeen times for the Welsh national team; now he had become America's foremost soccer evangelist. "I sell this game because once I believe in something and it makes sense to me, I will make it happen," he declared to *Sports Illustrated* in 1977. "This sport will take off. There is absolutely no way that it will not bypass everything else."

When Woosnam and the league's owners convened for their annual meeting in October 1976, it was with no less keen an expectation. Average attendance had increased by more than a third on the previous year, and several franchises seemed close to making money. At the same time, though, there were a number of lingering concerns—"certain unhealthy symptoms," in the league's idiom, "which were creating uncertainty about the security of our investment." The disparity between the best and worst franchises was growing; relationships with the U.S., Canadian, and international federations were strained; and the league's overstretched front office was failing to inspire confidence. More generally, there seemed to be a lack of consensus as to the league's priorities—or, put another way, an "absence of a common roadmap or plan against which member clubs can measure operating decisions."

There was a lot to get through at the meeting. Newspapers focused on the decisions to extend the regular season from twenty-four to twenty-six games, to turn the playoffs into two-match series, and to hold the following year's Soccer Bowl in Portland, Oregon. Largely forgotten among such material developments was the decision the league had also made to form a planning committee, one that would be tasked with (among other things) producing "a strategic plan for the growth and development of the NASL over the next decade."

This eight-man group included executives from seven franchises. Two of the most influential were Clive Toye of the New York Cosmos, an English expatriate who had famously brought Pelé into the league, and Lamar Hunt of the Dallas Tornado (see Chapter 2), an oil tycoon best known for his association with professional football and tennis but also one of the few to have remained with the NASL since its inception. The

Chicago Sting, Miami Toros, Minnesota Kicks, Seattle Sounders, and Washington Diplomats were also represented; Malcolm Bund, an external consultant, was the eighth member. Over the course of a year, the group set aside one weekend each month to work on the plan and presented its report to the league in October 1977.

The document, more than 250 pages long, included no fewer than fifty-three recommendations—on everything from the length of the season to player relations and the structure of the front office. It advised the NASL to "consider, evaluate and recommend some form of distribution system whereunder the world supply of rights to quality players would be more evenly distributed" among its teams; to "use every effort to apply for US and/or Canadian sponsorship of the World Cup in 1990 or 1994"; and even to "undertake as a separate but major full-time venture the financing and construction of Canadian and United States National Teams." There were prototype organization charts and pro forma budgets for the front office and the results of a survey it had conducted of club owners. It's hard to imagine such a blueprint for an emerging professional sports league ever having been produced before.

In its introduction, the report noted:

> While many signs are favorable, there is no guarantee that soccer will be popular and successful as a paid spectator sport in the United States and Canada, despite its popularity at the grassroots, participation level. What must be done, therefore, is to operate the NASL in such a way as to maximize public—and thus governmental—goodwill, present an extremely high quality product at competitive prices, and behave in a statesmanlike and customer-oriented manner, always recognizing that the NASL can only profit from what it creates and portrays, and that it is no better than the weakest of any of its franchises.

While it was hard to argue against this—the rhetoric certainly borrowed heavily from the NFL's winning philosophy at the time—the last clause in particular was something the league had struggled to address. The NASL of the mid-1970s defined itself by rising tides of interest in places like Seattle and Tampa and the phenomenon of Pelé and the Cosmos. Little consideration had been given to the plight of the Baltimore Comets, who'd often played before fewer than 2,000 fans on the campus of Towson State College in 1975, or the Boston Minutemen, whose owner had all but given up on the franchise in the middle of the 1976 season. The hasty disappearance of Philadelphia's Atoms, league champions in 1973, didn't seem too calamitous when Minnesota could attract nearly 50,000 for a playoff game; empty seats in metropolises like Chicago and Toronto were counterbalanced by raucous crowds in San Jose and Portland. When there was so much promise—and when the commissioner carried such an indefatigable optimism—dwelling on failure seemed perverse.

The strategic plan was less forgiving. Using a number of factors—"quality of ownership, capability of management, attendance and profitability, type of market and potential for future growth"—it had classified each of the NASL's eighteen franchises as either "standard" or "below standard." While not named explicitly, only ten were included in the former group: Dallas, Los Angeles, Minnesota, New York, Portland, San Jose, Seattle, Tampa Bay, Vancouver, and Washington. Of the eight classified as below standard, Chicago and Toronto had attendance problems; Fort Lauderdale and St. Louis were stuck in high school football facilities; and the likes of Connecticut, Hawaii, Las Vegas, and Rochester—only the latter of which would survive beyond the 1977 season—had, by the report's criteria, hardly anything to commend them.

For much of America, though, only one soccer team really mattered. Pelé's arrival in New York had transformed the Cosmos from one of the NASL's most poorly supported franchises into its principal drawing card. So, too, had the club's decision to move out of Yankee Stadium and into a gleaming new facility in the New Jersey Meadowlands. In June 1977, the Cosmos set a new attendance record for soccer in America when 62,394 turned up at Giants Stadium to watch them defeat the Tampa Bay Rowdies; two months later, they set another with 77,961 for a playoff game with the Fort Lauderdale Strikers. Even away from home, they were the team everyone wanted to see. The Cosmos played thirteen different teams on the road in 1977 and treated every one of them to their largest crowd of the regular season. By 1978, they were averaging 17,000 more fans than their nearest rival—and almost 35,000 more than the league mean.

Was this the future of professional soccer? "To a considerable degree, the Cosmos had created an illusion of success," Roger Allaway notes in his book *Corner Offices and Corner Kicks*. "Many American soccer fans today are puzzled by how a league drawing crowds of 70,000 could have foundered. They don't realize that those big crowds at Giants Stadium were the tip that appeared above the surface, but that the iceberg below was very thin." As Allaway points out, on the same day that 77,961 were assembling in Giants Stadium, a rather more humbling 5,295 were scattered inside the Los Angeles Coliseum for a playoff game between the Aztecs and Dallas.

Few could begrudge anyone the opportunity to see Pelé. But it had taken a lot of money to put him in a Cosmos shirt—and for better and for worse, it had widened the gap between rich and poor in the NASL. Warner Communications, the club's pretentious owners, would stretch it even further after his departure. No one spent money on players the way the Cosmos did, and no other city in America had so many fans it could tap. Yet the underlying assumption seemed to be that this was not unique, that what had happened in New York would soon happen elsewhere.

In 1978, the NASL expanded from eighteen to twenty-four teams. This was far more aggressive than the strategic plan had advised, which was to make only two additions that year and shore up at least two of the below-standard franchises. Twenty-four teams weren't envisaged until 1982.

Toye recalled in his book *A Kick in the Grass*:

Phil Woosnam was working on new franchises, at $3 million a pop, and when it came to a vote at the annual meeting, the idea of six new clubs coming in, with $18 million to be divided, was too strong a lure. I am sure it was not an easy sell but the Cosmos crowds, the glitterati, the attention paid by the media . . . the term Cosmos Country cropping up everywhere, go to Giants Stadium, feel the buzz, see Mick Jagger or lord knows who sitting a few seats away and, if you've got the money, it could be irresistible.

Each of the six new clubs did represent one of the major markets regarded as "imperative" in the strategic plan.* But none would survive beyond three seasons. Toye would later contend that most of the new owners, "to be kind, were the last sort of people we wanted." Yet there were others who regarded the likes of Peter Frampton, Paul Simon, and Rick Wakeman—all of whom took a financial interest in the Philadelphia Fury—as a "new breed" of owner. (The Cosmos, of course, had set something of a precedent with the Ertegun brothers, Atlantic Records executives who had helped launch the club in 1971.) "Rock music is American, and anywhere in the world you might go you can always find rock music," said a marketing executive for the Caribous of Colorado, whose ownership was also

---

* The report listed twenty "major markets" that at the time were without NASL franchises. In order of size, they were Philadelphia, Boston, Detroit, Cleveland/Akron, Pittsburgh, Montreal, Houston, Atlanta, Indianapolis, Baltimore, Hartford, Cincinnati, Milwaukee, Sacramento, Buffalo, Memphis, Kansas City, Nashville, Providence, and San Diego. Only eight of them would join the league in future.

connected to the industry. (The club's nickname, in fact, was taken from the name of the ranch and recording studio of one of the owners.) "Soccer, on the other hand, is the game of the world, played virtually everywhere but in America. This sort of brings the two together."

Others, mercifully, thought a little more deeply. "The sport itself is attracting people fundamentally in the same age and interest groups as those attracted to rock music," the Fury's general manager maintained. "Our own group is a good example, composed of not only the stars, but attorneys, concert promoters, managers, record executives, covering a whole spectrum of services that you must have to succeed in the entertainment area. These people know what it takes to promote, schedule, invest, whatever, and they're accustomed to success." The team, though, would bring them very little of that. After three seasons, the Fury was sold to interests in Montreal.

Clearly, there was more to promoting soccer than knowledge of the entertainment business, and some of it seemed to have been lost. John Best, president of the Vancouver Whitecaps in 1978, would recall in 1983:

> Early on the important thing was the challenge, building a foundation for the sport. Then the league began to swing from where involvement with the community, and especially youth, was most important, to the approach of promoter-type people, who had gimmicks to get people in the stadium. And it sounds odd, but winning became so important. You began to hear, "We must be totally professional," and suddenly players didn't have time for community work. That's okay for clubs like Liverpool or Real Madrid, where soccer has deep roots. It was not good here.

The product on the field had also come under scrutiny. The strategic plan had recognized that the soccer played in the NASL, and "particularly by North American athletes," was "inferior to that played overseas"; it also realized that importing established foreign talent was an expensive way to populate rosters but believed that a "spate" of high-quality native-born players would become available, somehow, within five years. To facilitate this, the plan called for each club to establish a reserve team, which could be put through its paces against its peers and other clubs outside the league. "As this program develops," the report advised, "the NASL by 1990 should consider the creation of a second division or minor league, each NASL franchise thereby operating two teams."

This was hardly an original idea. Back at the start of the 1976 season, the *New York Times* reported that several NASL franchises would field farm teams; they were to consist of fourteen players, at least seven of whom had to be native-born. But the paper didn't mention any clubs by name—and it never addressed the subject again. It's probably fair to say, though, that most owners perceived such teams as an unnecessary outlay rather than a legitimate source of talent. The strategic plan recommended that by 1984 the league restrict clubs to playing no more than six foreigners at a time, implying that reserve teams would make this happen without any drop in playing standards. It was only just becoming clear that the colleges could not be counted on to provide professional-caliber talent—and that strong Olympic and World Cup teams, stocked with NASL players, would work in the league's favor. But few felt able to invest in the future when Warner Communications kept upping the ante on the present. "I have an affectionate dislike for the Cosmos' operation," said Jack Bell, owner of the San Diego Sockers. "They go into a foreign country and pay, say, $500,000 for a player. I have to go in there next—and I can't afford it."

If the owners had given little notice to the strategic plan's advice on things like the size of the league and sources of its talent, when it came to television, they all but closed their eyes. The plan had warned:

> What a television network or NASL licensee pays for is a market. What it gives in return is access to its distribution system. Of course, a television network or manufacturer can, to a small degree, assist in creating or maturing a market for the product or, at the very least, expose the product to new markets. What they cannot do, however, is generate demand for the product in the first place.... [A]ttempts at securing a national television contract prior to the development of a market through increased local attendance would be wasteful and counterproductive. National television can provide access to markets; the NASL must deliver the markets. Unless these facts of life are recognized, the NASL could be seduced into a damaging arrangement.

In the report's view, the league could be selling national TV rights for $10 million by 1984, but the time wasn't right for a contract just yet ("Significant revenues from national television cannot be expected until the NASL creates its market by moving franchises to those cities where the number of television households is greatest"). The report also called attention to the fact that fifteen of the eighteen clubs had entered into arrangements for local television broadcasts of away games. Though in many cases the clubs themselves were responsible for putting the broadcast packages together, these seemed "to have generated sufficient advertising or promotional value to be considered worth the financial investment." In other words, local television could help put fans in the stands, but national television needed them to be there already.

And yet at the end of the 1977 season, Woosnam had declared: "Our absolute priority is a network television contract for a game of the week by 1979 and all three networks on board by 1980." The aggressive expansion in 1978 had been fueled largely by this ambition, and the undisguised inspiration was pro football: nearly everyone attributed gridiron's rise to its small-screen appeal. For 1978, the NASL had even arranged its clubs into two conferences of three divisions each—exactly like the NFL—in the hope, it was said, of fostering intra-divisional rivalries with which to tempt TV viewers.

Yet ever since the league's first season, the big three networks had been wary of soccer, even if the audiences it generated seem enormous by today's standards. CBS had attracted around 7 million viewers for telecasts of the league's predecessor, the NPSL, in 1967, but a year later the figure had slumped to around 4 million (which nonetheless is about twenty times what Major League Soccer telecasts averaged in 2010). Pelé's arrival rekindled the network's interest, though it proceeded with caution. It signed a three-year contract in 1976 but showed only one regular-season match that year, a 5–1 rout of the Cosmos by Tampa Bay. Fewer than 9 million tuned in—and when Toronto and Minnesota faced off in Soccer Bowl '76, the audience was even smaller. The network had been counting on the NASL for Nielsen ratings of around 6; for the biggest match of the year, it was lumbered with a 2.8. It didn't show another game. "We still think professional soccer will do well as a television attraction," said a CBS executive, "but it hasn't arrived yet."

The league was desperate to prove otherwise. But though it scrambled to find a replacement, all it could come up with was a six-match deal with TVS, an ad-hoc syndicate that offered sports programs to whatever local stations it could recruit. Interest was patchy. Some TVS affiliates delayed their NASL broadcasts until the middle of the night or even days later. A match between Seattle and Minnesota achieved a Nielsen rating of just 1.6. Even the audience for Soccer Bowl '77—Pelé's final competitive game—proved worse than what the NPSL had averaged ten years earlier. While in some cities the numbers had been healthy, it certainly wasn't what the NASL craved.

As TVS returned for a second helping in 1978, the league continued its pursuit of the major networks and late in the year emerged with its quarry: a three-year deal with ABC, a "tremendous landmark" in the eyes of Woosnam. In reality, it was really only a few toes in the water—five regular-season matches, three playoff games, and the Soccer Bowl—but the network was no less magniloquent, claiming that the time was right to put soccer on network television. Many disagreed, though, and over the course of the 1979 season, they would be proved right.

Taken as a whole—and with the considerable benefit of hindsight—the course the strategic review had charted was no less ambitious and much more pragmatic than the one the league had followed. Yet Woosnam had not been a member of the planning committee (something Toye later regarded as a mistake), and whatever interest he took in a plan he hadn't helped to draft was far from apparent. Chicago's Lee Stern, who was on the committee, maintained that Woosnam "just never paid attention to it." Toye claimed it was "abandoned in the snow without a second thought."

It was proving hard to discount the Cosmos' heady success—and the strategy the league seemed to be following was to harness it for all it was worth. "You force the growth as fast as you possibly can," Woosnam said toward the end of the 1978 season. "You could always get there in twenty years, but we've tried to develop the growth at its fastest pace. . . . We're trying to make every aspect of it go up together at the right pace, so that eight years from now we will be the world center of soccer and the number one sport in this country." The "right pace," it seemed, was the one being set by a decidedly singular team.

With the Cosmos attracting extraordinary crowds in New Jersey, the selection of Giants Stadium to host Soccer Bowl '78 had come as little surprise—and it was no less of a shock to see the home team there for the occasion. A crowd of 74,901, the second largest in the country's history, cheered New York to victory over Tampa Bay. A month later, Woosnam announced that Soccer Bowl '79 would also be held at the Meadowlands, doubtless entertaining hopes of an even bigger gate—this time emboldened by a network television audience of millions.

The home team was all but certain to be there. Into an already formidable squad of international talent—which included the likes of Franz Beckenbauer, Carlos Alberto, Vladislav Bogicevic, Dennis Tueart, and Giorgio Chinaglia—the Cosmos recruited a welter of reinforcements for 1979. From Brazil, they acquired Francisco Marinho, a goal-scoring fullback; from the French first division, Wim Rijsbergen, a key member of the Dutch national team; and from Iran, Andranik Eskandarian, one of the best defenders at the previous year's World Cup. They had also spent much of the winter trying to land two-time European Footballer of the Year Johan Cruyff but instead settled for another Dutch midfield ace, Johan Neeskens, who arrived in mid-season.

Other NASL teams were starting to spend handsomely on foreign talent—if not always wisely—but they were still catching up. A panel of experts rated the league's top players for *Sport* magazine: the Cosmos had three of the best four defenders, three of the best five midfielders, and two of the best six forwards. *Sports Illustrated* was no less awestruck. "To imagine any team other than the Cosmos emerging from Giants Stadium . . . as the winner of Soccer Bowl-79," it wrote, "requires a feat of prodigious fancy."

Before the season started, the league had approved two franchise shifts, both of clubs that had moved only the year before. The failure of the Caribous of Colorado had been "just down to a basic lack of dollars and cents," according to Woosnam—who nevertheless would have been pleased to see them reincarnated as the Atlanta Chiefs, the team he had left Britain to join in 1967 but that had folded a few years later. The other change involved the Oakland Stompers, which now became the property of Peter Pocklington, owner of the National Hockey League's Edmonton Oilers. "We'll put the same pressure on our new organization to win the cup as we would with the Oilers," he declared, before being informed there was no cup to win. "Well, whatever it is we have to win," he said, "we'll win it."*

Disorientation was perhaps forgivable. In four years, nineteen teams in the NASL had come, gone, or changed their identity. "I can't even name all the teams in the league," one public-relations director confessed to a reporter. "If I need a name I look it up. . . . If Phil Woosnam reads this, he'll kill me." But with twenty-four entries, a smattering of international superstars, and network TV, the NASL looked for all the world to be major-league. "The track record of sports is that they suddenly take off and for 6-8 years there's a phenomenal growth in media coverage, marketing attitudes, attendance, operating costs and franchise values," Woosnam claimed. "Now we're probably in the first or second year of that explosive period."

What sport was he thinking of? There had certainly been no explosive period for baseball, basketball, or ice hockey, and it had taken well over a

---

* At the time, Pocklington—or "Peter Puck," as he'd become known—was one of the wealthiest men in Canada. He moved to California in 2002 and, in the wake of several ill-fated business deals, filed for bankruptcy. He has since been charged with bankruptcy fraud in the United States.

decade for football to achieve its dominance. Its ascendance had also occurred during a fairly benign economic period, rather different from the late 1970s. All the same, the gushing optimism that had fuelled the NASL's rise to "the second-largest professional sports league in North America," as it liked to call itself, would reach its peak in 1979. Average attendance would increase marginally in 1980, and playing standards may have improved for a few years after that. But the momentum would be lost. The year 1979 proved to be the NASL's watershed: instead of when everything came together, it was when everything started to fall apart.

Come the day of Soccer Bowl '79, the Cosmos were nowhere to be seen, and neither were several thousand of their fans who'd bought tickets to what they assumed would be another coronation. The Vancouver Whitecaps defeated Tampa Bay in the championship game—and, a week earlier, had eliminated New York in one of the most dramatic and drawn-out matches in the league's history. "The times seem to be a-changing," *Sports Illustrated* reflected in the wake of the Cosmos' exit. Vancouver's victory offered "a fresh, cool breeze blowing through the league, and new realization of an old truth, that there are eleven men on every soccer team and that you cannot always buy your way to glory." But the glory of the new champions would prove short-lived. In little over a year, most of the members of the title-winning team would be gone—and the Whitecaps would never win the NASL again.

The 1979 season did not start well. Three weeks in, the players—or, at least, a few of them—went on strike, demanding that their union be recognized. On the surface, the grievance proved little more than a minor irritation to the league's owners, yet the near-inevitability with which it arose should have worried them. As early as 1975, Kyle Rote Jr., then the most famous American in the game, and Steve Frank, an attorney and former NASL midfielder, had canvassed support for a players' association. While the initial reaction was muted, the movement soon gathered steam, particularly when players who also appeared for the national team began to take issue with the arrangements the USSF had made—or not made—for them.*

---

* The national team had gone on strike in October 1976 during the middle of a World Cup qualifying campaign. It alleged that players were being paid less for their services than they had been two years earlier and that the USSF had not told them how much they'd get until the team had been training in Colorado Springs for several weeks. The walkout, which many perceived simply as a means of calling attention to the federation's inadequacies, lasted barely a day; the USSF wasted little time in putting together an improved offer.

Rote, Frank, and Al Trost, the national team captain, approached the NFL Players' Association for advice; they were offered the services of no less than its executive director, Ed Garvey. The NASL Players' Association held its first official meeting the day after Soccer Bowl '77; within the month, Garvey met Woosnam seeking recognition and ultimately a collective bargaining agreement. But the league pursed its lips, insisting that its clubs were independent employers and that negotiation needed to be taken up with each of them individually. That much of the NASL's ownership was drawn from non-unionized industries would not have been coincidental to its ambivalence; Pocklington, in fact, would seek the leadership of Canada's Progressive Conservative Party in 1983 on a virulently anti-union platform. But even after the National Labor Relations Board recognized the players' association—and ordered that the league do the same—the owners refused to change their minds. (As late as 1980, one club official would accuse the league of "handling the labor situation like everything else—like they expect a bolt of lightning to strike and make everything okay.") In the meantime, high-priced talent continued to arrive from overseas—and to command a greater share of the wage bill.

The intransigence came to a head on April 13—a Friday—when the association announced it had voted by more than two to one to strike. Given that the majority of players were foreign and stood little to gain from a union focused on the longer term, the margin was a surprise. But the imports had been advised that they would lose their visas and might even be deported if they worked during a recognized stoppage.

The league instructed its clubs to prepare to play with replacement players, though in the end, few were needed. The Portland Timbers had to use a complete team of them for their match with the Minnesota Kicks—who didn't field quite as many and won—but this was exceptional. Fewer than a third of the workforce actually walked out, and at some clubs, no one did at all. The Cosmos had backed the strike initially, but when the time came to visit the Atlanta Chiefs, they were all on the plane. Lack of support from the league's most visible club was a kick in the union's teeth, but the fiercest blow had been struck by the U.S. Immigration and Naturalization Service, which said it wouldn't deport foreign players who decided to play. Though the discontent remained, the strike ended less than a week after it had started.

Out in Vancouver, the Whitecaps didn't have to worry about any of this—Canadian law prohibited such industrial action—though their season got off to an embarrassing start of its own. The opening match, a home defeat by the Dallas Tornado, took nearly three hours to finish.

Ninety foul-strewn minutes of regulation play and fifteen minutes of sudden-death overtime failed to separate the teams, which left the outcome to be decided by the NASL's Shootout tie-break (a variant of penalty kicks in which the shooter was given five seconds to score from thirty-five yards away). The real embarrassment, though, was that the lights at Empire Stadium had failed twice, a hazard that came as little surprise to the Whitecaps' owner, Herb Capozzi. "When it was built in '54 it was one of the best facilities on the continent," he said. "Now it's the worst." That season, though, it would play host to a noisy, adoring crowd.

But the biggest gatherings were still reserved for the Meadowlands. A crowd of 72,342, larger than had ever attended a regular-season game in the NASL, turned out for the Cosmos' home opener, a 3–2 win over Fort Lauderdale. The defending champions had begun their campaign with three away games, and though they won them all, not everyone thought they'd deserved to. In the wake of a 2–1 overtime win against San Diego, losing manager Hubert Vogelsinger protested bitterly that the referee had disallowed a legitimate goal from his team. The NASL, he claimed, was "in awe, intimidated by the Cosmos," and the result had been "what the league wants—the Cosmos to win."

Win they did—seven straight victories to start the season, by which time it became clear that only the Washington Diplomats stood between them and another division title. Along the way, there had been the familiar moments of controversy: Beckenbauer blamed the AstroTurf at Giants Stadium for a knee injury that would sideline him for much of the season, and Marinho was benched for what the *New York Times* described as "social indiscretions involving women in his room."*

Then it came time for a showdown with the Cosmos' fiercest rivals, Tampa Bay, which not surprisingly was the match ABC chose to begin its series of telecasts. While the network had not needed to spend a fortune to land pro soccer, it treated its modest investment with respect. Heading its commentary team was none other than Jim McKay, whose enduring association with the network's *Wide World of Sports* and Olympic coverage made him for many the personification of international sports television. An avowed soccer fan, McKay kicked off ABC's campaign by fronting

---

* Later in the season, Chinaglia and several other players interrupted a practice session to start a fight in the stands with three abusive members of the Giants Stadium maintenance crew, one of whom ended up in the hospital. "Every time we practice, these people abuse the players," said a Cosmos official. "The manager at the stadium said these people have a lot of problems. It's a very sad situation."

an hour-long season preview and introduction to the game, given the bumper-sticker title *Soccer Is More Than a Kick in the Grass.*

The network's decision to pair McKay with a British expatriate proved more controversial, at least in certain quarters. Paul Gardner, a New York journalist, had worked on NASL telecasts for CBS and TVS and had lived in the United States since 1959. But at a time when Americanizing the league had become an intense topic of debate, his old-country voice grated on sensitive ears. "Gardner is very knowledgeable," *Soccer America* harrumphed, "but he's so dry you expect him to curl up and blow away at any moment. Plus, he carries an aura of patronism [*sic*] about American soccer that really makes you gag after awhile." The view may have been fueled by the fact that Gardner wrote for a rival publication at the time. But the magazine made clear its disappointment that ABC, having whittled its shortlist to two, had passed over Cliff McCrath, an American-born college coach who'd apparently lost out after he "stepped on McKay's lines" three times during his audition.

This, though, was hardly a major dispute and nowhere near as controversial as ABC's decision to gamble on soccer in the first place. Summer afternoons did not lend themselves to TV-watching, particularly for a sport that demanded a degree of patience and understanding. "I'm not sure the American temperament is suited for the continuing thrusts with no accomplishment," said Chuck Milton, who had produced soccer for CBS. "They want goals."

New York and Tampa Bay provided five of them that day, the Rowdies claiming a 3–2 victory. But when the winning goal went in, ABC had been caught up in the delights of Löwenbräu beer, an indiscretion of the type commercial broadcasters were always vulnerable to. Luckily, the embarrassments proved rare over the season, and for its coverage of an unfamiliar game, the network was widely praised. (*Soccer America* was impressed with, among other things, how "the shirt pulls, the vicious 'cleats up' frontal tackles, stood out in all their notoriety.")

Yet if goals were needed to hook Americans, ABC might have counted itself unlucky. A large proportion of those it got to show that season were confined to one match, a wild 6–5 victory for the Detroit Express against the Chicago Sting settled by a Shootout. Three of its other games ended 1–0. The ratings were weak—"lousy," a spokesman admitted—and over the season, they did not improve.

Vancouver recovered from their opening-day loss to Dallas to win eight of their next ten matches, then played Bristol City of the English First Division to a 1–1 tie. Their success was not unexpected. The man in charge, Tony Waiters, had been the NASL's coach of the year in 1978; beefing up a largely Canadian team with several English league professionals, he'd stormed to the best record in the league. "We brought over players who would not be seen as outstanding international players, but were good professionals," he recalled. "Everyone was trying to be a mini New York Cosmos. . . . [W]e went for guys who were good for the team. If you were on a budget and needed journeymen, you went with what you knew, which for us meant players from England."

They weren't all journeymen. Willie Johnston had gone to the 1978 World Cup with Scotland, though he was sent home for failing a drug test (allegedly because of tablets he'd taken to fight off the flu). Trevor Whymark had played over 250 games for first-division Ipswich Town of England and, but for an injury, would have turned out for them in the 1978 FA Cup final. Phil Parkes, an NASL all-star in 1979, had kept goal over 300 times for Wolverhampton Wanderers. Even some of Waiters's indigenous talent had a transatlantic flavor: Vancouver-born Bob Lenarduzzi had joined fourth-division Reading as a fifteen-year-old apprentice and made over seventy appearances for them.

The most illustrious name did not arrive until mid-season. Alan Ball, a World Cup winner with England in 1966, had joined the Philadelphia Fury on a summer loan from Southampton in 1978 and quickly established himself as one of the few bright spots in a feeble team—so bright, in fact, he ended the season as its coach. But when things didn't improve at the start of the following year, the club deemed him expendable ("His stats aren't terribly strong," one executive insisted)—and Waiters pounced. "It did not go unnoticed that in Ball's first practice session with the Whitecaps, it was something just over two minutes before he took over," *Soccer America* wrote, "with Waiters and coach Bob McNab beaming approval."

When Ball arrived in British Columbia, the Whitecaps were on a high. A few days earlier—and before 32,372 at Empire Stadium, a record crowd for soccer in Vancouver—they'd thumped the Cosmos, 4–1. While even in their prime, an occasional heavy defeat was part of the Cosmos' constitution, in this instance there may have been mitigating circumstances. Two weeks earlier, the club had sacked Eddie Firmani, the coach who had brought them championships in each of his two seasons there and seemed on the way to a third. A club official insisted that the Cosmos were "not playing as a team and not improving" and that their 9–2 season record was "deceptive." Not that anyone believed him. Many suspected the club's notoriously hands-on front office had taken issue with Firmani's team selection and his aversion to the heavy of schedule of exhibitions. (The Cosmos were due to host World Cup winners Argentina a few days later and would lose, 1–0.)

Firmani's assistant, Ray Klivecka, was named as his successor, but a few days later the club announced that Julio Mazzei, a former assistant and longtime friend of Pelé's, had been appointed to the position of "technical director." In truth, no one could be sure who was ever in charge of the team. There were several candidates in suits and ties and one in particular on the field. Firmani's initial appointment in 1977 was widely ascribed to interference from Chinaglia—and many believed his dismissal stemmed from a decision he'd made all of a year earlier to substitute him in a league game.

Under Klivecka, Mazzei, or whoever was running them, the Cosmos closed out the regular season with eight straight wins. A crowd of 57,223 watched a 4–1 defeat of Minnesota, the team with the second-best record in the conference, and 70,042 were on hand to see them avenge their televised loss to Tampa Bay, 4–3.

Before this streak began, though, they had faced Vancouver a second time—and once again they lost, 4–2, in a match that exposed their notorious arrogance for all it was worth. The referee, Keith Styles, had been kept busy all night, whistling for no fewer than forty-eight fouls, but it was with nineteen minutes to play that the full force of the champions' wrath came crashing down on him. After chasing for a ball, Johnston and Eskandarian came to blows and triggered a mass brawl. Styles issued red cards to the two instigators and then to Chinaglia and Vancouver's John Craven. At that point, according to *Soccer America,*

> Chinaglia charged Styles and appeared to grab the card from the official's hand. Chinaglia was restrained while arguing continued between Cosmos' players, coaches and the referee and linesmen. Chinaglia started towards the home bench when, according to Chinaglia, Trevor Whymark yelled an obscenity at him. That prompted Chinaglia to go after Whymark. . . . Round Two of the brawl began as Pelé, who was sitting on the Cosmos' bench, followed Chinaglia running onto the field. Pelé went after Parkes, who was dancing around with his clenched fists in the air. Numerous fans jumped onto the field and Chinaglia's business manager Pepe Pinton grabbed ahold of Styles. After delaying the hard-fought match for 14 minutes, the ejected players left the field, some fans were arrested and the match resumed.

It was hardly the first time American soccer had succumbed to such gro-
tesque behavior, but rarely had it been witnessed by 32,000 fans. The
Cosmos were incensed by what they perceived as Styles's failure to protect
them sufficiently ("We're not going to play ice hockey. People come here
and try to kill us"). Inevitably, they lodged a protest, and though the
league threw it out, it suspended Chinaglia for just one match.

Since their formation in 1974, the Whitecaps had faced New York six
times; they had lost to them only once. "The Cosmos used to hate playing
against us because we didn't give them any respect," recalled Derek Pos-
see, one of Vancouver's English imports. "Some other teams would think
'Oh, my God. We can't beat the Cosmos.' We said, 'Screw it. We can sort
them out.'" The key to their success was probably their defense, which
employed a system of zonal marking ("When we lose possession we have
eleven defenders," Waiters claimed). But in the best tradition of English
teams they also hustled and harried the opposition all over the pitch.

Victory over the San Jose Earthquakes in the penultimate match
brought them the division title; the Cosmos had won theirs with three
games to spare. But the "explosive period" Woosnam had forecast for the
league had failed to materialize. Attendance increased in 1979, but only
by around 1,000 a game, and cities like San Jose and Tulsa continued to
outdraw teams in much larger conurbations. The Cosmos' average was
down from the previous season, but at just under 47,000 it was still well
ahead of what NASL teams in the next three largest markets could manage, even when put together. Clive Toye, who'd left the club and was now
in his second year with the Sting, had maintained that four cities—New
York, Chicago, Los Angeles, and Toronto—would make or break the
league. In three of them, there was still a lot of work to do.

Some of the problems were grave. The Philadelphia Fury were hampered by their mediocre team, but even that couldn't excuse the crowds of
a few thousand rattling around Veterans Stadium (just 3,337 turned out
for a playoff match). Much the same applied to New England, whose Tea
Men had been forced out of the football stadium in Foxboro owing to
scheduling conflicts with the adjacent racetrack. They ended up on the
campus of Boston University, where few were prepared to watch them.
Down in Houston, the second-year Hurricane were surprise owners of
the best record in the American Conference ("I really don't know why
we're any good," their coach had confessed), but they played in an Astro-
dome that was usually more than four-fifths empty.

The follow-the-leader strategy wasn't working. Many clubs searched
for a Pelé to call their own, only to discover there wasn't one. Few names

in soccer were bigger than that of Johan Cruyff, and the contract he signed with the Los Angeles Aztecs was said to be worth $700,000 a year (not including a $600,000 payoff to the Cosmos, who owned the rights to him). But while the Aztecs' gates did increase with his arrival, it was only to an average of around 14,000, and there were no Pelé-size crowds greeting him at the Rose Bowl or anywhere else. In Fort Lauderdale, the Strikers had signed Bayern Munich's goal-scoring ace Gerd Müller, reportedly for $300,000 a year, but his impact at the turnstiles was even more limited.

As the strategic plan had emphasized, attendance was crucial to the league's success—not just reducing the empty seats (and on average, NASL stadiums had been more than 70 percent empty in 1979), but filling them with loyal fans prepared to pay the going rate. How many of them were there? Group outings, door prizes, and fireworks displays might have suggested there were many, but not everyone with a ticket became a fan.

Some thought the league was treading the wrong path. They remembered how in 1973 the Philadelphia Atoms had won the NASL championship with a team that featured nearly as many Americans as imports; even their coach, Al Miller, was native-born. The city, in turn, had responded with enthusiasm, at least for a few seasons before the franchise disappeared in 1976. Unquestionably, the Fury were stocked with better talent than the Atoms, but hardly anyone went to their games.

Miller was now the coach of the Dallas Tornado. "I just can't carry the American banner anymore," he confessed. "The foreigners have just proved too good. . . . You take a kid who grew up with seven pairs of soccer shoes and his mom driving him to practice, and when the going gets really tough, he'll let you down. The foreigners play the game with guts and blood. You can rely on them." The Pennsylvanian had learned his lesson the season before, when he routinely included four or five native-born players in his team and failed to make the playoffs. There had been no such indulgences in 1979; Americans in Dallas made way for Germans and Brazilians. New Jersey-born Glenn Myernick had started nearly every game for Miller in 1978, but in 1979 he was usually on the bench. "At least the foreigners coming over here now are top players, not guys who've lost so many steps at home that they can't compete," he said. "We're going to look at them, take what we can from their experience and skills, and soon we'll take over the league."

This was precisely the NASL's thinking. In 1978, it increased from one to two the number of North Americans who had to start each match (with at least six to be carried on the roster). But most coaches treated this as a maximum as well as a minimum—and many of Myernick's peers were not as philosophical. Foremost among them was New York's Bobby Smith:

> Who's looking out for the Americans in the NASL? The owners? They can't get their faces out of the trough long enough to be moral. The coaches? They're so scared of losing games they won't take a chance on us. The foreign players? With a few exceptions like Chinaglia and Rodney Marsh, who will help out an American? The old guys who were over the hill in Europe or South America are too insecure with their starting positions here. As a result, we're getting the shaft right here in our own country. We're the window dressing. They keep telling us to wait, to take our time. Well, we've heard those lyrics before and we want it now.

One of the victims of Miller's de-Americanization process was Kyle Rote Jr., who'd been traded to Houston, where he played sparingly. For him, the league had restricted itself in the wrong direction:

> I think our league has two purposes: to showcase the best talent in the world and to develop American players for our Olympic and World Cup teams. We're doing an incredibly good job of the first. It's unbelievable, the names and the quality that are here. As for the second, we're standing still or falling back. We could remedy it with a simple formula: that each team could bring in only five players. We could still get the best 120 in the world. We've got to legislate to force the coaches to work with the American player.

But the league was intensely fearful of a drop in playing standards, and in the quest for victory even the most sympathetic clubs took a dim view of native-born talent. At Hartwick College, Myernick had been collegiate player of the year in 1976 and Miller, who'd once coached there, had taken him first in the NASL draft. "Glenn could have been at a high level earlier and could have been playing and making money earlier had he not gone to college," Miller claimed. "Now he could be further ahead. He developed certain habits we would like to break. In college he was far superior to most. Now he is inferior to most, and he faces the test of rising above that."

The limitations of the native-born player—and of the colleges many expected to develop him—had come into sharp focus at the 1978 NCAA final, which paired San Francisco against Indiana. The coaching philosophies of the two schools could hardly have been more different: San Francisco's Steve Negoesco recruited almost all of his players from overseas while Indiana's Jerry Yeagley played so many Americans—and made such liberal use of the colleges' free-substitution rule—he couldn't get his hands on enough of them. "Yeagley's tactic is the one he has to use with mediocre American players," Negoesco contended. "The name of his game is substitutions. What his kids lack in finesse, they can make up by burning themselves out for a few minutes. . . . He just grinds opponents into the ground with his depth." Yeagley—the colleges' coach of the year in 1976—was unrepentant. "It's just a different value system," he claimed. "I want to develop the American player, and to do so I have to substitute. . . . When American kids get more skills, we'll cut down on the subbing." San Francisco won, 2–0, their goals coming from a Norwegian and a Nigerian.*

There was, of course, an American eleven fans of all persuasions could rally behind, but even at the height of the NASL's popularity, the U.S. national team remained little more than a footnote. The prospect of a confrontation with the Soviet Union in soccer-friendly Seattle may have been enough to send Henry Kissinger to the Pacific Northwest in February, but it couldn't tempt more than 13,000 to the Kingdome. A rematch in San Francisco a week later drew barely half as many. Even in the Meadowlands, the national team wasn't much of an attraction: an exhibition with France in May—which the United States lost, 6–0—attracted fewer than 21,000.

Not everyone was convinced that the NASL needed to put more Americans on the field. In 1976, its three best-supported clubs had been Minnesota, Portland, and Seattle, who had barely a native-born player among them. Indeed, the only team that had featured Americans in any number was the St. Louis Stars—and such was their drawing power that they moved to California in 1978. Was the fault with the league for failing to include native talent, or was it with the lower reaches of the game for failing to develop it?

Flag-waving fans may have needed patience, but patience was anathema to the NASL. "Over three years the Cosmos went from 5,000 to a 50,000 average," Woosnam had noted. "If it can happen in one city, it can be done in others." But could it really? It was one thing for New Yorkers

---

* The school was forced to vacate the title in 1980 after discovering that one of its Nigerian players had "submitted an altered transcript at the time of his application for enrollment."

to embrace Pelé, and quite another for the people of Fort Lauderdale to warm to the likes of Gerd Müller. Talent in the NASL may have reached an unprecedented level in 1979, yet it consisted of names that meant little to those in the stands.

All but eight of the league's twenty-four teams qualified for the play-offs in 1979, even Philadelphia, which won just ten of thirty games. Vancouver had won twenty and was paired with Dallas in the first round, giving newspapers in Texas the opportunity to recycle comments attributed to Al Miller earlier in the year that the Whitecaps were "thugs" and "would get into a kicking match with a team of nuns." But the only controversial moment of the series proved to be the resignation of the Tornado's general manager shortly before the first match. Vancouver advanced with wins of 3–2 in Dallas and 2–1 at home. The Cosmos, meanwhile, eliminated the Toronto Blizzard, a team Bogicevic had referred to at the start of the season as "donkeys and horses ... English and Scottish big zeroes." The losers were somewhat less disparaging. "Obviously, I wouldn't be surprised if the Cosmos won it again," said Keith Eddy, the Blizzard's coach, "but right now I'm picking Vancouver. If they play to their utmost potential, Vancouver is the only team that can beat the Cosmos."

The Tulsa Roughnecks came close to proving him wrong. For the first game of their second-round confrontation, New York traveled to Oklahoma and lost, 3–0. Three days later, though—and with over 76,000 shouting encouragement at Giants Stadium—they were a different proposition. It made for a late night at the Meadowlands. The loser of the first playoff game needed to win not only the second but also a thirty-minute "mini-game" that immediately followed, with the prospect of two Shootouts if both ended in ties. But the Cosmos, who had secreted themselves in a hotel the night before to focus on the task at hand, blanked the Roughnecks 3–0 and followed it up with a 3–1 win in the mini-game. "They played with heart," said Alan Hinton, Tulsa's coach, "and when you add this to their skill, they are unbeatable."

On the West Coast, Vancouver wrestled with a mini-game of their own, having thrown away a 2–0 first-match lead in Los Angeles with just eighteen minutes to play to lose, 3–2. The Aztecs had been the only team to beat them twice during the regular season, and the fact wasn't lost on the anxious crowd that filled Empire Stadium to capacity three days later. ("They were hardly cheering because they were as nervous as we were," Waiters recalled.) But a parsimonious defense came to the rescue—and the fans eventually roared themselves hoarse. The Whitecaps advanced with a pair of 1–0 victories.

Soccer America reflected on a memorable night:

Coach Rinus Michels, who had earlier won the grudging admira-
tion of Caps' boss Tony Waiters ("He's a bloody good coach you
know, that Michels. He doesn't miss a trick does he?") was over-
heard in the Los Angeles dressing room to observe that "no one
should mind losing to a team like that." It was a game that drew
superlatives from case-hardened sportswriters because of its inten-
sity, its finesse and the high caliber of soccer on the part of both
teams. It might well have been the crowd that made the difference.
One veteran English writer noted: "This is a more English soccer
crowd than an English soccer crowd." For the singing, the chant-
ing, the scarf and flag-waving were all there, in a spontaneous out-
pouring of affection for their team.

The results left only two teams standing in the National Conference:
the Cosmos and the Whitecaps, who now met for a place in the Soccer
Bowl. The first encounter took place in Vancouver on a Wednesday night.
It attracted a feverish crowd of 32,375—and more of the champions'
histrionics.

The first half passed off with no goals and little in the way of controversy; New York was missing the injured Rijsbergen and Neeskens and
spent most of the period trying to contain Vancouver's industrious forwards. With twenty-five minutes to play, the Whitecaps took the lead
after Johnston headed in a cross from Ball. But when in the eighty-fifth
minute Whymark raced free to score a second, the Cosmos protested ani-
matedly that he'd been offside. Scarcely had their tempers eased before
referee Peter Johnson showed the red card to Eskandarian for a rash challenge, effectively suspending him from the second game.

As the final whistle sounded and delirious Vancouver fans celebrated
yet another victory over the champions, Cosmos players and officials
descended on the men in charge. Johnson noted in his match report that
a verbally abusive Carlos Alberto threw his shirt and spat at them. The
player's recollection would prove rather different ("I just gave a linesman
my shirt and said, 'Here, remember the Cosmos'"), but unhesitatingly,
Woosnam suspended him for the rest of the season.

The Cosmos were not known for graceful reactions to perceived injus-
tices, but their response on this occasion was outré even by their own
standards. One league official recalls that Steve Ross, the brash chairman
of Warner Communications, threatened "to pull the Cosmos not only

out of a game but out of the league entirely, then just out of the playoffs" over the suspension. The *New York Times* reported that the club threatened to file suit against the NASL, claiming that Woosnam had made his decision before receiving the match report. The Cosmos also questioned—without any apparent irony—the impartiality of the Canadian referee. "We've always had trouble with this guy Johnson," said Rafael de la Sierra, their executive vice-president. "First of all, he's from Toronto. How can the league allow him to officiate in a crucial game like this where a Canadian team is involved?" De la Sierra even claimed that the league had wanted "a result like this" in Vancouver to heighten the tension for the second game, which ABC was televising. But probably the only people in the world who believed the league was biased against the Cosmos were the Cosmos themselves. "They don't think it is possible for them to lose," said Waiters. "They have a sort of arrogance which is almost naïve."

The stage was thus set for what many regard as the greatest match—or afternoon of soccer, to be precise—in the NASL's history. Certainly it did not lack drama or suspense, though from the outset it also carried an air of disappointment. No other team in the league would have minded pulling in 44,000 for a playoff match, but for the Cosmos this was below their season average—and the smallest crowd Giants Stadium had managed for a post-season game. Blithely, the club and the league attributed the empty seats to the busy Labor Day weekend and the presence of ABC's cameras (the match was not blacked out in New York). But they should have been worried. When supporters of the league's flagship franchise weren't prepared to turn out for their team on such a crucial occasion, just how popular was their club—and how strong was the NASL? If the league had a single turning point, if it's possible to point to the day when its fortunes went into reverse, it's hard to look past the 32,000 empty seats in Giants Stadium on September 1, 1979.

Vancouver had doubted whether Woosnam would stand up to the Cosmos and go through with Alberto's suspension. The decision wasn't finalized until the evening before the match, but it had stood: the Brazilian was out, and so was Eskandarian. This still left the champions with plenty to choose from, of course, and what many regarded as the essence of the team—the invention of Bogicevic and the finishing of Chinaglia—combined after eleven minutes for the first goal of the afternoon. The Whitecaps came back seventeen minutes later, with Craven finding the net after Ball's free kick, but Chinaglia struck again before halftime. The score remained 2–1 until the eighty-fifth minute, when Johnston got his head to a Lenarduzzi cross for the final goal of the match.

The home team could consider themselves unfortunate that two of their better players, Tueart and Neeskens, went off with injuries and had to be replaced. But when the fifteen minutes of sudden-death overtime failed to produce a goal and left the match to be decided by the Shoot-out, fate seemed to be with them. Vancouver had won only one of five tie-breaks that season, and New York had lost only one of five. The Cosmos duly leveled the series when just one opposing player managed to find the net.

Already play had lasted nearly two hours, and in near-ninety-degree heat, on an unyielding artificial surface, even the fittest man had been pushed close to exhaustion. But the mini-game was now to follow. Woosnam had always rejected suggestions that his league revert to the two-match, total-goals system favored by the rest of the world; he feared teams would turn defensive in the second leg if they won big in the first ("Our whole league is based on scoring").* At the same time, though, there wouldn't have been many at the Meadowlands or watching on TV who understood how the system worked; it wasn't even covered in the NASL's media guide. Was the mini-game sudden death? Were substitutions permitted? And what if nobody scored?

Sure enough, nobody did score, though on another occasion, with another set of officials, it might have been different. As it was, the mini-game served largely to underline the Cosmos' petulance. Early in the first period, a strike from Vancouver's Carl Valentine crashed off the underside of the crossbar and bounced on the goal line. Clive Gammon watched the melodrama unfold for *Sports Illustrated*:

> On the line? Or just over the line—as it had to be for the goal to count? The referee apparently had no doubt. He immediately pointed to the center of the field, indicating a score. The decision drove the Cosmos berserk. Led by Giorgio Chinaglia, they rushed across to the linesman, who would have been consulted by the referee had there been any doubt in the ref's mind. Chinaglia roughly grabbed the official by the shoulders—an offense that would have meant immediate expulsion from the game anywhere else in the world. The referee came over, not to eject the Cosmos' star but apparently to join in a discussion. And somehow, after several minutes the ref was persuaded that he was entirely wrong, that no goal had been scored.

---

* The league would drop the mini-game format in 1981 in favor of a best-of-three series.

If ABC's cameras indicated that the ultimate decision was correct—the ball was shown to have struck the line—they also seemed to confirm what the likes of Hubert Vogelsinger had suspected at the start of the season: the NASL was in awe of its biggest club. *Soccer America* noted that once the linesman appeared to indicate a goal had been scored, the Cosmos rushed toward him, "with Chinaglia grabbing [his] neck, and later picking up one of the sideline markers and holding it like a spear."

Officiating had always been a thorn in the NASL's flesh, and in hiring several "guest referees" from other countries, the league had tacitly admitted as much. (Keith Styles, center of the midseason storm at Giants Stadium, was from England.) "People make comparisons all the time, they say the officiating hasn't kept step with the player improvements," said the league's director of officials, Keith Walker. "And that may be true. After all, 85 to 90 percent of the players are foreign, and 90 to 95 percent of the officials are home-based. There's a big difference. I've been told I should try to get fifteen or twenty foreign refs, but I'd rather try to motivate the people here. Part of my job has been to upgrade the American officials."

But being part of an educative process was of little comfort to clubs chasing a title. Hardly a week of the season passed by without one of them filing a protest or being fined for something that was said or done toward an official. "I'd say there's about eight percent of the total games where there's an element of doubt," Walker claimed, "and some club executives have pointed that out vociferously, I'd say. But this year I have introduced twelve new referees. Seven have worked out well, five not so well. I expect a lot of turnover."

Having disallowed Valentine's goal in the first half of the mini-game, the referee at Giants Stadium—Toros Kibritjian, who was not Canadian—would do the same to the Cosmos in the second. Mark Liveric's effort was ruled out after a Vancouver player had been sent to the turf. Liveric protested his innocence, but the mini-game ended goalless—and with play well into its third hour, the participants were now asked to negotiate another Shootout.

In the wake of this match—these matches?—Woosnam would come under considerable criticism for the design of the playoff system and would admit being open to suggestions "to make things better." But it was of no consolation to the two enervated teams. "We haven't been able to have any decent training for the last while because of the constant travel," Vancouver's assistant coach Bob McNab said after the match. "If we looked fresher against the Cosmos at the end, it's because our players dug deeper inside their souls."

Beckenbauer and Rick Davis missed two of the Cosmos' first four Shootout efforts; only Bob Bolitho failed for Vancouver. With one round to go, New York's hopes of survival rested at the feet of New York's Brazilian fullback, Nelsi Morais—and what for all its contrivances had been an afternoon of riveting drama continued literally to the last second. Morais pushed the ball past the advancing Parkes and into the net, and Giants Stadium erupted with delight. But Kibritjian waved off the effort: Morias had exceeded the five-second shooting limit. The goal didn't count; the Whitecaps had won.

They won again the following week in Soccer Bowl '79, beating Tampa Bay, 2–1. But the showpiece occasion had been shrouded in anticlimax. Sixteen thousand ticket holders failed to show up; many of those who did filled the air with frustrated chants of "Cos-mos." When the time came to present the trophy, Woosnam, the villain of the Meadowlands, was forced to make an embarrassed plea over the public address system for quiet "in respect of the performance of the two teams here today." Some did applaud the Whitecaps as they took their victory lap, and there were a few hundred from British Columbia who cheered rather more ecstatically. But the champions returned to their hotel, only to discover they'd been thrown out of their rooms; the league had assumed Cosmos players would be occupying them and wouldn't be around that night.

Back in Vancouver, perhaps 60,000 were waiting to honor the new champions. One Canadian paper noted that the players, "swilling beer and champagne in the backs of pickup trucks, [took] more than an hour to inch their way over a three-kilometre parade route." But they weren't as happy as they might have been. The club's owners had refused to match the NASL's playoff bonus of $54,000 for the winners to divide, claiming it was against league policy. That did not sit well with the team. ("Our guys were on 36,000 Canadian dollars and the New York players were on about 360,000," McNab maintained. "The Cosmos spent more on program sellers than we did on players.") Such had been the level of discord that, in the days leading up to the Soccer Bowl, players talked of boycotting the match. But the owners also claimed the season had lost them around a third of a million dollars.

Vancouver's plight was a microcosm of the NASL's difficulties: if a no-frills team playing to decent crowds couldn't make money, who could? Even at clubs with deeper pockets, bets had been hedged. Among the changes in ownership that had taken place in 1979 was that of the Washington Diplomats, who'd been sold to the Madison Square Garden Corporation, the entertainment arm of Gulf and Western's vast conglomerate.

The club president, though, was still the same man who had assumed the role in 1976, Stephen Danzansky, a lawyer—and one of the eight members of the league's planning committee. In Washington, as Woosnam would discover, the strategic plan had not been abandoned in the snow.

The chairman of Madison Square Garden was Sonny Werblin, one of the biggest sports impresarios in the country and most famous for having brought Joe Namath to the New York Jets. With the weight of a major investor behind them, many expected Werblin and the Diplomats to, as a rival club executive posited, "crank the whole thing wide open." Yet the club spent only modestly in 1979. "We still haven't determined whether we just want this to be an NASL franchise or make it an international power," said Jack Krumpe, the corporation's vice-president.

Before the season had ended, though, the reasons for such hesitance had been laid bare. "The league has been the most negative thing we've come across since we've taken over," Krumpe declared, with an arrogance worthy of the Cosmos. "I guess there have to be reasons for why they do things the way they do but I still haven't figured them out."

He pulled no punches:

> The only way to improve this league right now is through attrition of franchises. . . . There should be ten, maybe twelve teams at most, certainly not twenty-four. The best thing for this league would be to have twelve franchises, each one committed to budgets of at least $3 million a year. Each and every game should be an event, an extravaganza of some sort. Instead of playing two or three games a week and hoping to average 12,000–18,000 fans a game, let's play one or one-and-a-half games a week and try to average 40,000. . . . For North America this is a major league. But in Europe it wouldn't be. It isn't good enough yet and it isn't professional enough yet. We have to build it to that point. I just don't think it's being gone about in the right way right now. This league isn't nearly as profitable as it could be.

Woosnam fought his corner. "In every league you are going to have good franchises and struggling franchises," he maintained. "But the struggling ones learn from the good ones and get better." Was that true, though? Atlanta had averaged 6,961 fans a game in 1967; twelve years later, they were averaging 7,350. Dallas and Portland had lost almost half their support in two years. Rochester's Lancers had endured for ten seasons without ever averaging more than 9,000; by the end of the 1979, they were contemplating a move to Montreal. Across the league, not a single club had finished in the black—and total losses were said to be around $20 million.

It was as much through luck as judgment that the NASL returned in 1980 with exactly the same teams in the exactly the same places, the only time this would ever happen. Memphis's Harry Mangurian, who also owned the Boston Celtics, had spent virtually the whole of the 1979 season trying to offload the Rogues, even advertising them in the *Wall Street Journal*; Sonny Werblin had considered transplanting them to Milwaukee before he'd zeroed in on the Diplomats. New England's owners met with the governor of Rhode Island with a view toward moving out of Boston. Even ostensibly healthy entities in Portland, San Jose, and Seattle had changed owners. Minnesota, once hailed as a blueprint franchise, would be put up for sale in June; its owners had spent the 1979 season watching attendance plummet from an average of nearly 31,000 to under 25,000—for a team with the third-best record in the league. ("We've created no excitement here for the last couple of years," a spokesman said. "That intangible factor is missing.") All the same, as the 1980 campaign began, few were casting any doubts as to the league's permanence. **N.A.S.L., Stable and Star-Studded, Enters 14th Season**, the *New York Times* had proclaimed.

Naturally, the Cosmos were still the team to beat, though in 1980 it looked as if they might be having company. Madison Square Garden had brought Johan Cruyff to Washington, reportedly paying the Aztecs $1 million and the player $1.5 million for a three-year contract. Cruyff's presence in the capital proved more consequential than it had in California: the Diplomats' average crowd rose from under 12,000 to more than 19,000. But the owners were far from happy. Instead of rejoicing over the 53,000 who'd filled RFK Stadium for a mid-season match with the Cosmos, Werblin had fumed: "We could do that three or four times a year if they would give us a chance."

The year before, the Diplomats had also made clear their feelings about the contract with ABC. "I think we sold our souls to national television and we've gotten very little in return," Krumpe had complained. "Why should we agree to let them put games on at 2:30 P.M. on Saturday in the middle of the summer? That just isn't worth a darn." Others had also been skeptical—even the chairman of the league's own television committee, Ed Blair. "I had a very different view of our television potential than the other team and club members," he recalled. "They wanted an instant network contract and I said we will go on television and fail, then they will blame soccer. . . . I wanted us on anthology shows, like *Wide World of Sports,* with standings, players, saves, goals, player-of-the-week, to build all the intrinsics of the sport and only put the championship game on television. I was overruled."

There was actually very little about the NASL that seemed to please the likes of Werblin and Krumpe, right down to the format of its schedule. The arrangement of six divisions and two conferences included just one home and one away game with the other three teams in the division, interspersed with much cross-country travel. The Diplomats were said to favor splitting the league geographically into three conferences, with each team limited to playing the other teams in its conference during the regular season. But as this effectively meant most of the clubs wouldn't get to play the Cosmos, and as the clubs themselves needed to approve any such change, the idea never stood a chance.

Cruyff had even weighed in with criticism of his own. At the ceremony honoring him as the league's most valuable player in 1979, he had upset a number of club executives by accusing them of failing to Americanize the game. "They won't have farm clubs or reserve-team schedules," he complained. "Pretty soon no one will be able to afford foreigners. If you bring up your own talent, you don't pay transfer fees." Needless to say, the Dutchman would be named to the league's all-star team again in 1980—and just as predictably, each of the other ten selections was also foreign.

The Cosmos won their third Soccer Bowl in four years in 1980, defeating Fort Lauderdale (ironically, on the Diplomats' home turf). But their aura was fading. Never again would they attract as many for a league match as the 70,132 who turned up for the visit of Fort Lauderdale in June of that year. Average attendance fell by nearly 4,000 a game, and nobody seemed to know why. "Maybe we've taken people for granted," an executive mused.

Madison Square Garden, meanwhile, could no longer afford the Diplomats: two seasons in the NASL had set them back $5 million, they said, and their patience was nearly up. "Don't bet on Sonny for 1981," one source told the *Washington Post*. "He's had it with this league. If they aren't ready to change, he'll get out."

He did. Toye recalled:

[Werblin and Krumpe] turned up at an annual meeting of the league, at L'Enfant Plaza in DC, to make the Big Bang argument. Guys (and I paraphrase this but this is guts of [it]), we have some good clubs, well-financed and we have a bunch of weak sisters, ill-financed. We have to get rid of those and then we can go forward successfully, knowing we will succeed. That's the Big Bang, get rid of all the weak sisters at once, and we'll move our club to Shea

Stadium, buying that territory from the Cosmos, and build a fantastic rivalry in a strongly financed League. If we do not do this now, then we will lose people bit by bit along the way . . . that's the Little Bang. The support he gained was not enough; Warner Communications wanted $4 million for the territory east of the Hudson River, a ridiculous sum, and the Big Bang theory began and ended with Sonny Werblin's words.

The majority ruled in the NASL. Woosnam may have been possessed of his own vision, but he was beholden ultimately to the twenty-four owners. "Not everybody believed in expansion, but I think there are ulterior motives in those who questioned it afterwards," he reflected later. "All the owners knew exactly what was going on. They had to approve everything we did. If people say now we shouldn't have gone to twenty-four, well, so what? They voted for it." But they were hardly likely to agree to things like a reduction in their own numbers.

Moreover, in giving each club an equal voice, expertise in the NASL had been marginalized. Toye recalls the league meeting in advance of 1980 season in which the league had voted to change its executive committee so that each of the six divisions had a representative. The old committee, he recalls, "was swept aside and with it the years of experience and caring and mistakes-not-to-be-made-again. I remember turning to my neighbor and saying 'there goes the league.'"

Madison Square Garden's withdrawal left Woosnam in a mad scramble to find owners for "one of our best franchises." But the strategy of forced growth he'd for so long expounded was unraveling. Half the league's clubs had lost fans; four had lost more than a quarter of them. Houston and Rochester folded; the Diplomats were saved only at the expense of Detroit. Now the headline in the *New York Times* read **N.A.S.L. No. 1 Goal: To Save the League**. Clearly, there was to be no "explosive period," no imminent parity with the NFL, no proliferation in franchise values. And when ABC, lumbered with dismal ratings, announced it would show only the Soccer Bowl in 1981, there would also be little in the way of the "absolute priority" of network television.

In the quarter-century since its demise, the NASL has been subjected to no end of post mortems. Almost all list several causes of death, and many of these the strategic plan had warned against: hasty expansion, the rush for network television, a failure to develop native talent, the wrong kind of marketing. But other ailments were less easily remedied. Foremost among them was the naïve assumption that the millions of children who had discovered the fun of playing soccer wanted to watch others play it—or that their parents would even let them. "My father used to take me to Yankee Stadium," Kyle Rote Jr. recalled. "He'd say, 'Watch Mickey Mantle do this,' or 'Watch Tony Kubek make the double play. See how he gets out of the way of the sliding runner.' The father is comfortable teaching his children. In soccer, it's just the other way around. It would be a fair comment to say that kids know more about the game than parents do. That can be tough to handle from the ego standpoint."

A decade after covering the tribulations of the NASL's Washington Whips for the *Washington Post,* Andrew Beyer made his own comparisons to baseball:

> The problem, simply, may be that too many Americans do not like the game. We are too oriented toward fast-paced, high scoring sports such as football and basketball to appreciate soccer's more deliberate tempo. We want action. Perhaps it would be a more accurate, less harsh indictment of the game and its American audiences to say that we have not learned to understand or appreciate soccer. Our enthusiasm for baseball proves that we do not need nonstop action in our sports. Baseball's appeal lies in its subtleties; there are times when an intentional base on balls may have so many ramifications that an aficionado can be mesmerized by a play of total nonexcitement. Soccer is similar, a game in which the movement of eleven players on the field involves an enormous amount of subtle strategy.

Other challenges the planning committee couldn't possibly have foreseen. Foremost among them was indoor soccer, which would spread like a rash during the early 1980s. At the time the planning committee printed its report, the Major Indoor Soccer League (MISL) had yet to be conceived; by 1979, its brash commissioner, Earl Foreman (a onetime NASL owner) was throwing down the gauntlet. "Outdoor soccer has never been able, after thirteen years, to capitalize on making outdoor soccer a spectator sport," he proclaimed. "But after thirteen years of organized professional soccer in this country, we're still saying, 'In ten years, we'll be here.' They won't."

Foreman was right, though his league would perish in 1992, at an earlier age than the NASL. But as the 1980s progressed, it looked for all the world as though his was the game Americans preferred. (Sonny Werblin had admitted being more excited by indoor soccer.) From an average of under 4,500 a match in 1978, attendance in the MISL rose to nearly 8,000 in 1982, while the number of franchises ballooned from six to thirteen. The St. Louis Steamers would average over 17,000 fans in 1983, more than any National Hockey League or National Basketball Association franchise—and better than all but two in the out-of-doors NASL. Its team was also mostly U.S.-born, something Foreman eagerly drew attention to. "American kids want to relate to American players," he said. "Who would they rather see play, Werner Wolfschnagel, the greatest soccer player in the world, who's going to get on an airplane and go back home at the end of the season?"

Although as far back as 1973 the NASL had staged an indoor tournament, the success of the MISL soon forced it into devoting entire winters to the game. It went head to head with its rival in the winter of 1979, albeit with only ten teams; come the following season, almost all the rest had joined in. By 1983, the league was shortening its outdoor season and playing more games inside than out. But in the intervening four years, it had also lost half its clubs, and the Cosmos had lost more than a third of their fans.

And Woosnam had lost the dance floor. The owners had hired a new chief executive, Howard Samuels, believing that his business sense, rather than any feel he had for the game, would revive the league. Under this new, austere regime, roster sizes were shrunk and a salary cap brought in; many thought the rot would stop. "The game isn't in trouble at all," Toye insisted. "It's individual NASL owners who are in trouble, and nine times out of ten they're in trouble because of themselves."

But it was difficult to turn around the listing ship, and there was no consensus as to how to do it. Woosnam would later insist that the salary cap had come too late and might have saved the league ("We had no means of controlling how much the Cosmos spent, and that scared the other owners"); Stern believed wrangles with the players' union probably had more to do with the league's demise than anything else. Others, rather desperately, blamed the decision of FIFA in 1983 to hold the next World Cup in Mexico after Colombia relinquished its hosting rights, a choice the governing body had made in the face of strenuous lobbying from the NASL and its friends.

The real reasons for the league's decline—and the intractability of its position—were broader and more subtle. A month before the end, in February 1985, Paul Gardner wrote in the *New York Times*:

> Pitifully few of the NASL's owners ever displayed more than a superficial grasp of the essential nature of soccer. They saw it first and foremost as something that was widely popular elsewhere in

the world, a commodity that could be marketed for the American audience. Soccer is not a commodity. It comes with a 100-year history of intense human involvement. It is a sport that seems to call for a peculiarly intimate and passionate involvement with fans. But there is no such thing as instant intimacy. It takes time to develop, it needs a history. And that was something that the American public could not bring to soccer. It is just that intimacy that allows the world's soccer fans for forgive their sport its excesses and its aberrations, to overlook its shortcomings. The aberration that American owners could not forgive was that soccer was too *inconsistent* a game. When it was good it was very good, but when it was bad it could be deadly dull.

Those who look back at the league as folly are mistaken. It may have sewn the seeds of its own demise, but it planted others that grew heartily. Many ten-year-olds who fidgeted in NASL stadiums in the '70s were adults sitting still for the 1994 World Cup. Glenn Myernick—who died in 2006—may have struggled to establish himself as a professional player, but at the 2002 World Cup he was an assistant coach of the U.S. national team. Nothing before the NASL, and perhaps nothing since, introduced the sport to so much of America. Whether Major League Soccer can be classified as a success may still be a matter of debate, but it enters its sixteenth season in 2011 in far healthier shape than the NASL at its peak. It is doubtful it could have assumed this position without studying its predecessor's mistakes and learning from them. It has profited from the NASL's groundwork—and has even offered it, if belatedly and begrudgingly, a tip of its hat. It is not a coincidence that MLS's franchise in Seattle is called the Sounders or the one in San Jose, the Earthquakes—or that both names arose largely from the protestations of fans who remembered. The league's new entries for 2011 are known as the Portland Timbers—and the Vancouver Whitecaps.

The team representing New York, though, is named after a soft drink, and though it plays in New Jersey, in a purpose-built stadium, it does not attract crowds of 70,000. There was, it seems, a time and a place for the Cosmos and the NASL, and for better and for worse it has passed. But the time for soccer in America has not.

Index

Note: "FC" is sometimes used in this index for the avoidance of ambiguity; it does not always form part of the club's official name. Page numbers in italics refer to illustrations.

DAVID WANGERIN was born in Chicago, grew up in Wisconsin, and moved to the United Kingdom in 1987. He is the author of *Soccer in a Football World: The Story of America's Forgotten Game* (Temple) and for more than twenty years has contributed to the British soccer magazine *When Saturday Comes*. He lives in central Scotland, where he has developed an affection for Raith Rovers.